AF230887

Wanderwest :: The Old World

Michael Dustin Youree

For information regarding permissions and other, email Lionheart Group Publishing: permissions@lionheartgrouppublishing.com

Paperback ISBN: 978-1-938505-57-7
Hardcover ISBN: 978-1-938505-58-4
Library of Congress Control Number: 2021947862

10 9 8 7 6 5 4 3 2 1
First Edition ~ December 2021

Published by Lionheart Group Publishing, Colorado, USA
Printed in the USA ~ All rights reserved.

Visit us on the web at www.lionheartgrouppublishing.com

Wanderwest

WITH MICHAEL DUSTIN YOUREE

For more than two decades, I have chased *the Old World*.

This compilation of images, words, and doorways was created to share
my nomadic experience that it may inspire yours.

Within are a few blank pages and spaces. Their purpose is for the pen. If
you find it blank, write a letter to someone who might like this taste of
the Old World and pass it on.

Or perhaps you have a better idea.

If you find it painted. Put it on your coffee table. Take it with you when
you travel. There's plenty more blank space to add as you see fit. Art is
never done and the journey carries on.

As for those doorways, they, too, are living things. Like my map of
Europe, it is far from complete.

I hope *the Old World* brews new thoughts.

old is relative — 02

glocalism — 18

learning bagpipes — 24

the way of my heart — 36

travel torture — 60

forever a novice — 70

in the end — 86

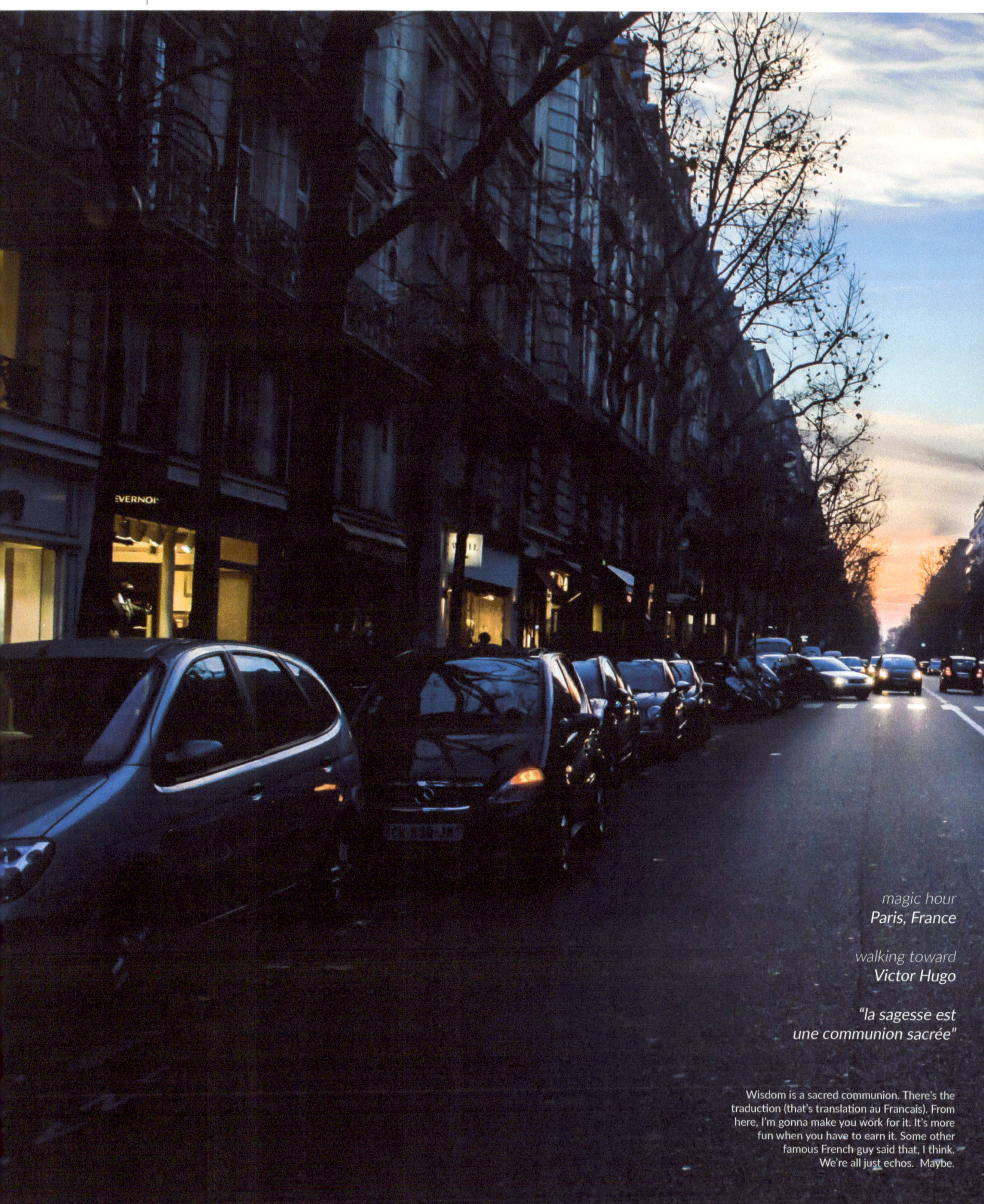

magic hour
Paris, France

walking toward
Victor Hugo

"la sagesse est
une communion sacrée"

Wisdom is a sacred communion. There's the
traduction (that's translation au Francais). From
here, I'm gonna make you work for it. It's more
fun when you have to earn it. Some other
famous French guy said that, I think.
We're all just echos. Maybe.

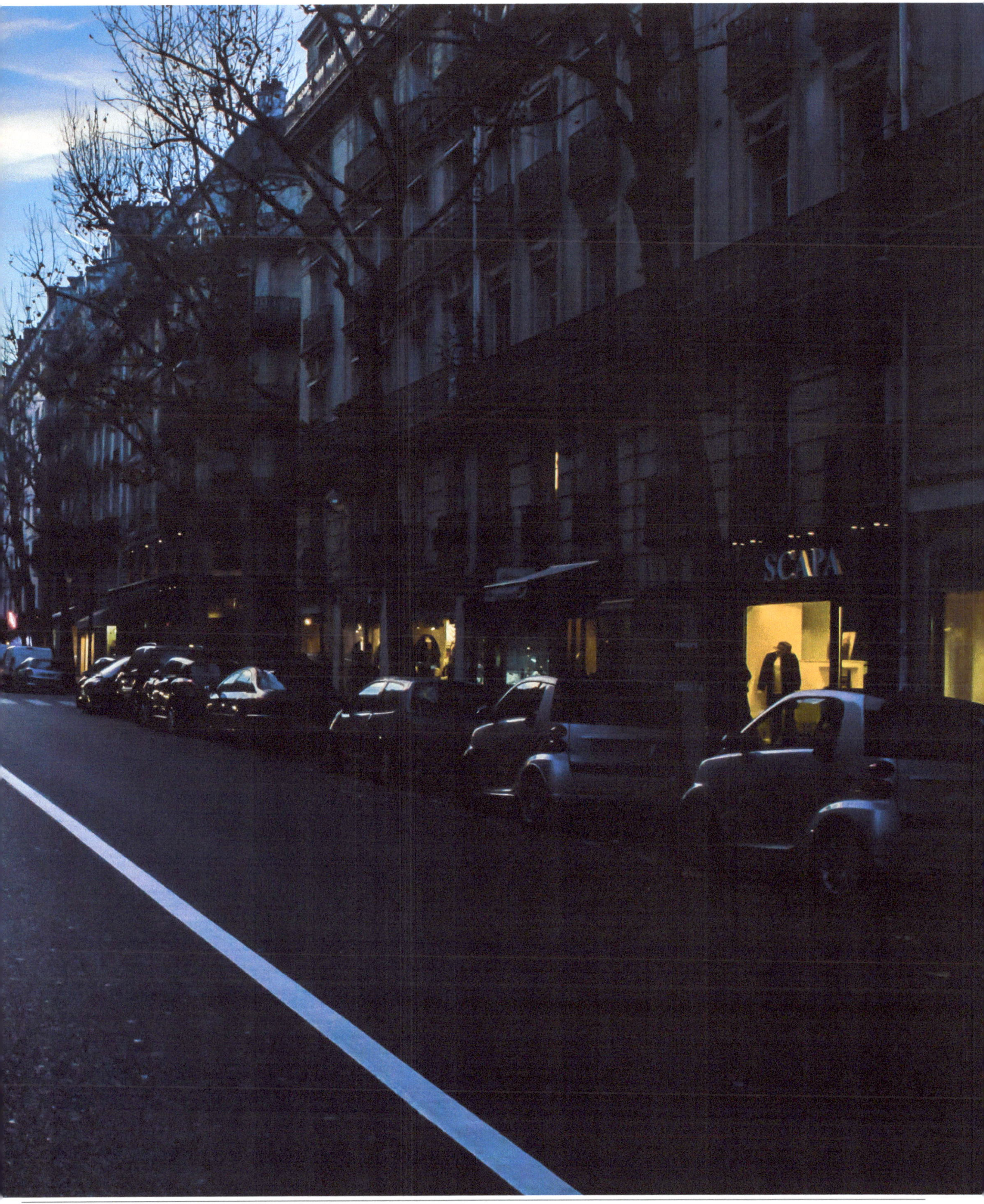

old is relative

Where I grew up, a building that's stood for 40 years is old. In most cases, we just demolish and replace it with something shiny and new. Our sense of old things is like our family trees—we can't really see beyond our grandparents.

Would we like to? I guess so. My mamaw always told me we were related to William Henry Harrison (perhaps the most forgettable president... odd brag, Mamaw) and rumor has it my great grandmother was Cherokee. I like the idea of that.

Enter genetics testing. No surprise. I'm mostly European. Perhaps that's why I feel such an *Old World* connection. I wonder if some Musketeer version of me guides my feet through ancestral streets of hand-laid stone a thousand years old. Perhaps my soul is bound to Cardinal Richelieu and the intergenerational karmic experience. Or maybe I'm just an American cliché. Paris is neat.

I'd been to Europe a couple times before I found the City of Light—a high school choir trip to London and a summer tour around Austria in college. During the latter, my friends and I had a few days off and popped over to Venice. That's when the *Old World* magic hit me like Pavarotti singing *Ave Maria*.

Apparently, I have a thing for cities with canals. More on that in later pages if you're paying attention.

As a graduation gift, my uncle funded a return to Italy. Unfortunately, the recipe of life at that time had me lonely and homesick after the first week. I decided to return to the USA earlier than scheduled and rerouted my trip through the practical choice of Paris. The change fees were cheap. And Paris is supposed to be nice, right?

I can't recall exactly where I stepped out of the metro for the first time, but if feels like Tulleries, a garden and promenade surrounded by the sprawling architectural majesty of the Louvre.

What I can remember clearly is that my gloom evaporated in the glory of Paris.

I was inundated with *Old World* beauty. Everywhere I turned was another magnificent structure that whisked me away down avenues of enlightenment like Franklin and Jefferson (who both have statues in Paris, btw). Before this baptism, I scoffed at the idea of touring the Eiffel Tower.

It's just a giant steel structure. How cool could it be?

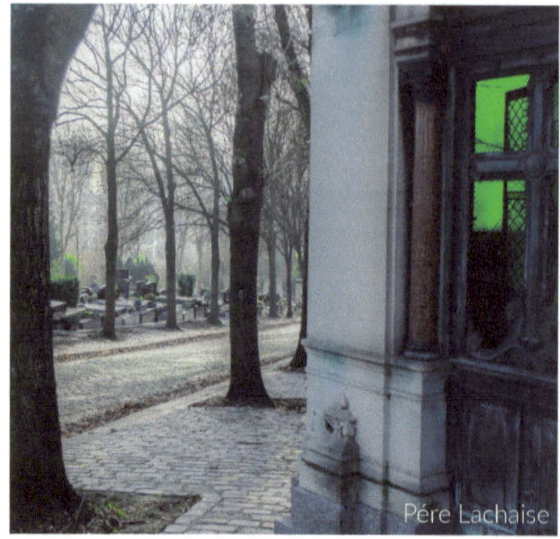

Well, my little bubble of naivety burst as I sprinted up winding steps of the iconic structure, so in love with my experience nothing could tire me. Kitted up in my new Henry Arsenal jersey, I blasted past strangers. They stared. "What is that guy on?" I was high on the *Old World*.

Paris became the centerpiece of my infatuation. A year and a half later, I spent all the money I had to go back.

Paris showed up. Trying to find the way back to the hotel on our last night, my buddy and I accidentally strolled past Notre Dame (because that's what you do in Paris).

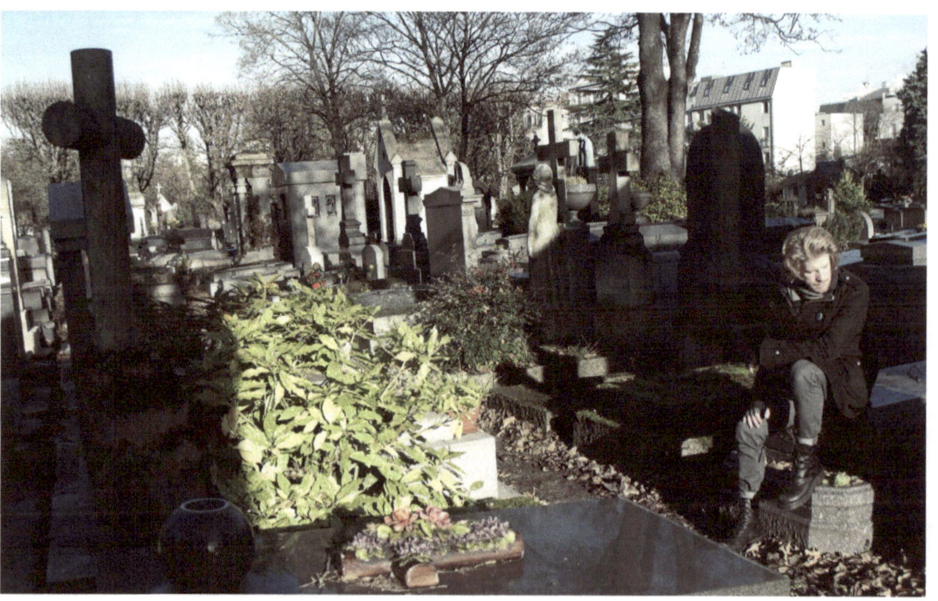

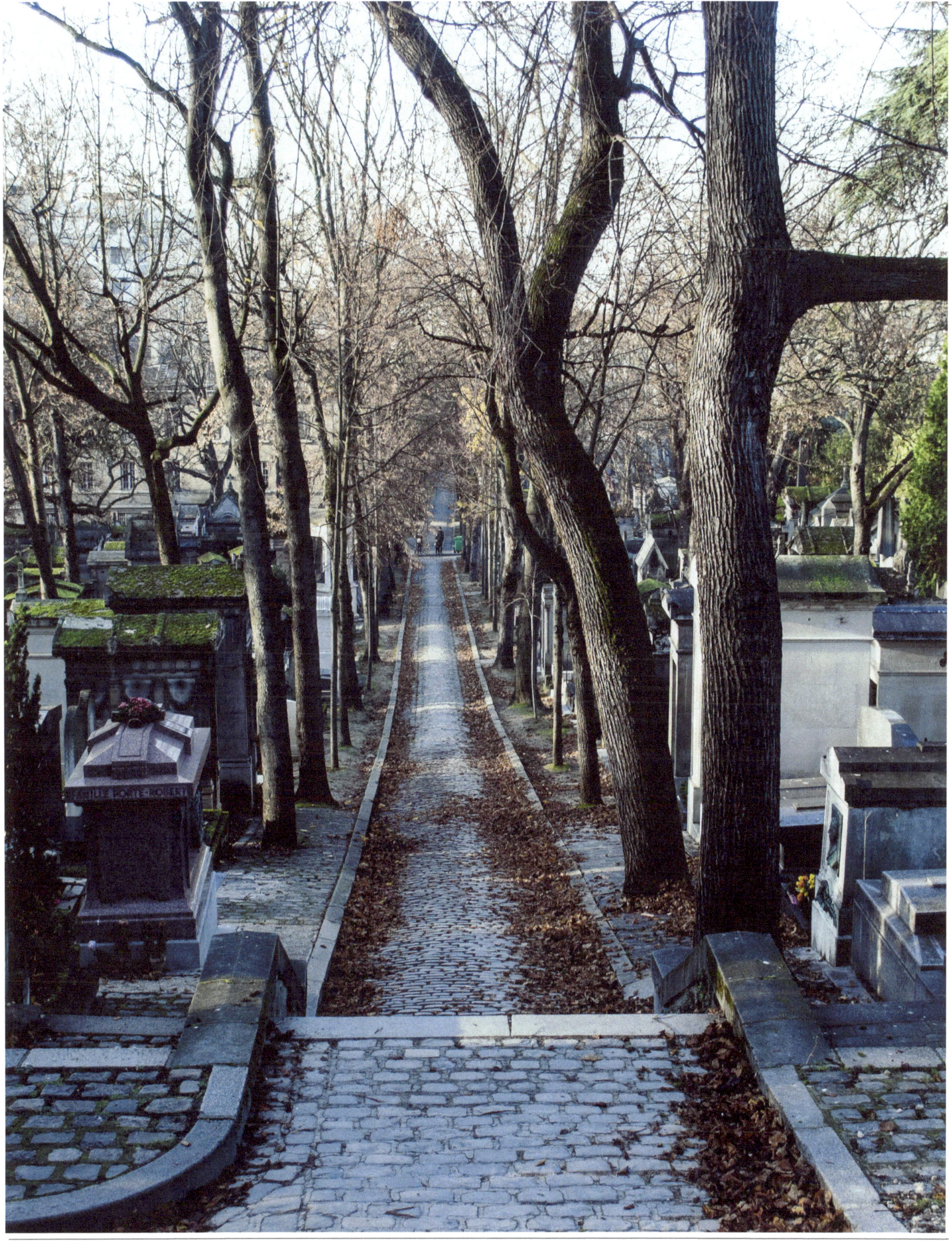

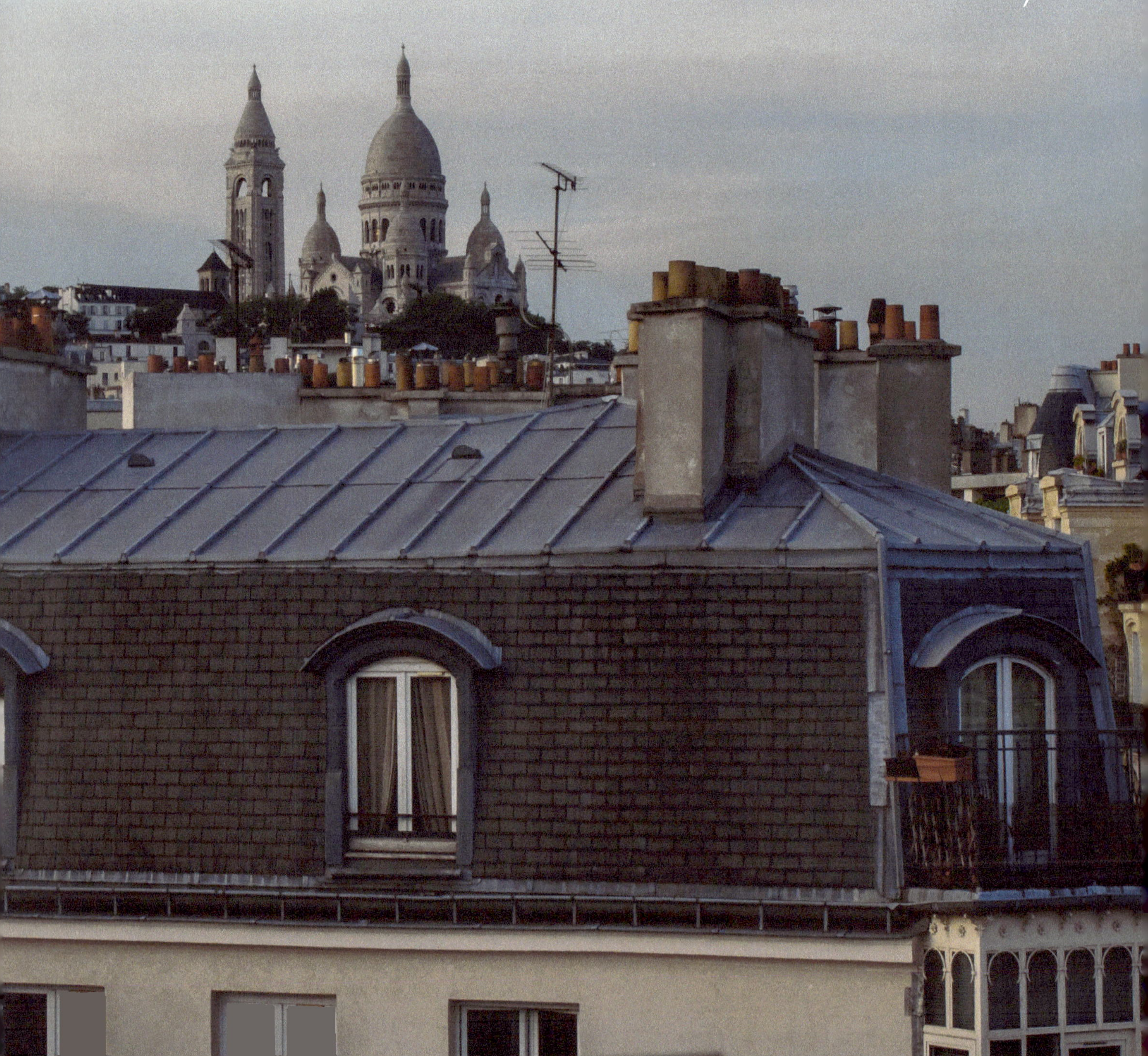
home of sacred hearts

"que jamais par la force on n'entra dans un coeur
et que toute âme est libre à nommer son vainqueur"

Molière

We noticed two dudes lying down at the main entrance of maybe the most famous cathedral in the world. It was late. No one else was around. Everything was shut. They noticed us. Five minutes later we're all on our backs at the feet of Notre Dame, staring up at the faint Parisian glow, passing a bottle of wine and having deep conversations I've long forgotten, but still feel. In the end, the local lads guided us back to our hotel, and then disappeared into the fog of my Parisian lore.

Around the same time *Paris, Je T'aime* came out—a collection of short films expressing the old world spirit that had captured my imagination. One story in particular struck me, that of a frumpy, middle-aged American's solo trip to the city she'd always wanted to visit. Entirely done as an inner monologue in French, she explores alone, contemplating the experience in her painful American accent (though impressively fluent and contextually charming).

Immediately, I connected to her thoughtful loneliness and curious independence.

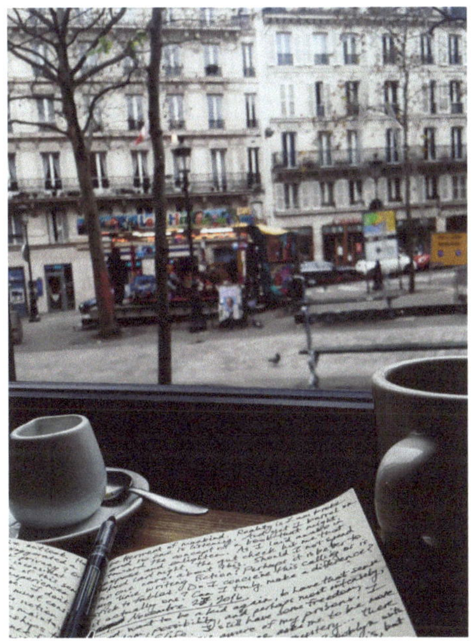

bleeding ink at
Pratz and KB CaféShop
Pigalle

What the story came to articulate is a bittersweet emotion so perfectly fit for Paris: melancholy.

A city filled with the drama of its history, the radical terror of revolution subtly soaks into your senses standing in the Place de la Concorde where Marie Antoinette and her king lost their heads. It's a conflicting sensation of pleasure and pain that pours through the Parisian streets like blood from the guillotine in 1793.

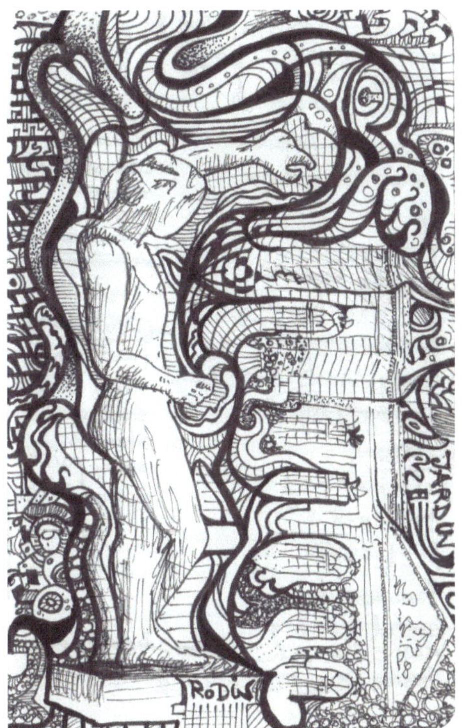

Like beloved children Simone de Beauvoir and Jean-Paul Sartre, Paris can't escape her existential crisis, and, therefore, is a gold mine for artists, thinkers, and soul searchers.

Heck, the original thinker lives in Paris and was created by a Parisian (you know, that sculpture of the guy in the quintessentially deep-thought pose). Visit him and find yourself contemplating the clouds in yet another hidden Parisian garden.

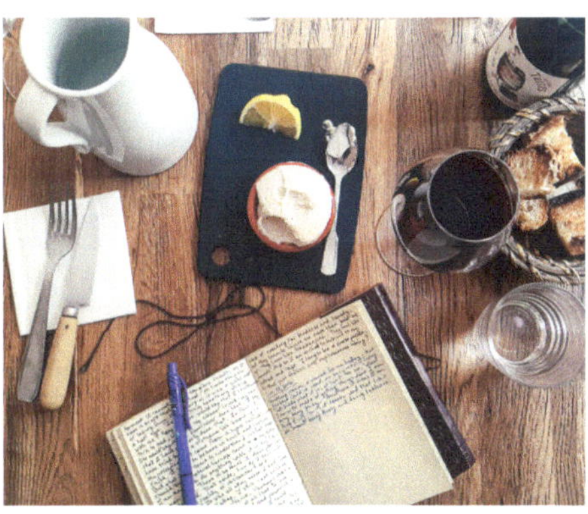

Chasing the ghost of American Parisian Ernest Hemingway, I walk through the Latin Quarter to Montparnasse and let my mind drift through the idealized melting pot of creativity found in Paris after The Great War and before the Nazi occupation stirred its sorrows once again. It's no wonder why Jim Morrison's enigmatic legend found its resting place in Pére Lachaise.

She's a classic film noir, standing outside the Moulin Rouge in a lace negligee. Painted red lips whisper to you in a foreign tongue that sounds like sex, and yet the smeared black eyeliner speaks of tears and trauma too heavy for this pretty thing. She takes a long drag from her freshly rolled cigarette, kisses you the way the French are famous for, and then eats your heart out.

A love affair with The City of Light is a rendezvous with your shadow.

She's a bitch. You have to deal with it. If that puts a kink in your conscious, she's probably not for you (unless you're into the other kind of kink).

Paris is the kind of place where you walk into the boulangerie speaking English and they speak back in French, but if you walk in speaking French (however terrible), they'll speak back in English. It's an important lesson. Be aware of your surroundings. You're in France, asshole. Make an effort. Learn how to say *"bonjour."*

Paris is the place to be a voyeur. Back in that original encounter, I remember being impressed by how the chairs were arranged at outdoor cafes all over the city. They aren't across from each other, but side by side. You're meant to sit and observe.

As far as I'm concerned, Paris invented the art of people watching.

The eye feast is a vampire bite that holds a mirror. Like creatures of the night that captivate our macabre fantasy, I am drawn to the alluring horror found in the furnace of introspection.

It's melancholy, this *bal-musette* with Paris. At times, I was done with it. On my third trip to Paris I found myself complaining about how sleepy the city seemed. Unlike the metropolis I called home at the time, New York, the Paris streets are empty well before midnight. *This town is drab.* Or so I thought.

I would later come to understand Paris is actually like a giant speakeasy. I recall one particular party on the edges of Paris where the house was rammed with people and the band played all night, but step outside to get a reprieve from the smoke, sweat, and sin, and you're suddenly in a ghost town.

Before I finally leapt into being nomadic, Paris was the citadel of my fantasy. Now, nearly a decade into life without a place I call home, Paris is one of those places where I can feel at home. I haven't lived there, per se. Just passed through a lot. More than I can count. And I've certainly done quite a bit of living in Pigalle, Le Marais, Oberkampf, and San-Germain des Prés. But now I'm just being a pedantic dick. How French, right? Consider it inside information.

The wannabe Parisian in me relates to the morose satisfaction found in a city always battling itself. Spend a day walking and you're bound to find a protest. They happen all the time.

Revolt is part of the cultural fabric.

The blood that runs through these streets will keep pumping, and you'll find yourself staring into the mirror of Paris saying, *I'm not sure I like myself (but these fangs are kinda sexy).*

In the turmoil, I find a connection to my own American culture of persistent metamorphosis.

Simultaneously adoring and despising ourselves, we shame slave-owning founders while clinging to the enlightenment ideals they enshrined (and that gave Paris its "city of light" nickname). It feels satisfying and uncomfortable at the same time.

Perhaps I'm being too melancholy. Not all of us are weirdos like the Emperor of Montmartre, Salvador Dali. I know. What the hell does that mean, anyway? I've already lost you several times here. Okay. Fine. Let's take a step back.

Discovery is a long romance, and it doesn't matter how well you dance at the start.

I remember sitting on the bus to Newark, en route to Paris for the umpteenth time. The woman in front of me was headed there, too. It was her first time. She bragged on the phone of her dinner reservation overlooking the Eiffel Tower. Finally, she would be visiting the Louvre and Musée d'Orsay as she'd always dreamed. It was cute.

Even though my vampire looks up at the charred remnants of Notre Dame with some sort of *vie de merde*, metaphorical satisfaction, basking in self-loathing and sophistication while scoffing at the bourgeoisie taking selfies, I still turn down unknown Parisian streets and think, *golly gee, that sure is purdy.*

The veneer of Paris lives up to the hype. If you're not awestruck you might have the Stars and Stripes shoved so far up your ass you can't taste the freedom fries anymore.

Too dark? Relax. It's a joke. All I'm saying is that if Paris doesn't make your jaw drop, you're probably biased and didn't learn how to say "*bonjour.*"

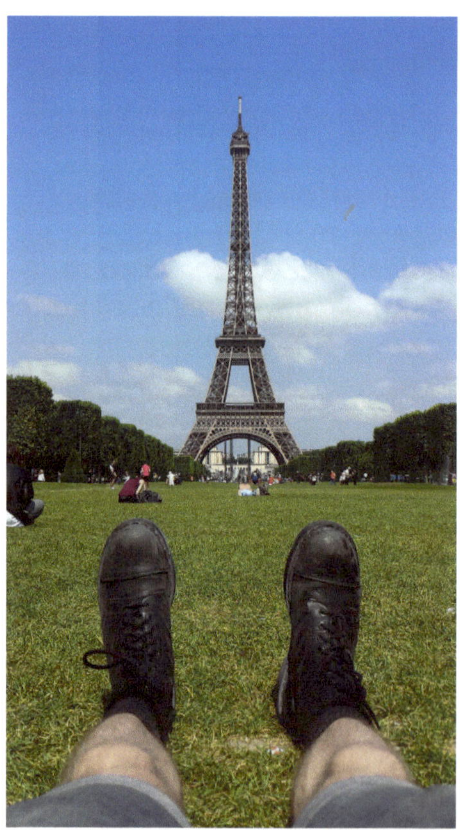

the shoes I wore every day
and other things

I identify with Alceste.

Here I go being pedantic again. For those of you who don't have a useless degree in theater, he's the main character from the most famous play of France's Shakespeare. Moliere is dead in a Pére Lachaise box, but his misanthrope is alive and well. He just might be the perfect Parisian, disgusted by petty prattle and basic bitches, but charmed by simple pleasures and youthful beauty nonetheless. That's pretty much how I feel every time I walk down the Champs Ellysees. *I hate this. I love this. WTF is wrong with me? I'm an idiot. This is great. Maybe I should go into exile.*

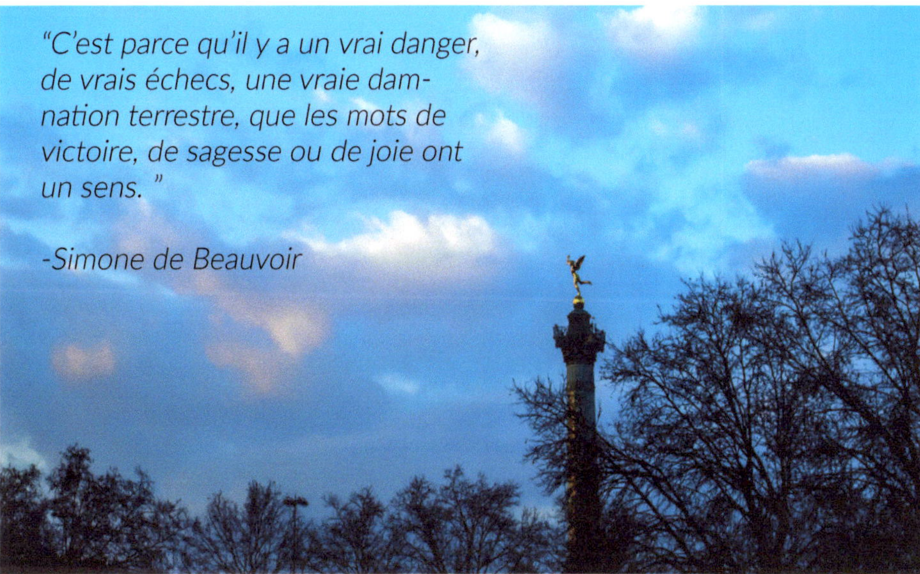

Do I sound crazy? It's how I feel trying to articulate my experience of Paris and how she expresses a fundamental aspect of my connection to *the Old World.*

I consulted a friend: "Paris. One word. Go!"

"This is stupid," he replied, "But the first word that came to mind is croissant."

Fair. French pastries are legit. The *croissant almonde* changed my life. Or maybe it was the *pain au raisin*. The classic *pain au chocolate* never fails.

It's worth a trip to Paris just for the bread.

You might also be amused seeing "pain" written on the door where you find pleasure for your mouth. Bread is pain. More French lessons for that fat ass.

Back to the inquiry, my buddy eventually arrived at a place you might find simultaneously unfamiliar and familiar, Pére Lachasie.

"I love to grab a baguette and just hang out there," he said.

The notion of a joyous picnic in a dreary cemetery might seem odd. But in Paris, it makes perfect sense. Do you feel me yet?

Let's bring this to a close, shall we? Or at least find an end to this beginning.

According to my 23andMe results, my old world ancestors are 25.7% "French & German", which seems like a bizarre pairing considering recent history, but the more you dive into *the Old World*, you discover Europe is just as hodgepodge as the USA. Even more so in some ways. A trip to Alsace (a few hours from Paris and just before Germany) will teach you such border towns are both countries and neither.

In robot speak, the density at which this cross-pollinating phenomenon exists matched with the longevity of its collective civilizations is what makes Europe so special. The internet says it has more World Heritage Sites than any other continent. Cold, hard data that helps me rationalize my argument.

I call it *the Old World* because, love it or hate it, the empires of Europe are my mommy and daddy.

Let's be clear, I'm not trying to convince you to visit Paris. This is the land of Le Miserables and forlorn hunchbacks. The melancholy is not for everybody. What I am suggesting, as the Street Musician of Amsterdam recommended (we'll get there, don't worry), is that you get out of your shitty town and see the world. The mindfuck will do you some good.

Paris helped me understand the nuance of loving and hating something at the same time. Can you handle the kink?

children of the universe can never grow old

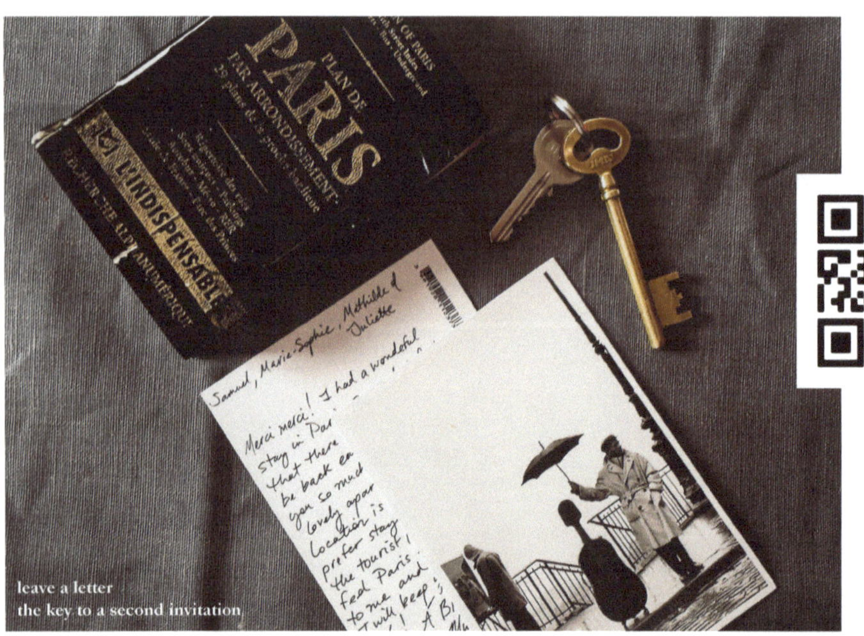

leave a letter
the key to a second invitation

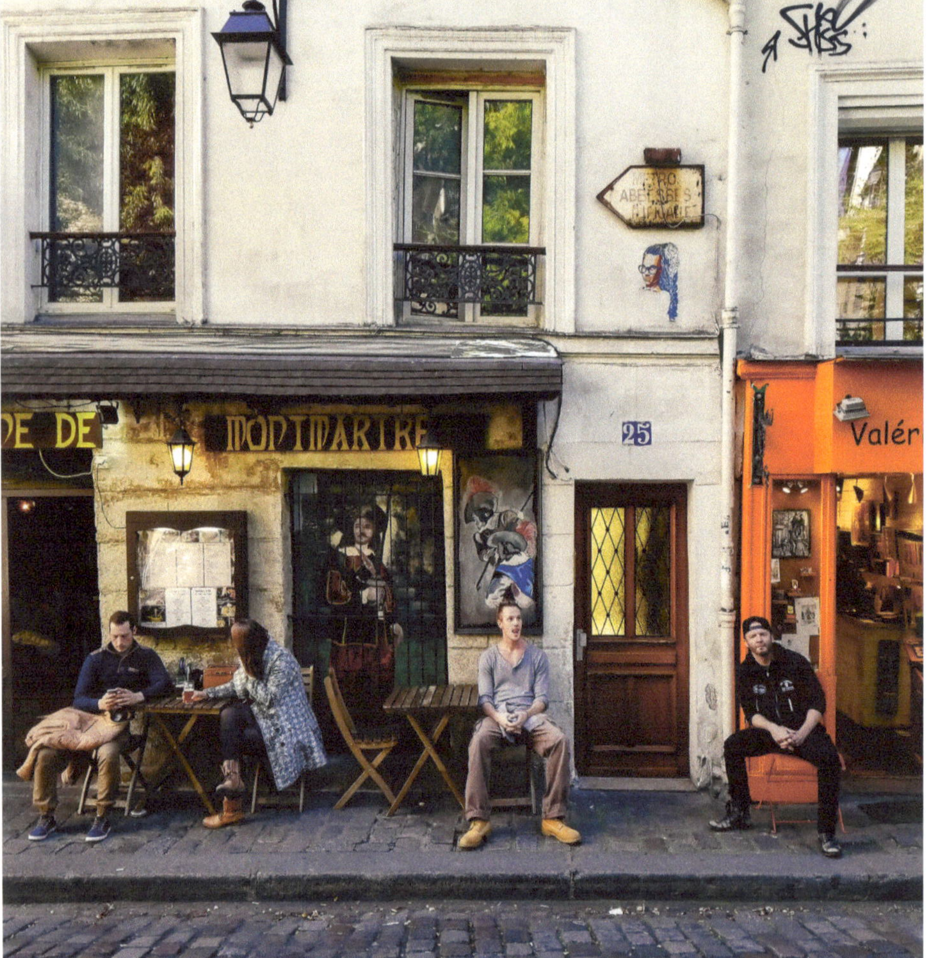

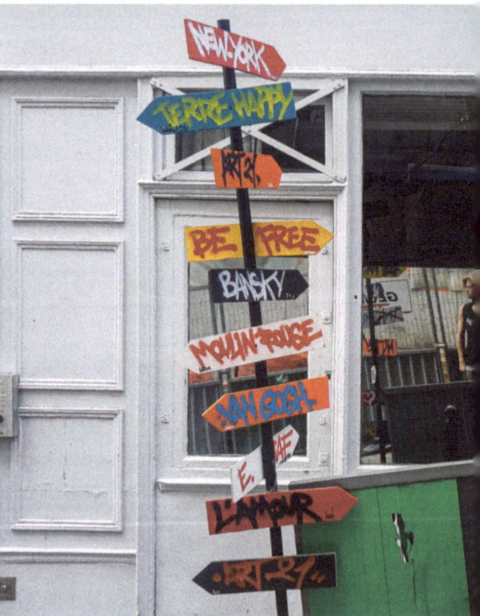

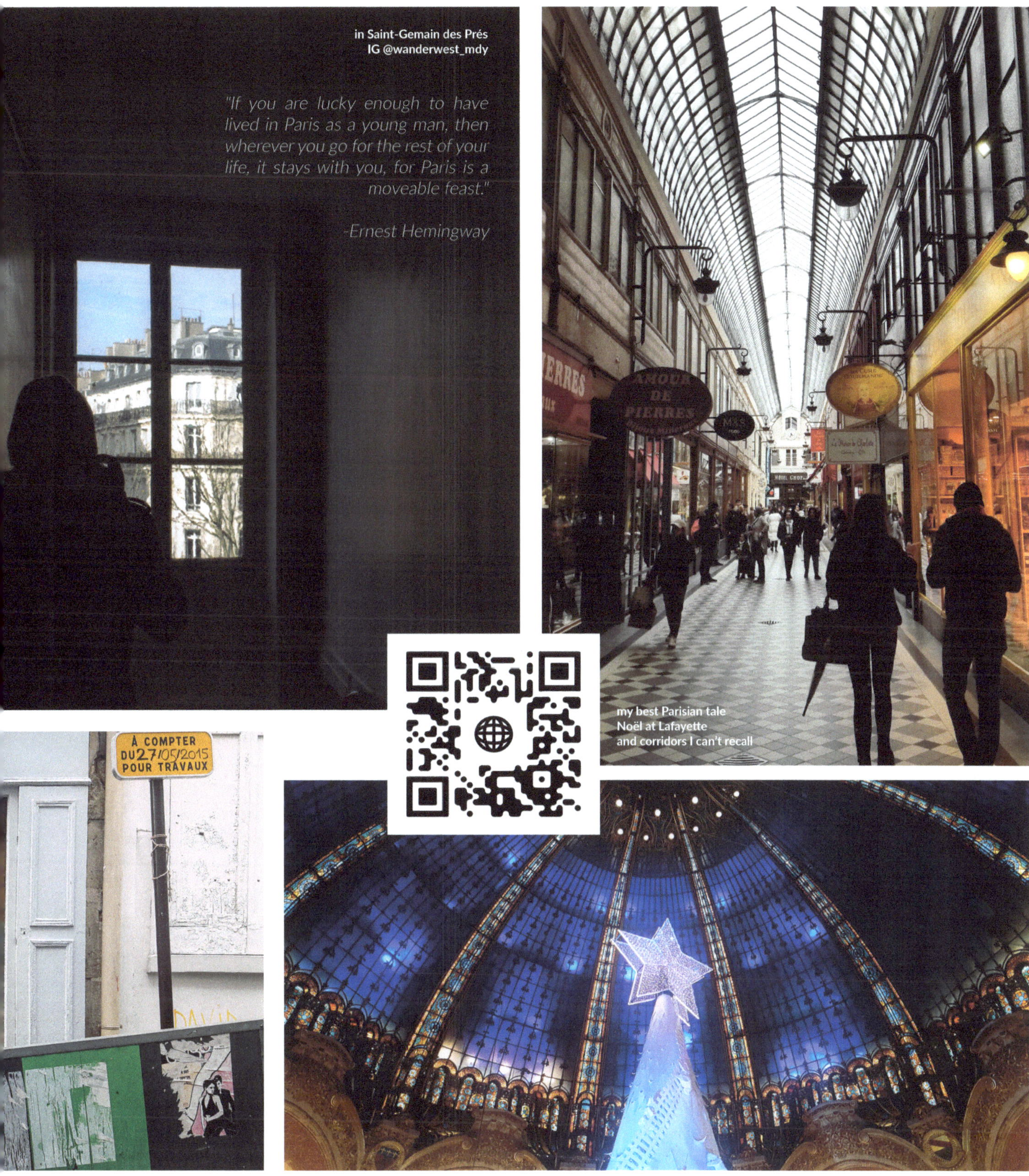

in Saint-Gemain des Prés
IG @wanderwest_mdy

"If you are lucky enough to have lived in Paris as a young man, then wherever you go for the rest of your life, it stays with you, for Paris is a moveable feast."

-Ernest Hemingway

my best Parisian tale
Noël at Lafayette
and corridors I can't recall

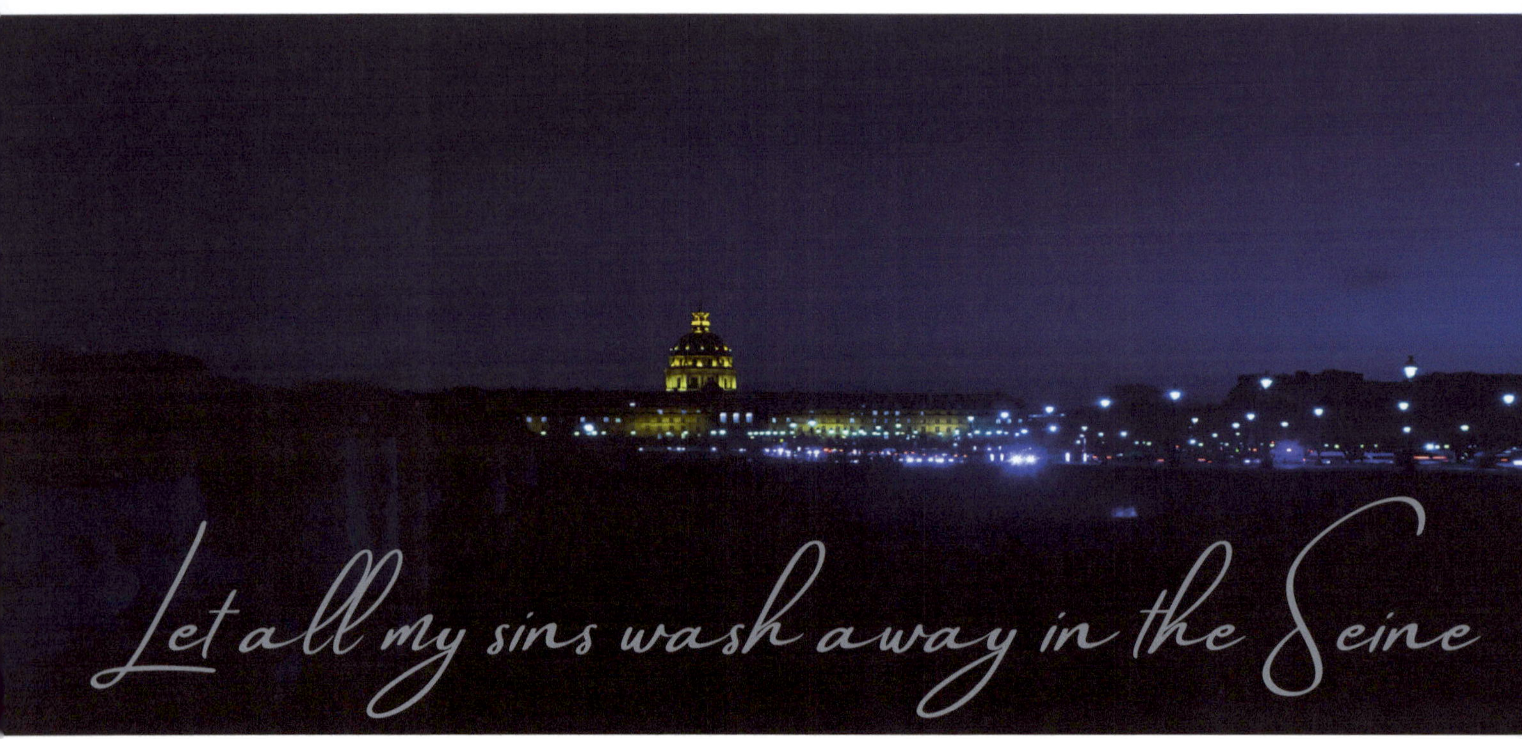

Let all my sins wash away in the Seine

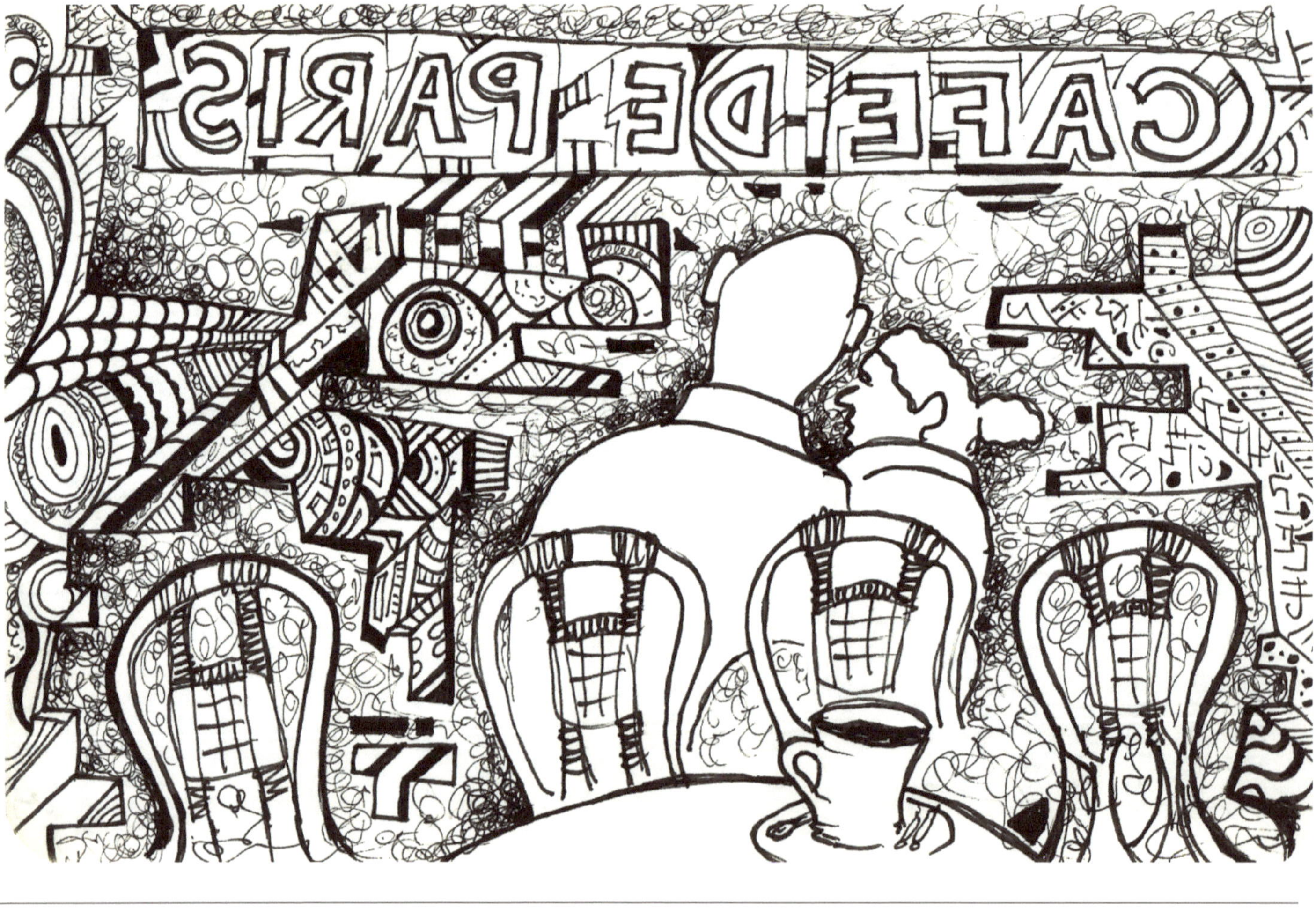

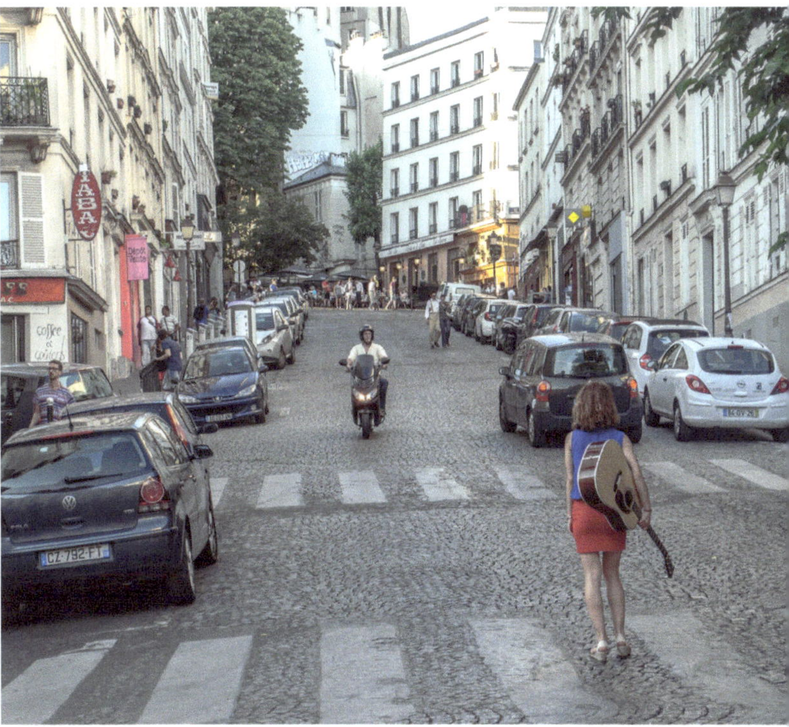
MAKE
ART
NOT
WAR
MAKE
ART
NOT
WAR
LA NUIT
J'
CRAINS
PLUS
VENIR
DEMI PORTION
NOUVEL ALBUM
LES HISTOIRES
25/11/13 DANS LES BACS
Châtelet 15 mn
Luxembourg 25 mn

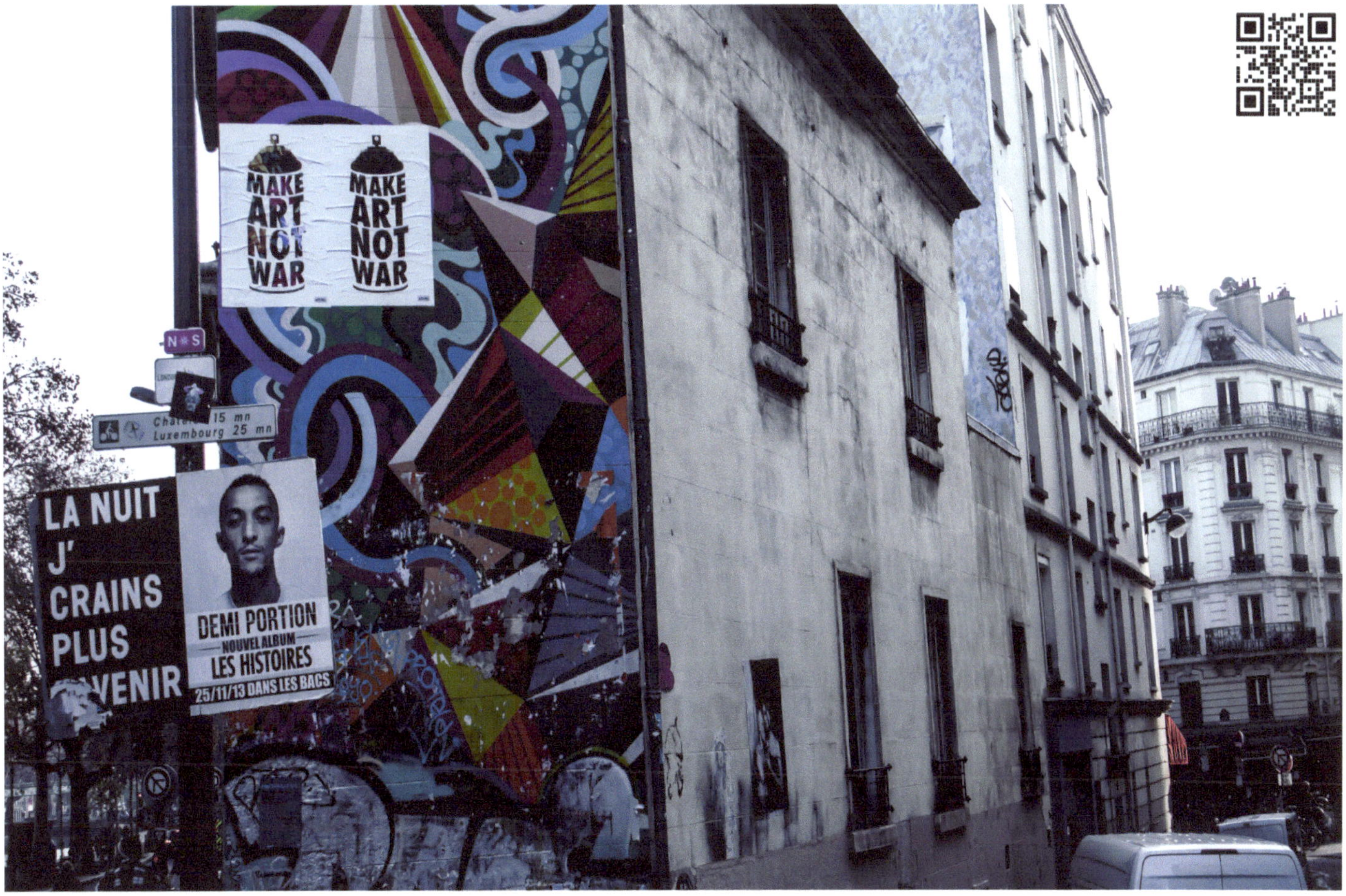

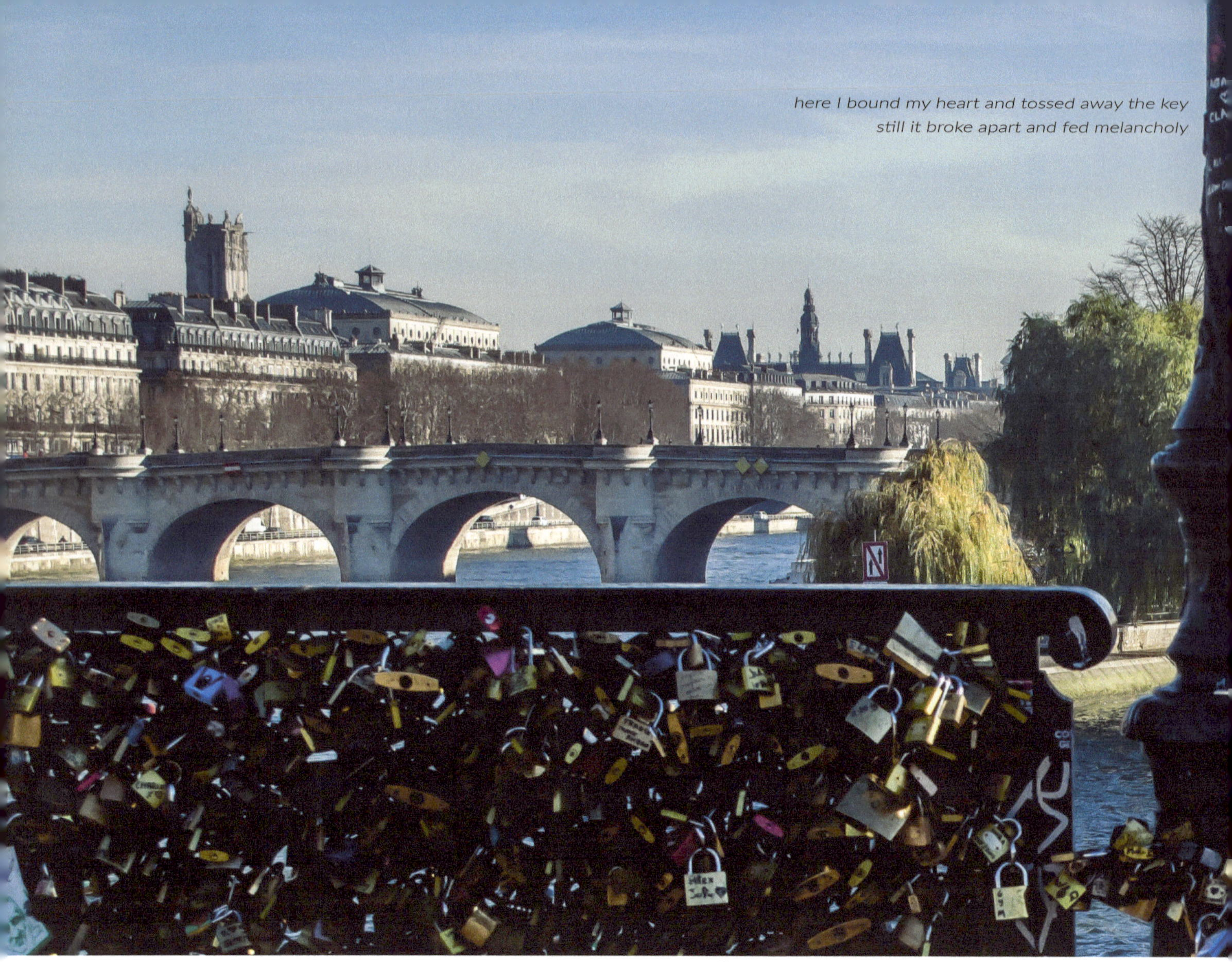

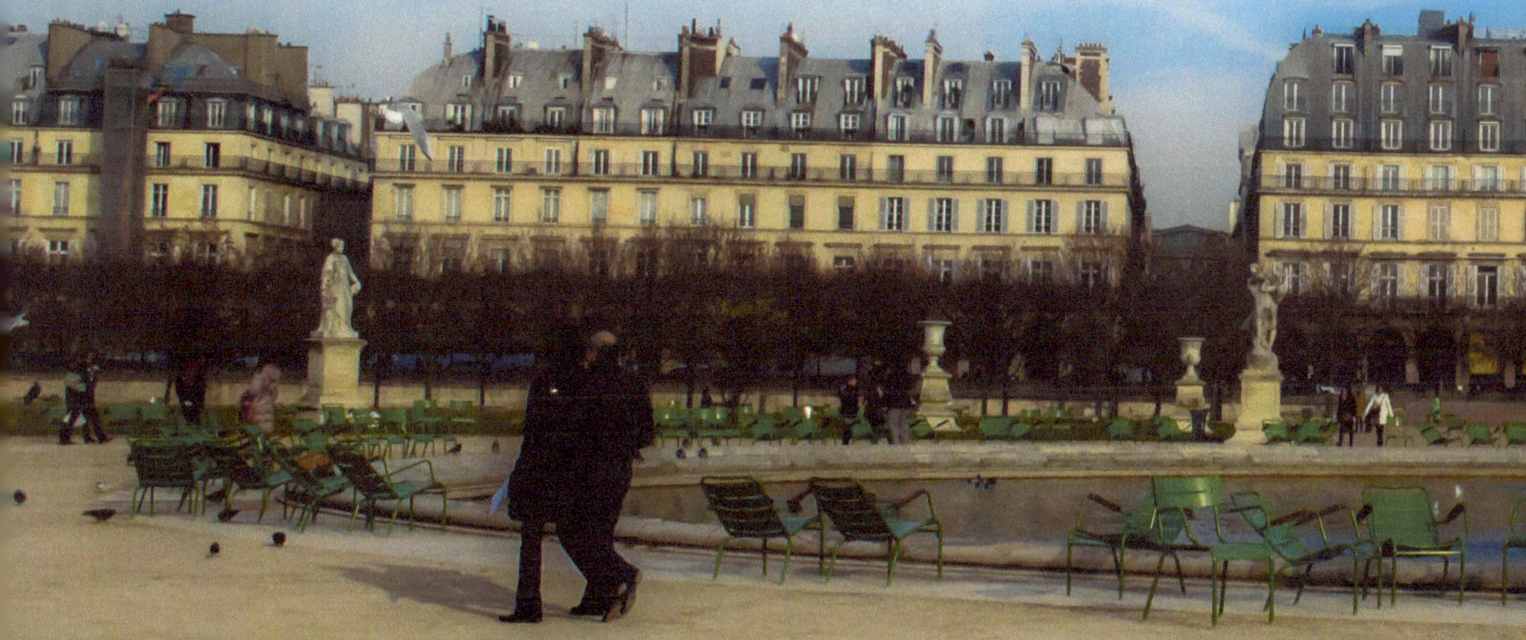

"When good Americans die,

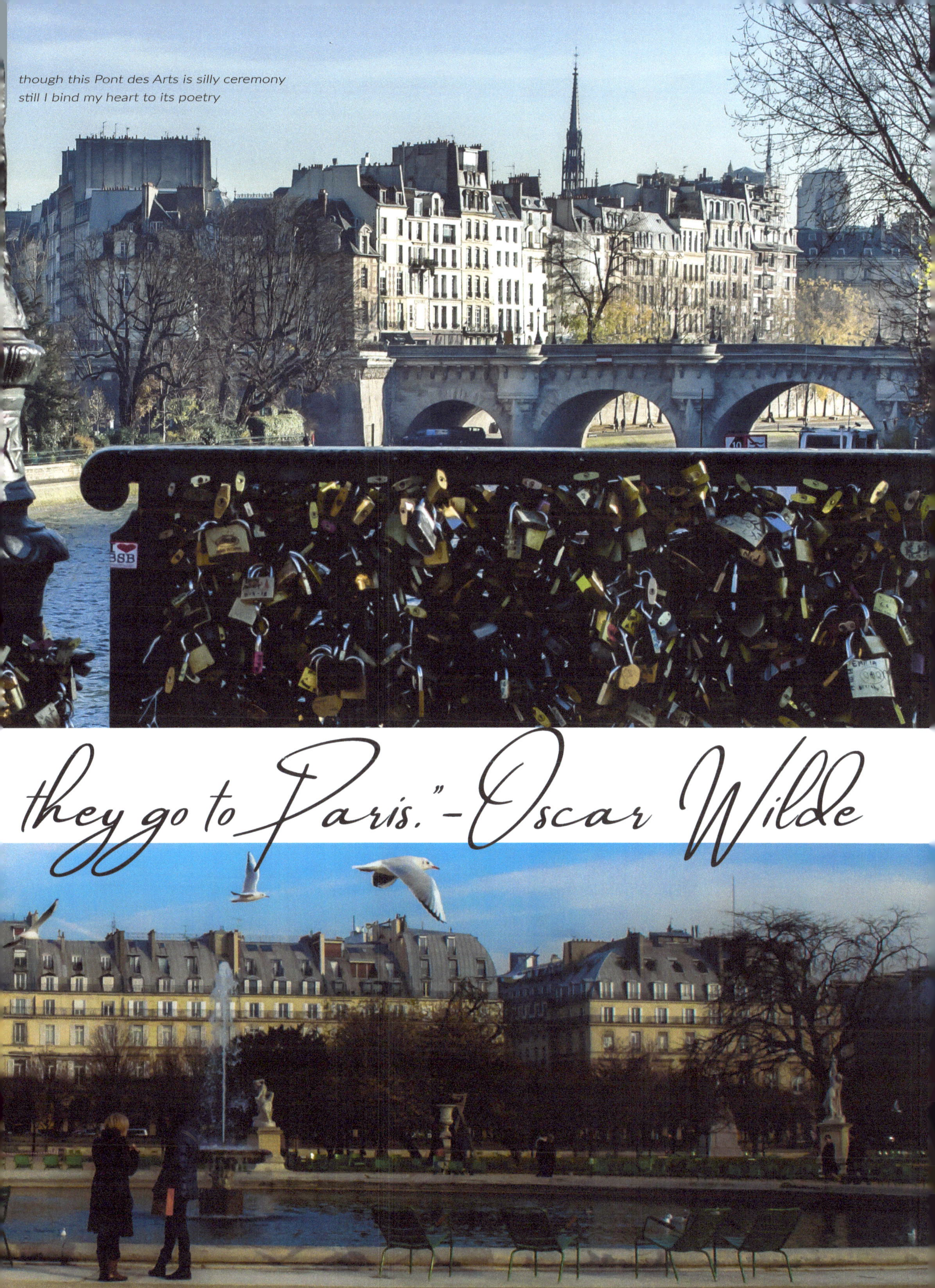
though this Pont des Arts is silly ceremony
still I bind my heart to its poetry
they go to Paris." -Oscar Wilde

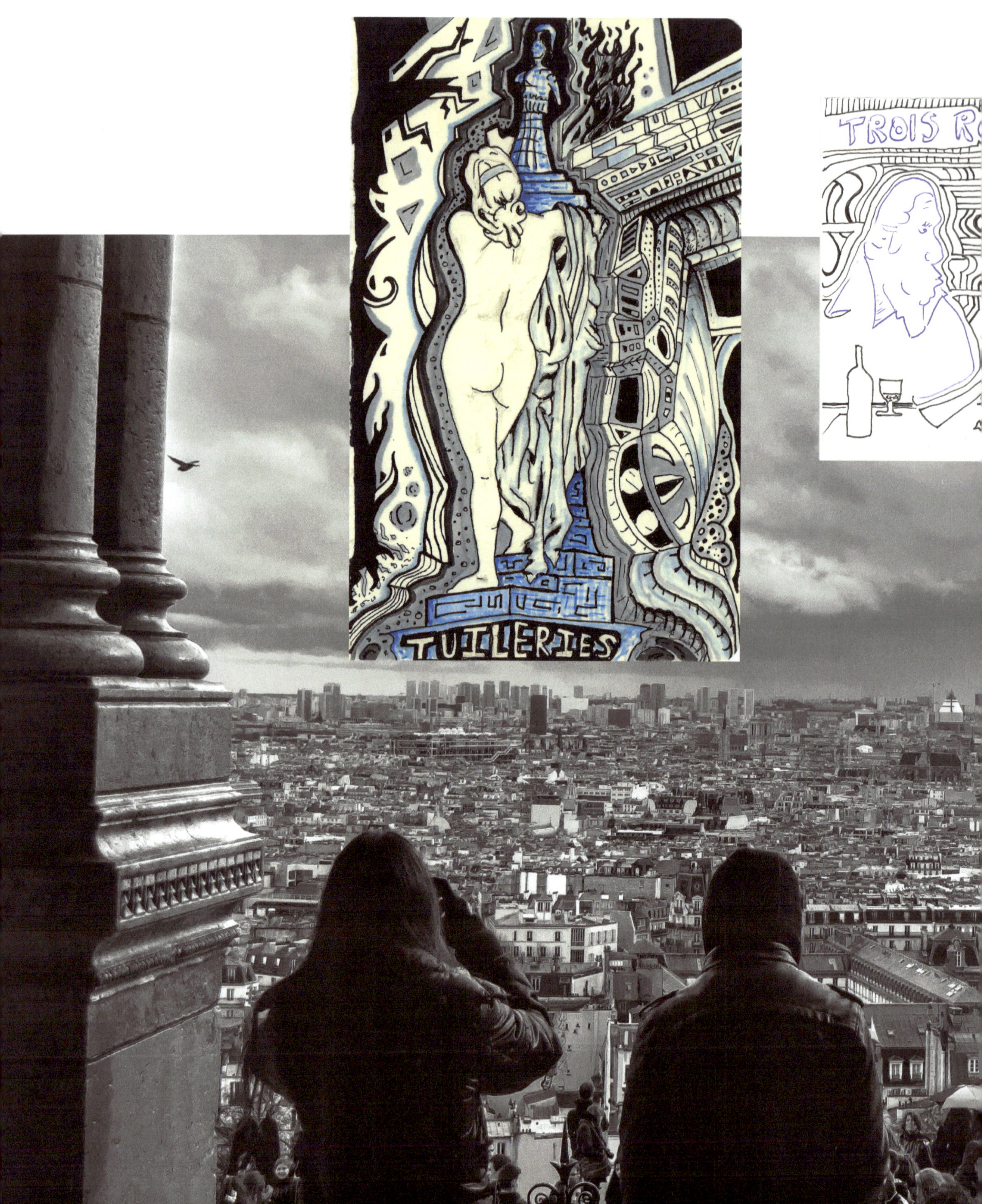
TUILERIES
TROIS R

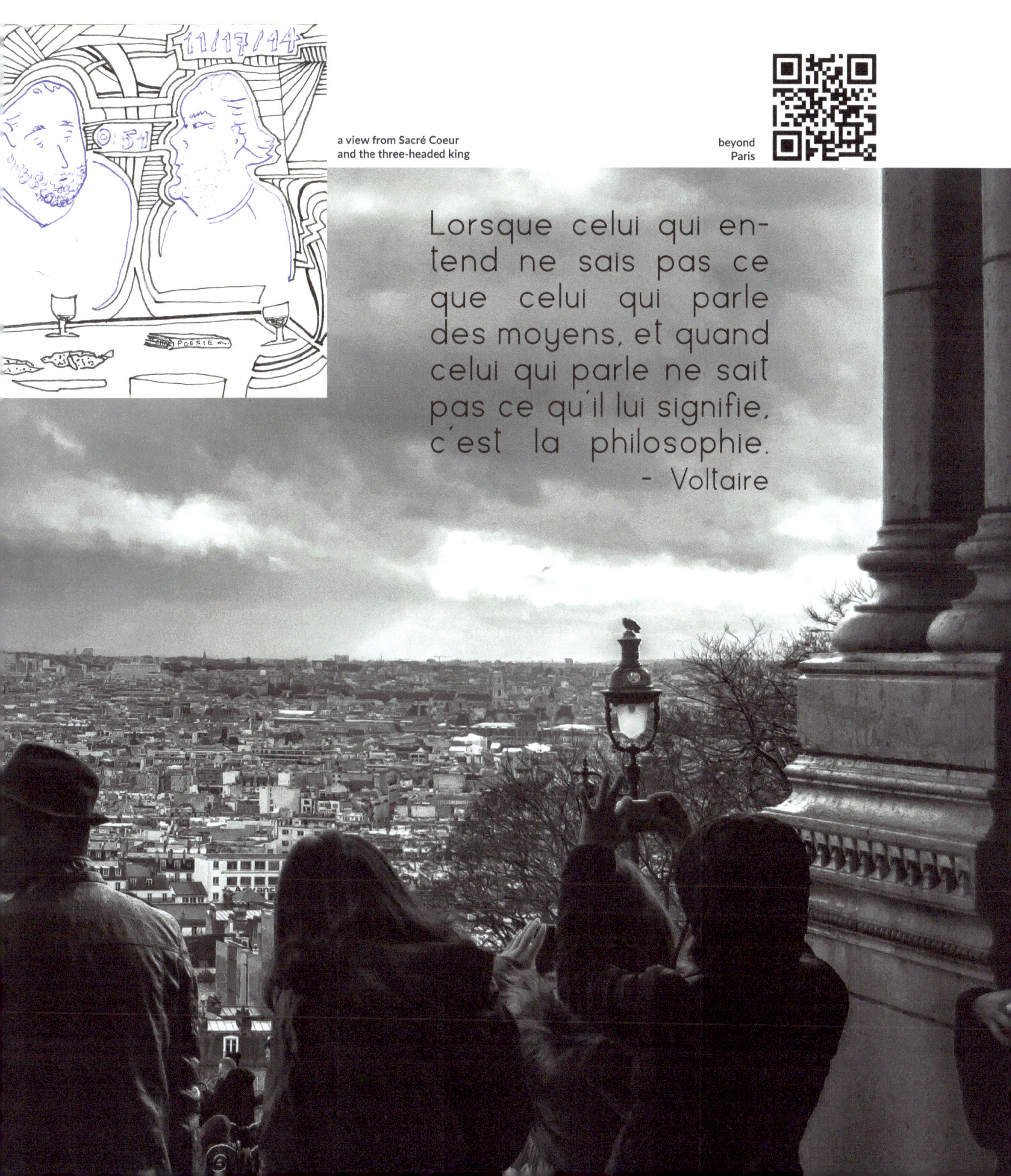

a view from Sacré Coeur
and the three-headed king

beyond
Paris

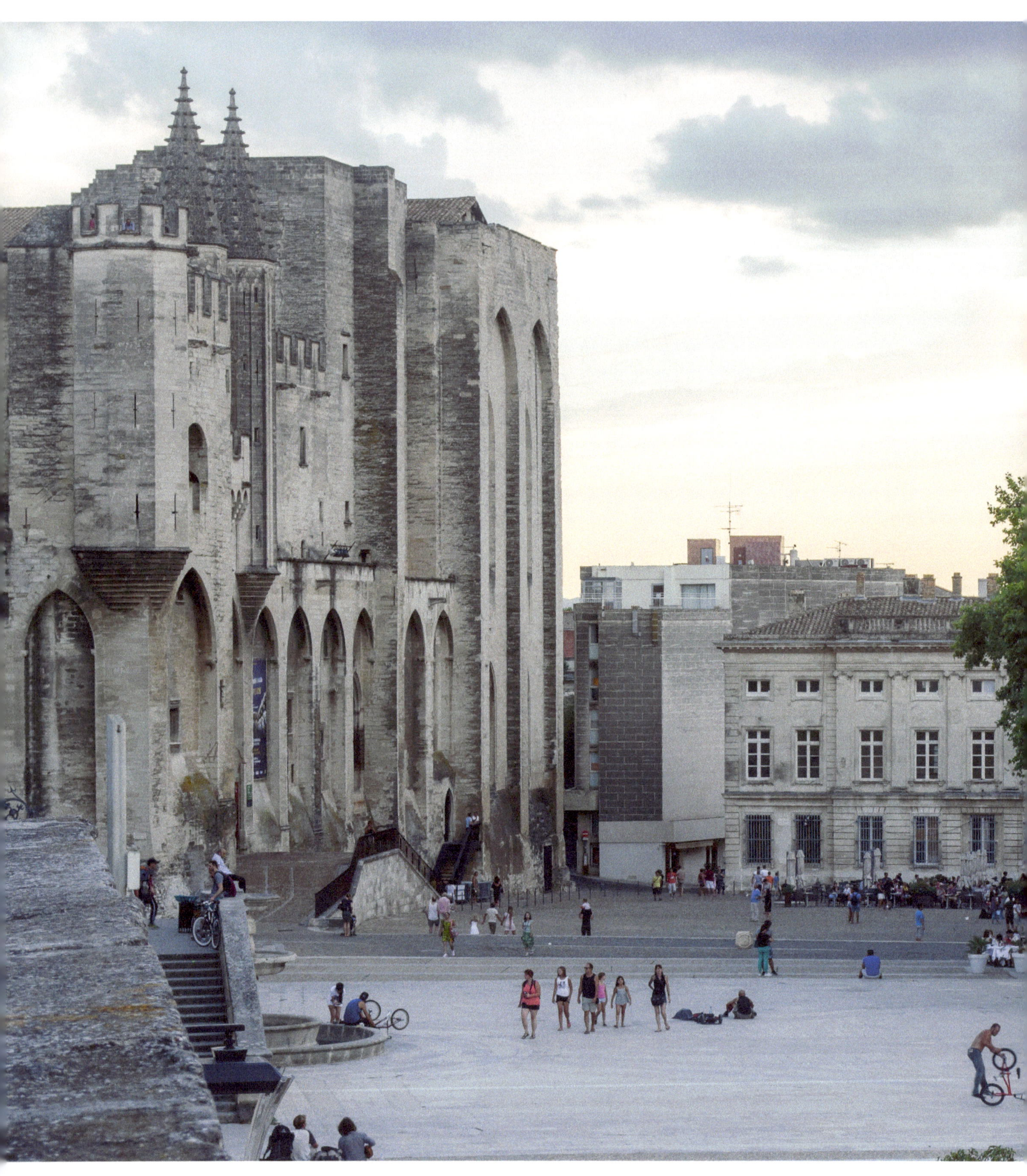

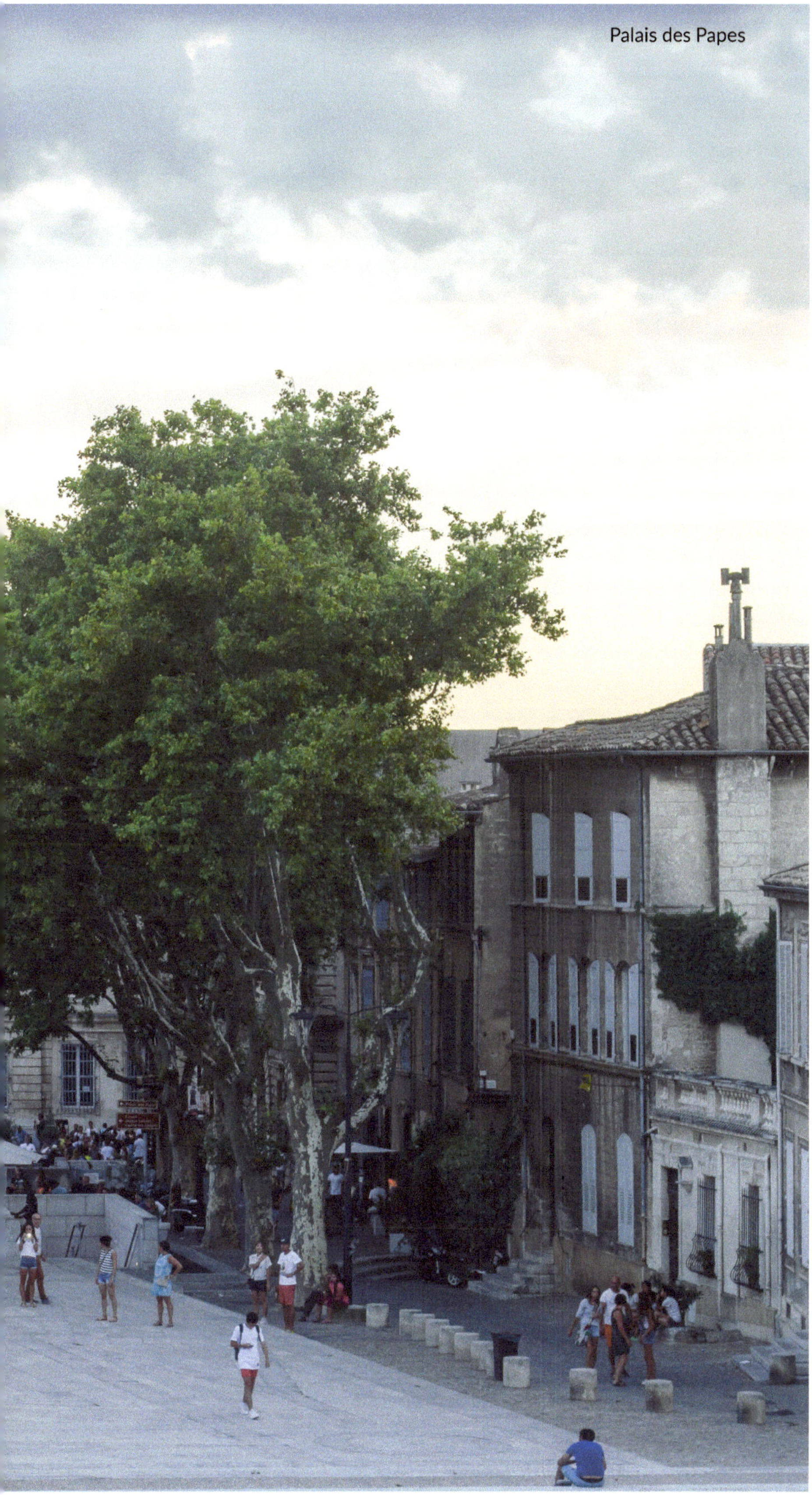

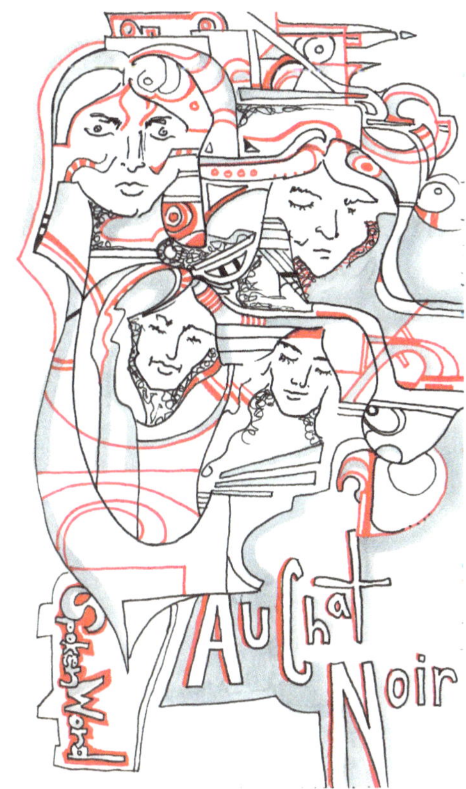

Palais des Papes

We are all trapped in Purgatory
Not you, not I; but we
Though the story may differentiate
The state is the same
The poor still laugh
The rich feel pain
There is no peak without a valley
For you, for me, for all life is folly

My love for you is like the heavens
Vast & varied beyond comprehension
A mansion of stars beyond my understanding
The suspension of all things I thought I knew

It seems to me growing up is
never ending, I'm allways the child
into the wild, chasing the man I
think I am, but it seems to me the
boy I was is no longer me, caught
inbetween infancy & infinity, out
of innocence into making sense

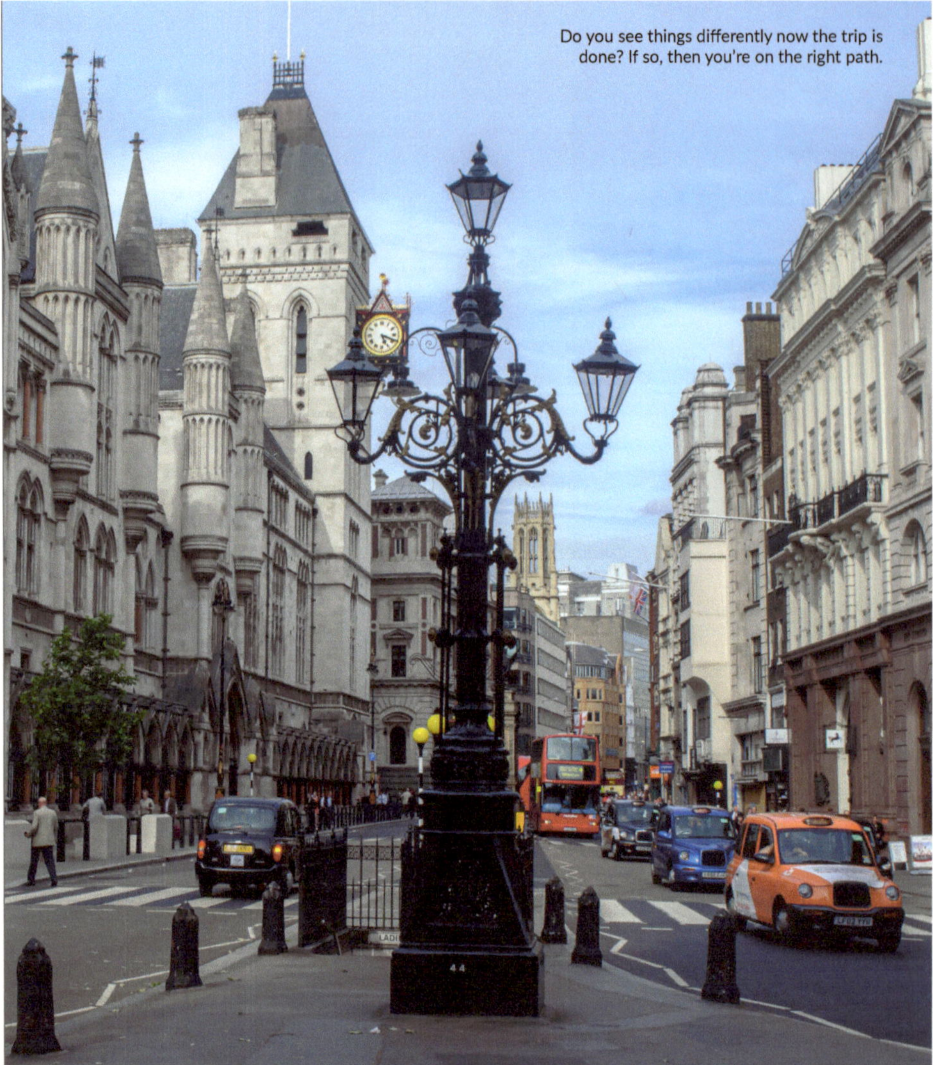

the City of London

not to be confused
with Londontown

It's my original travel tenet, a fundamental rule for nomads (or those seeking to be).

It wasn't scratching through a bucket list that guided me to destinations across the world, but invitations (and a bed). I followed friends who would let me stay.

It's because of this practical fact that I was able to push aside the veil of tourism and experience Paris, Amsterdam, Valencia, and so many old world treasures from the inside out.

Before I got philosophical about it, glocalism was simply a way to celebrate my transient, global wanderlust while recognizing the culture I craved was deepest felt in experiences I could only have through the guidance of a local.

I recall the story of an eager explorer determined to be the youngest person to visit every country on Earth. By 27, she achieved her goal with an average of three or four days in each country. At first glance, you may consider this human well traveled. Well, that's just about all she did—travel.

The question is: did she ever really stop anywhere?

I don't think so.

There's a long running debate between a friend and me. On a train from Paris to Amsterdam, we briefly got off and stood on the platform while the train took a ten-minute pause in Brussels. My friend says he's been to the Belgian capitol. I've made that same trip at least ten times since then. As far as I'm concerned, I've still yet to go to Brussels.

Make friends. It's the only shortcut.

the glocalist challenge is to stay on the move, but stay long enough to be moved.

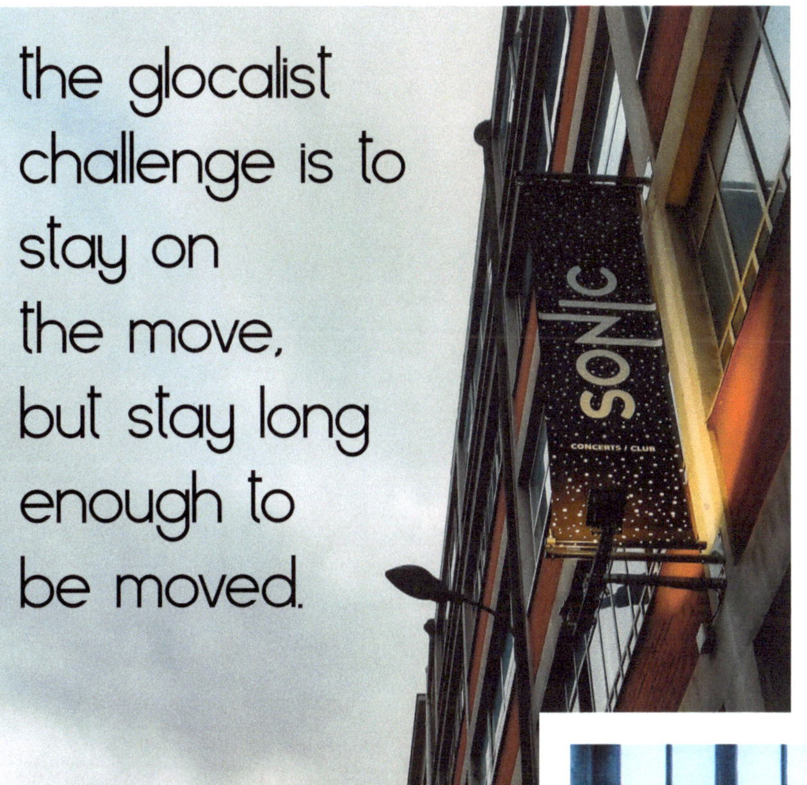

a dispatch from year one

venues in Paris I once played

an angel found in Versailles

Traveling is not about the countries counted, but the experiences collected. It's new perspectives, not stamps in a passport.

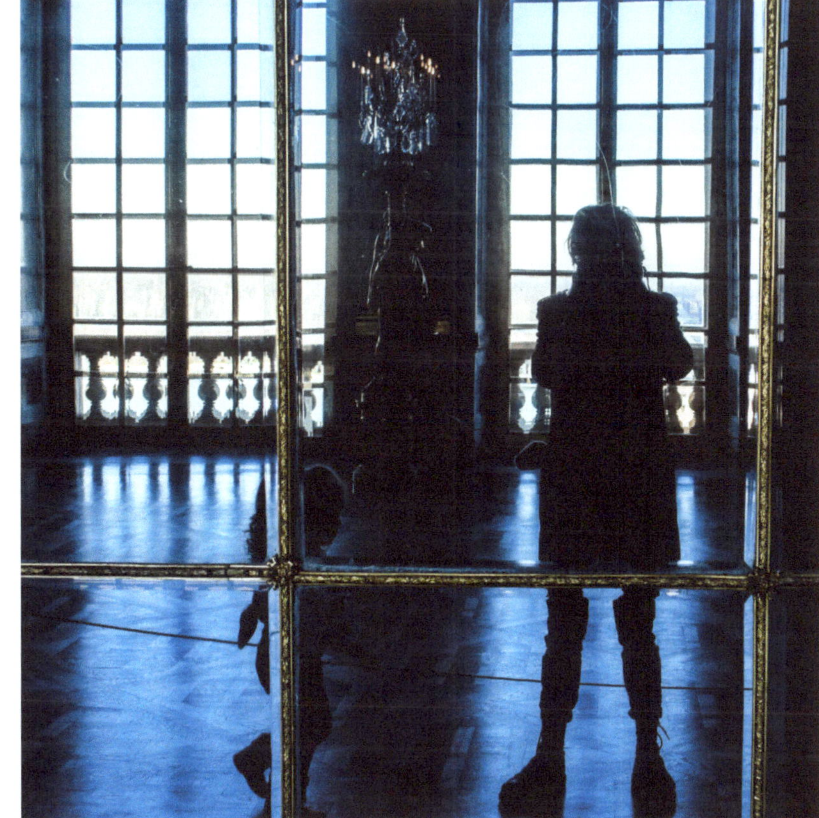

Are you picking up what I'm putting down? The goal of a glocalist is not to see as much as possible, but to dive as deep as possible. You might say it's to travel without traveling.

Does the Red Light District define Amsterdam? Does the Colosseum define Rome? Um. No. If it's a true cultural experience you want, don't spend your European vacation trying to do four countries in two weeks, as if you can cram thousands of years into an Instagram post. Go to Berlin and stay there. You might actually start feeling like an insider.

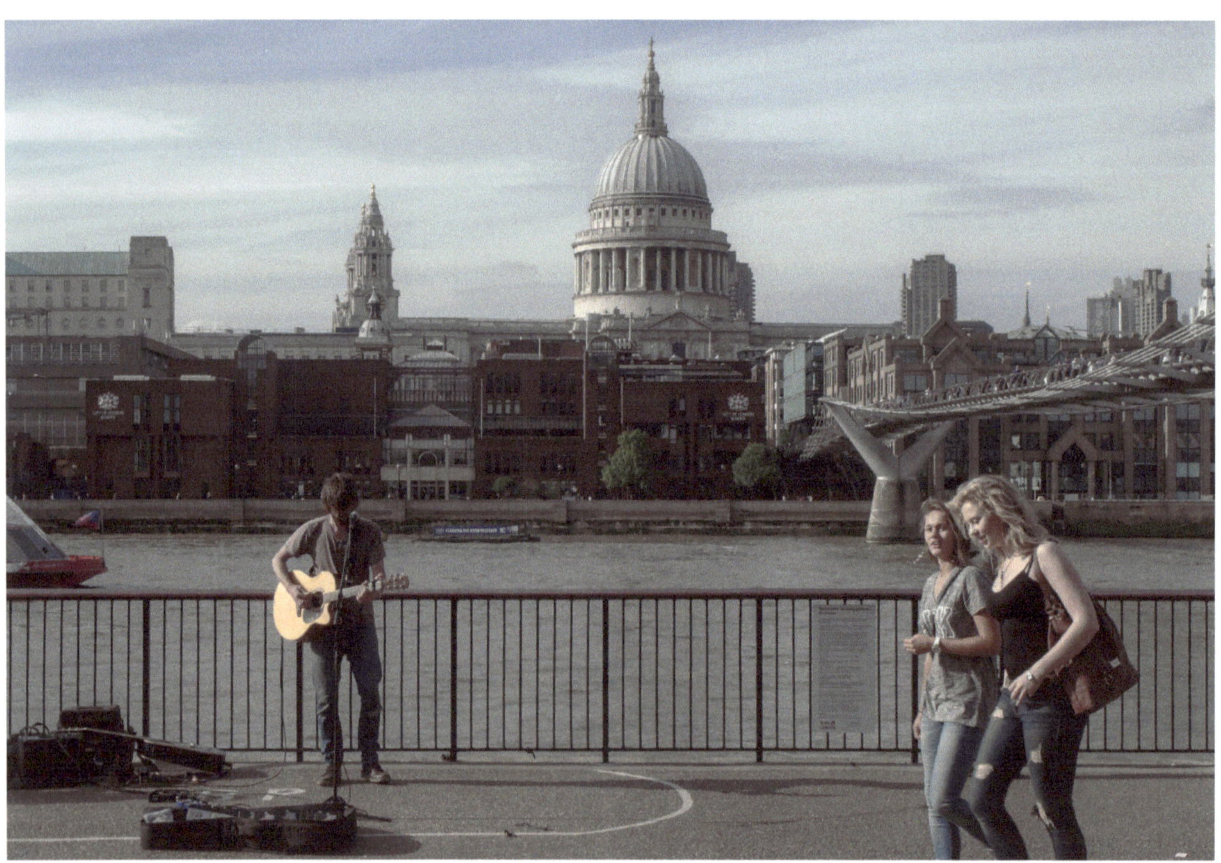

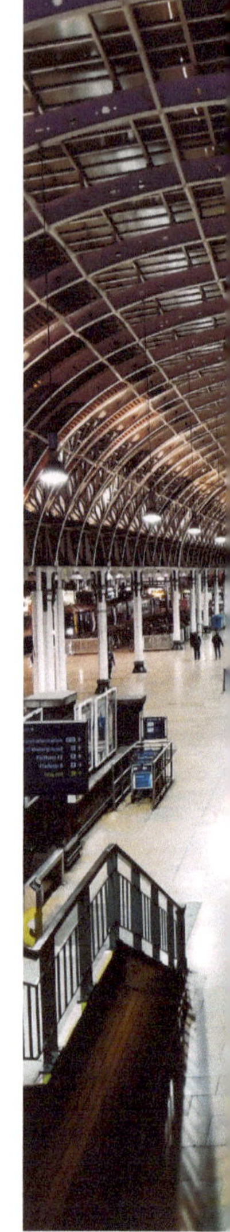

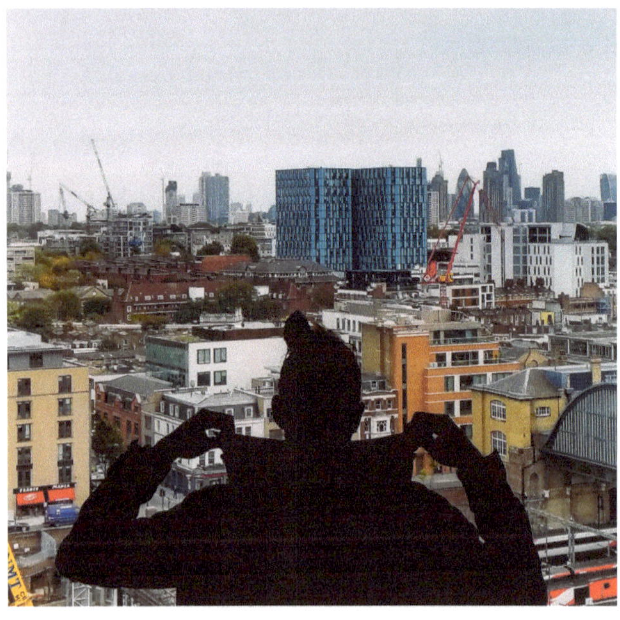

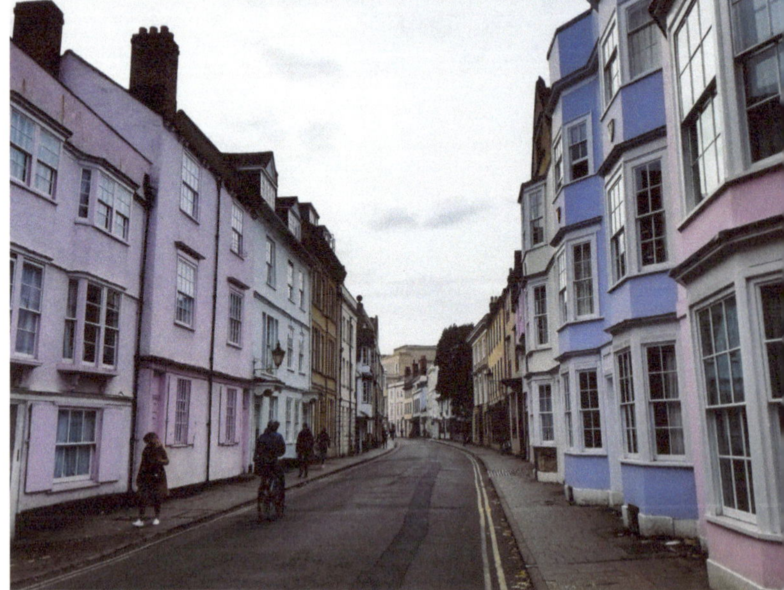

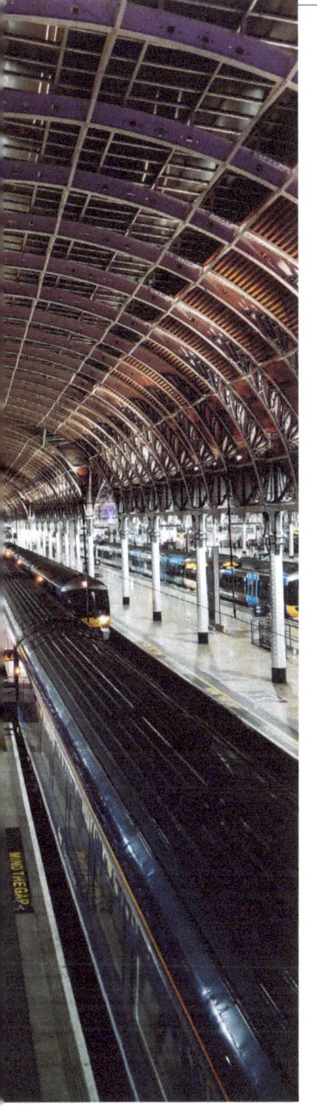

*kingdoms
unite*

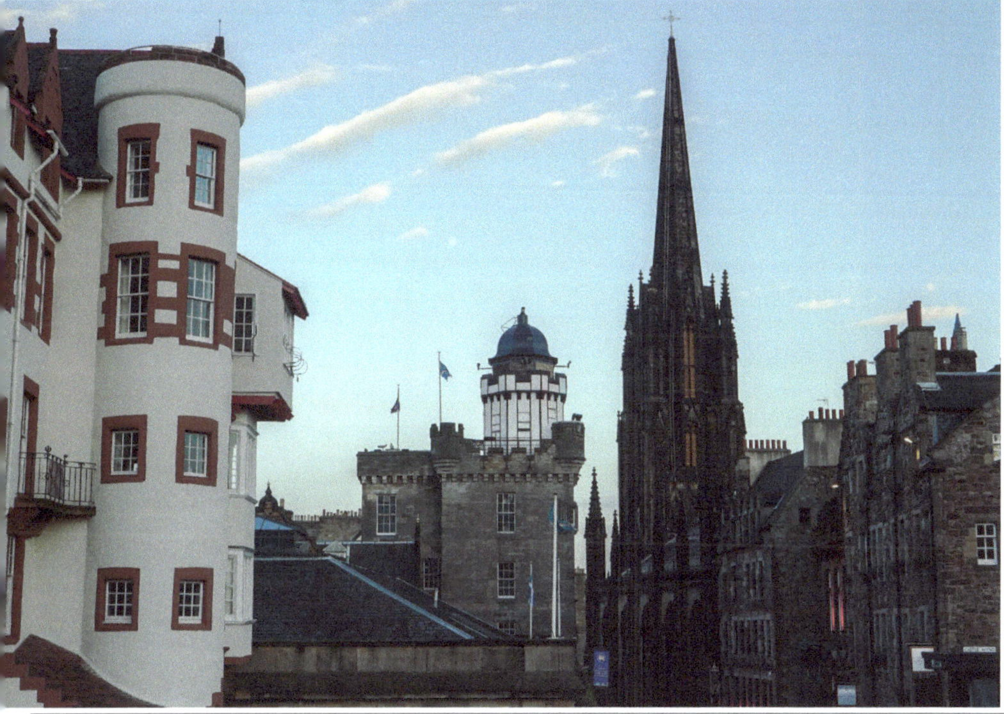

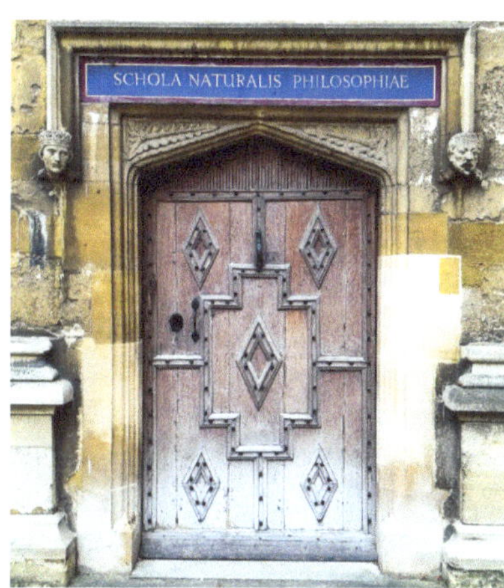

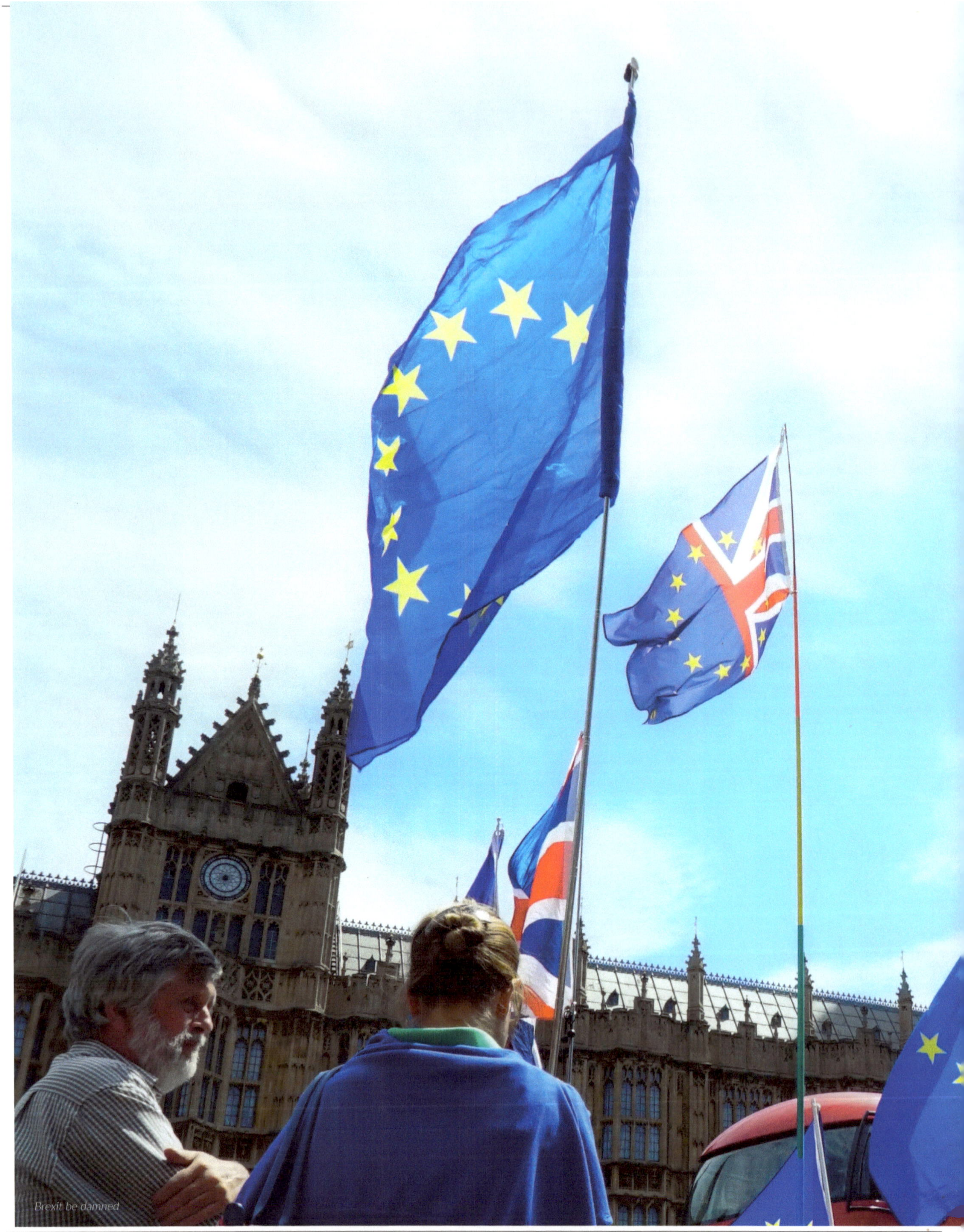

Brexit be damned

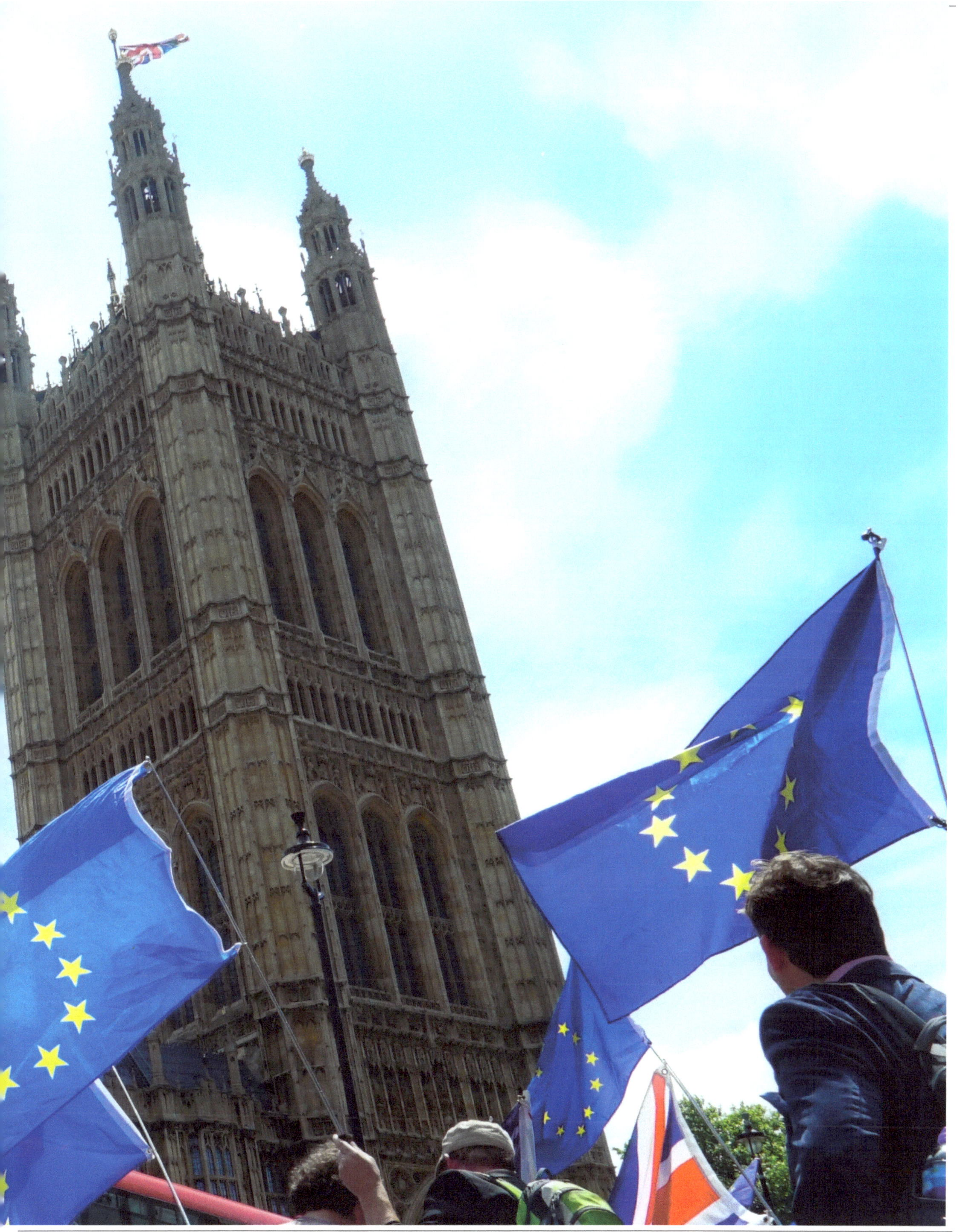

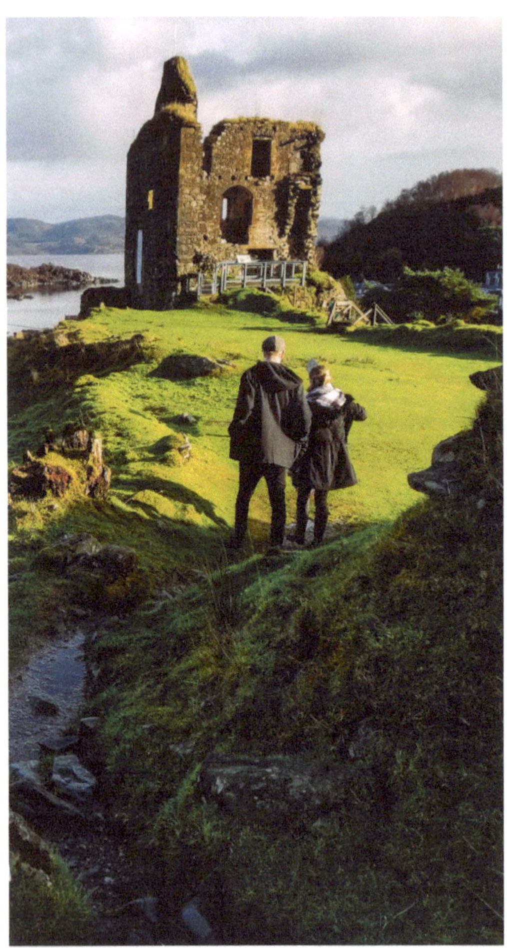

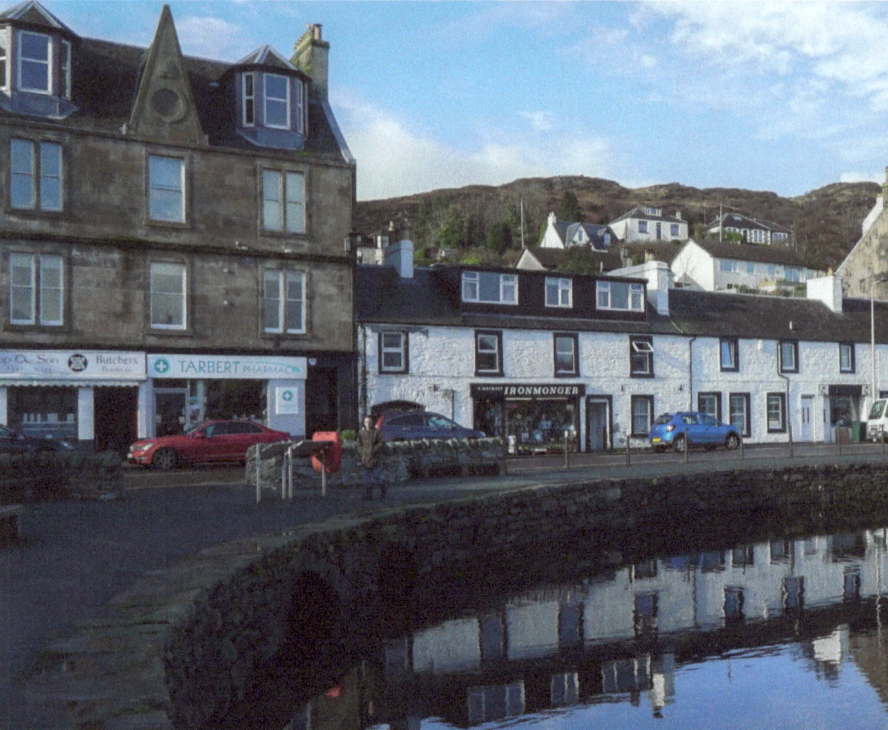

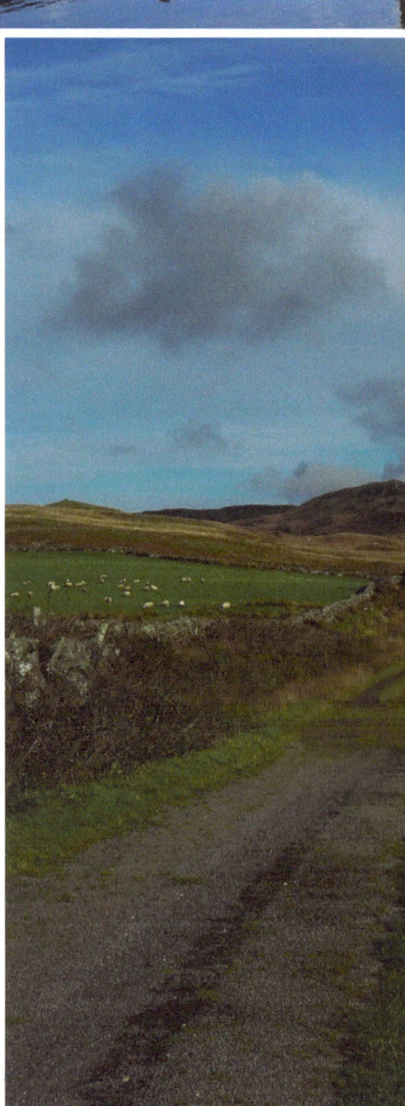

I never cared much for the screeching sound of bagpipes.

The few random times it (or is it they?) showed up in my life before actually being in the land of this obnoxious instrument, I might have plugged my ears. There're faint memories of a high school gymnasium. Bloody awful. And that's saying something. I'm a culture junkie musician. I should like these things.

Scotland is a different story.

It always had appeal. But being a glocal-ist, I needed a reason beyond my William Wallace wanderlust to travel to this edge of *the Old World*. It came in the form of a wedding. I already had plans to be in England, so it was easy enough to pop up to the land of kilts and whiskey.

I was picked up at the Glasglow airport and we headed west to a little port town called Tarbert with its rural Gaelic charm and token castle ruins. You get used to these in *the Old World* (albeit never over it).

The next morning a bus picked up the wedding party and drove us to the cere-monial grounds along the coast. Up and down pebbled roads through rolling hills of deep green that eased into the rough, murky Atlantic we went. Small farms spot-ted the rural terrain with fluffy, free range sheep roaming in packs.

It was a beautiful autumn day, but when the marine winds whipped across the treeless open, we were reminded: this is north country.

As we pulled up to the venue, I noticed a bloke in full Scotch regalia waiting to wel-come us. And, of course, he had the damn bagpipes ready to blow. *OMG, I've arrived in a theme park*, thought the inner cynic with a self-righteous eye roll.

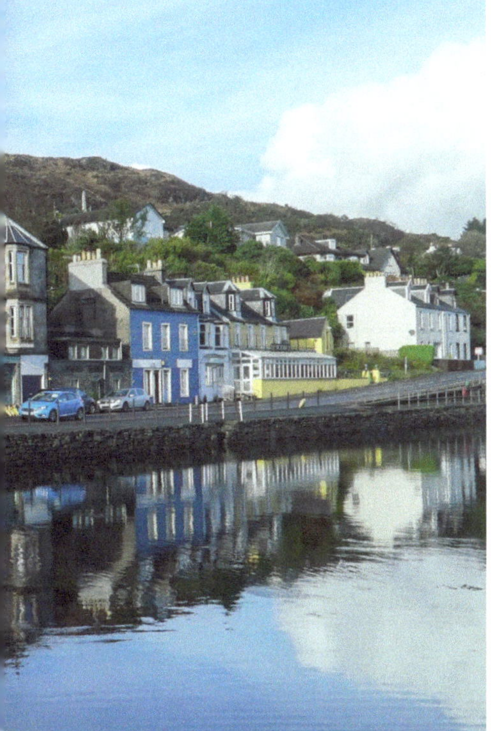

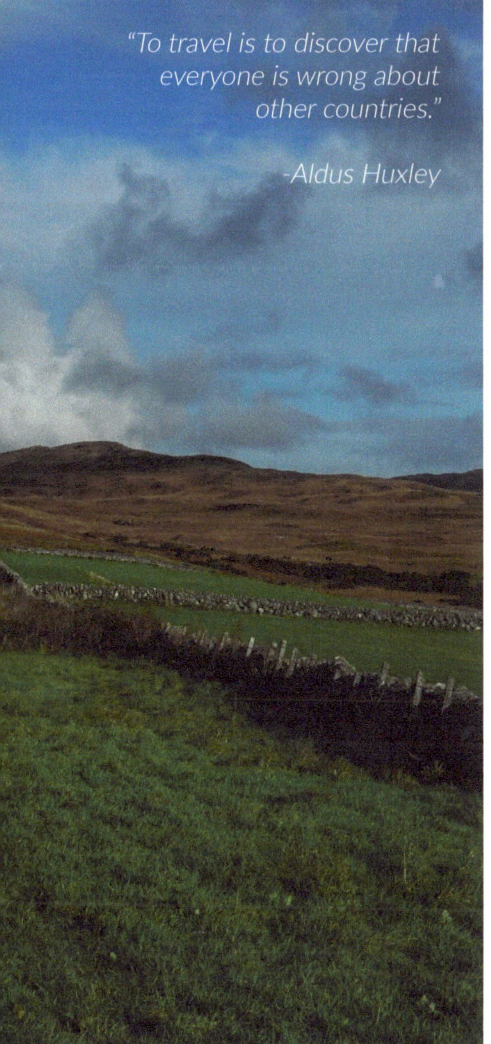

"To travel is to discover that everyone is wrong about other countries."

-Aldus Huxley

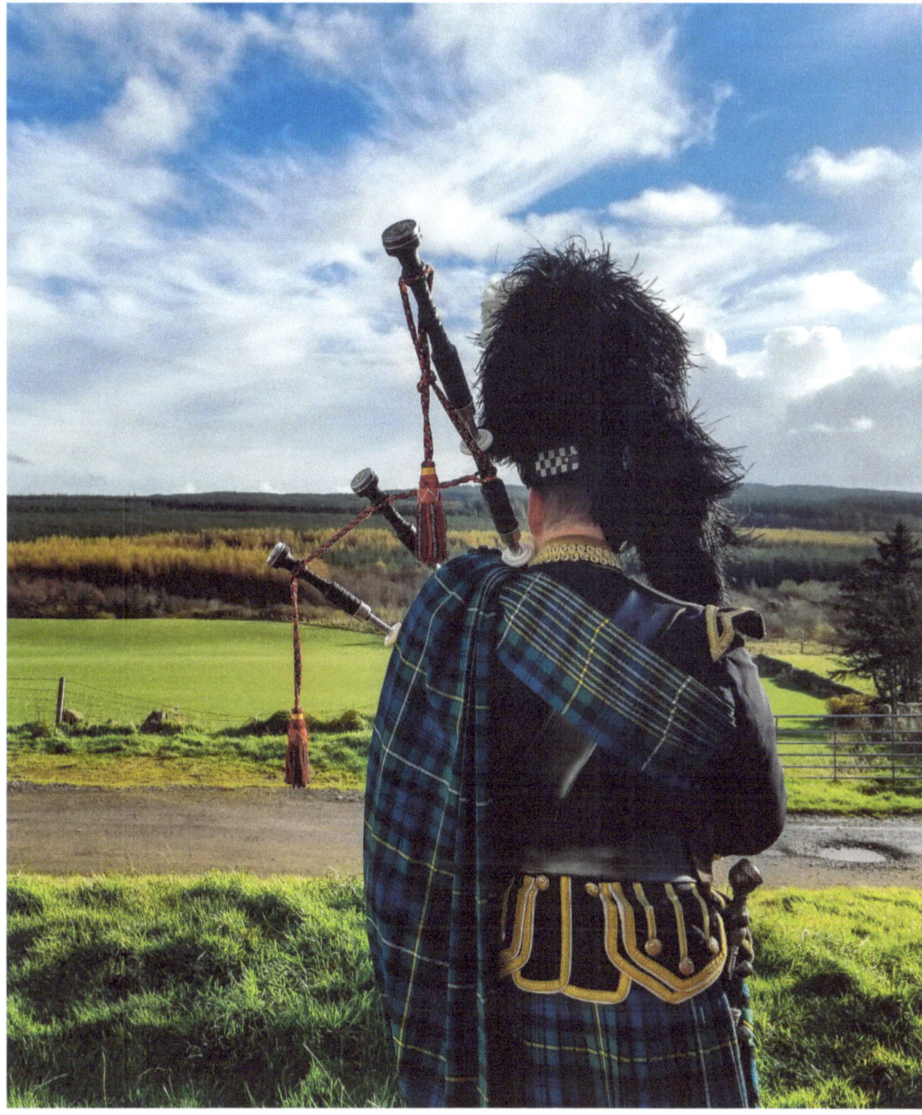

However, my bias met the unexpected. It wasn't the screeching annoyance I remembered. To the contrary, I stood stoic next to him, soaking in the drone and melody long after everyone else went inside.

It's as though you can't really hear the bagpipes unless you are there, in Scotland, where the sound of sea and blustery bite are part of the band, where the empty landscape allows its piercing vibrations to dissipate into the sprawling horizon. I was so moved by the moment, tears flowed down my face.

I was connecting to something essential in this highland Earth, tapping into the clans who have inhabited it for centuries.

It's like that Huxley quote. The more you explore, the more you break down stubborn pathways of the mind. It doesn't happen consciously, but circumstantially. Before I stepped foot off that bus, the bagpipes still sucked. I wasn't necessarily wrong about that. The concrete hull of a gym isn't the right recipe. It's like I was wearing blinders, running a race of thought without any peripheral vision.

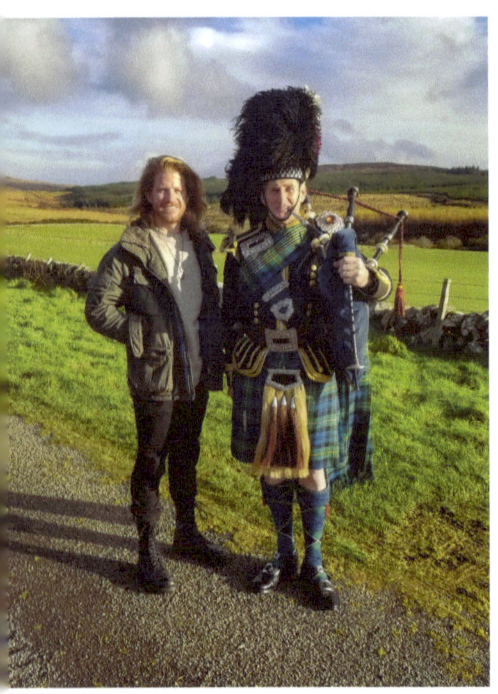

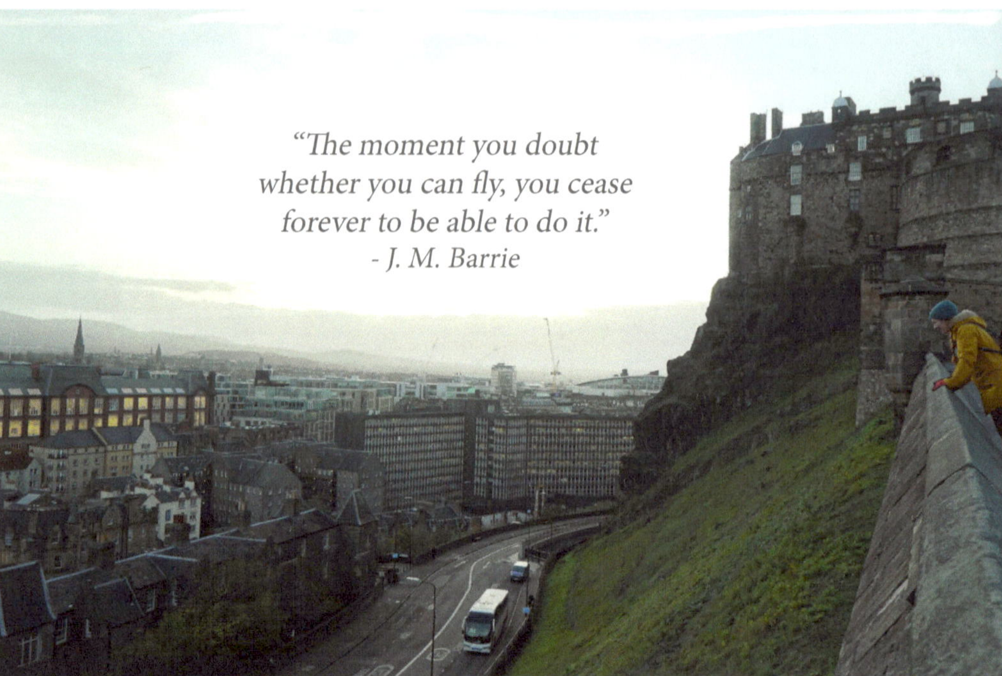

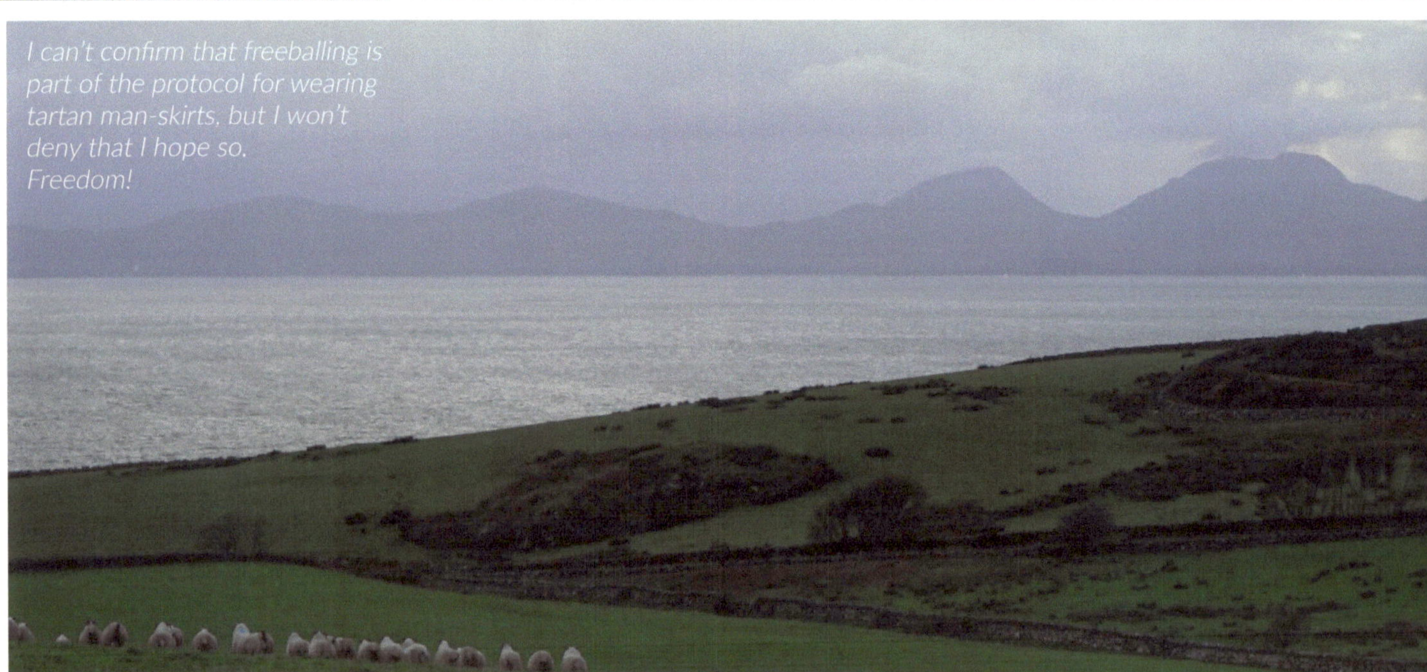

I came to find that the product of my epiphany was a great-grandson of the last battalion of bagpipers who marched into the battlefields of the first world war.

That's a helluva family legacy.

If I were wearing a kilt, I might go full on William Wallace and give my younger self a flash of my bollocks.

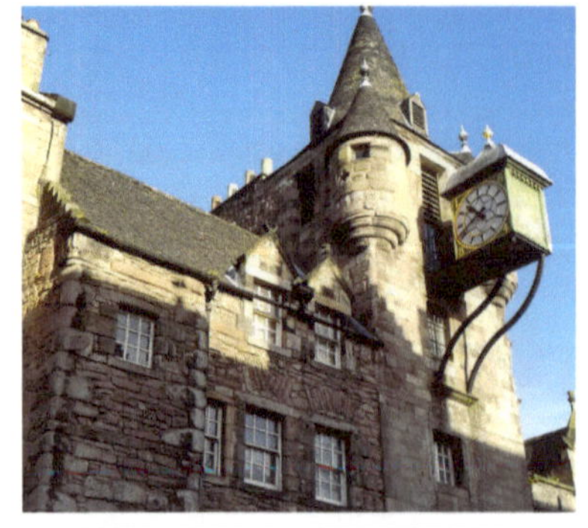

It's as the bride eventually said to me, noticing my revelry in the days that followed traveling across Scotland, "I think you have highlander in your blood."

Maybe so, but that's also the elation of discovery as it kicks out old concepts and builds new bridges in your mind.

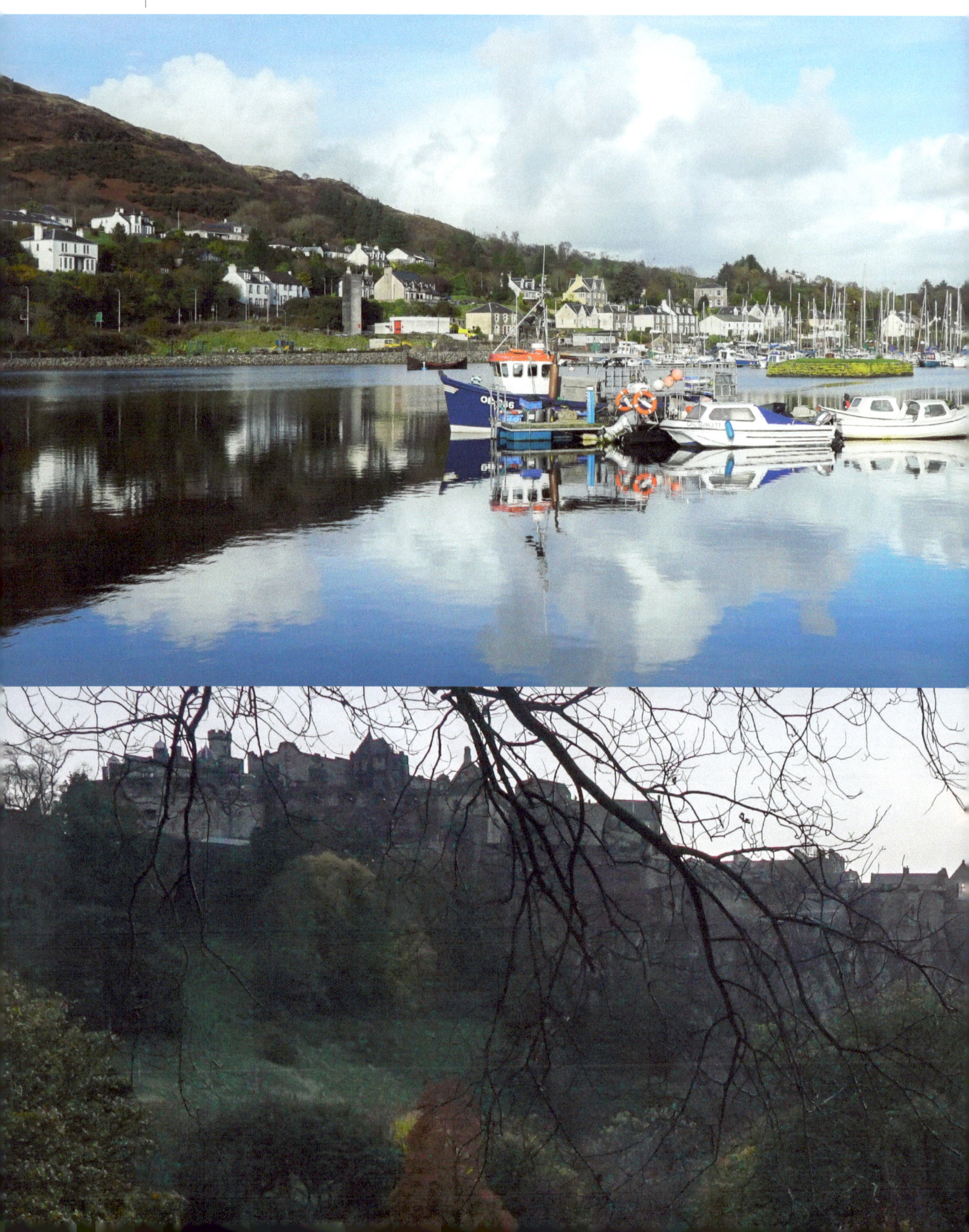

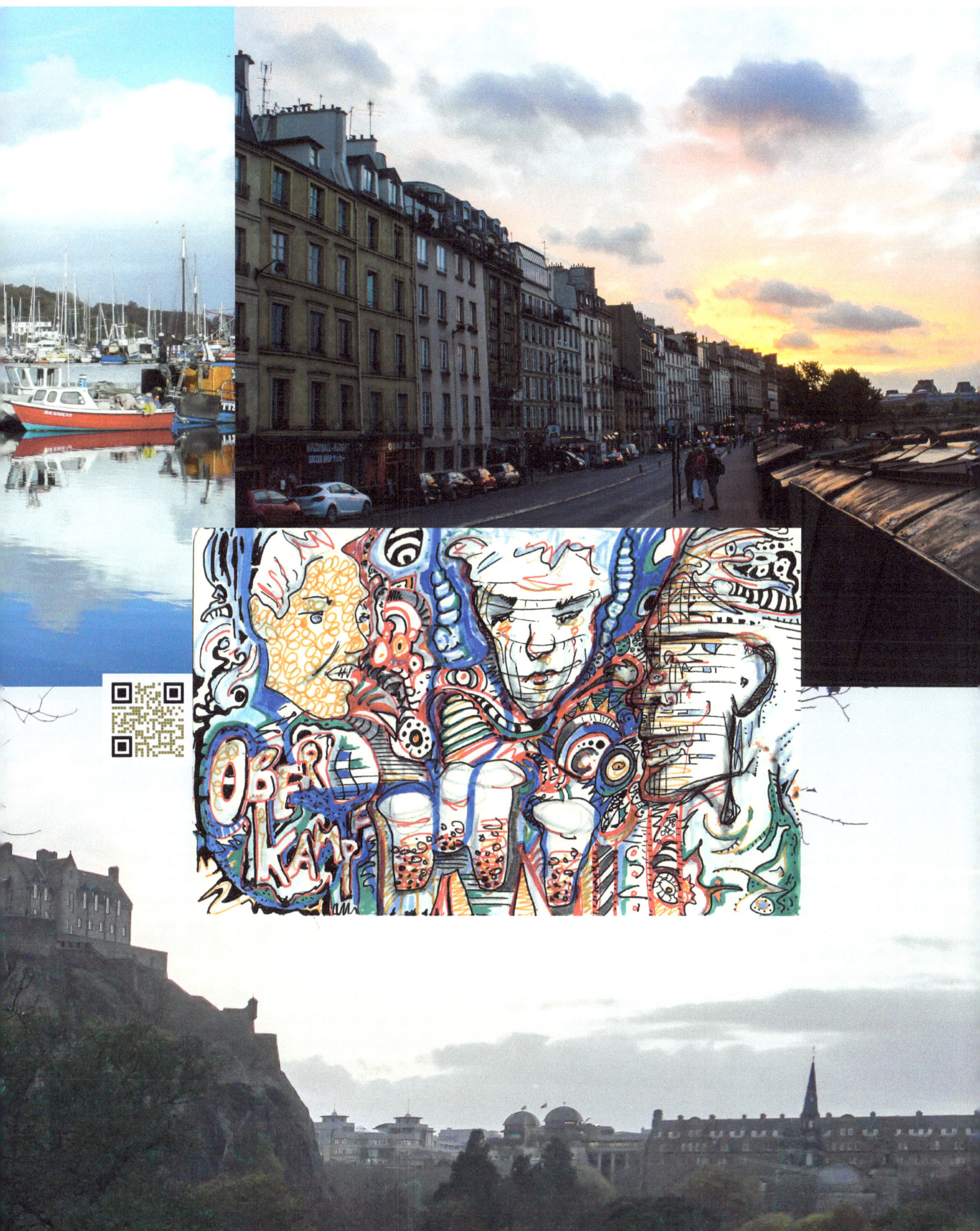
OBER
KAMP

When I think it over I'd rather be a sailor
Than sitting by the fire never changing
I'm a boat out on the ocean
~~Never knowing~~ unsure of where I'm going
Take me where'er the wind is blowing
And I'm gone sailing

Tired ~~of think over~~ what I could have done better
Life is like the weather – ever changing
To live is like the thunder (full of fear & wonder)
There's never enough cover, we all one day go
under, might as well go sailing

I don't care much for fate
Or a God marking my mistakes
I fall and fear it feeds the doubt
~~for going~~ on, did I turn out all wrong?
Should I have listen more to my old man

I do ~~think life is~~ see life as living like your
destiny is dreamed
You're a king or your own theif
If there's a god, the more I know I, not dint
know, but there's magic this I'm sure
So I will ride like I'm the hero in this
fantasy)
come on bring it on
Tragedy is just lessons to be learned

Wake up to nobody & nowhere
~~Not a sound only silence I see~~
~~No~~ Silence the sound
only white light I see
~~Close~~ This night be heaven
But I still feel like running
Am I dead or just lost in my head

In the end we begin again
At the finish we replenish
To desolve is to evolve
As winter becomes summer over & over
So we revolve
Not here to there but everywhere
Conclusion is an illusion
Amiss the myth of genisis
We persist forever

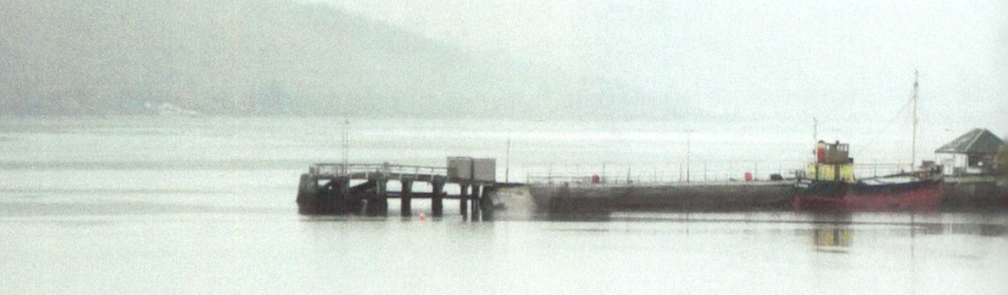

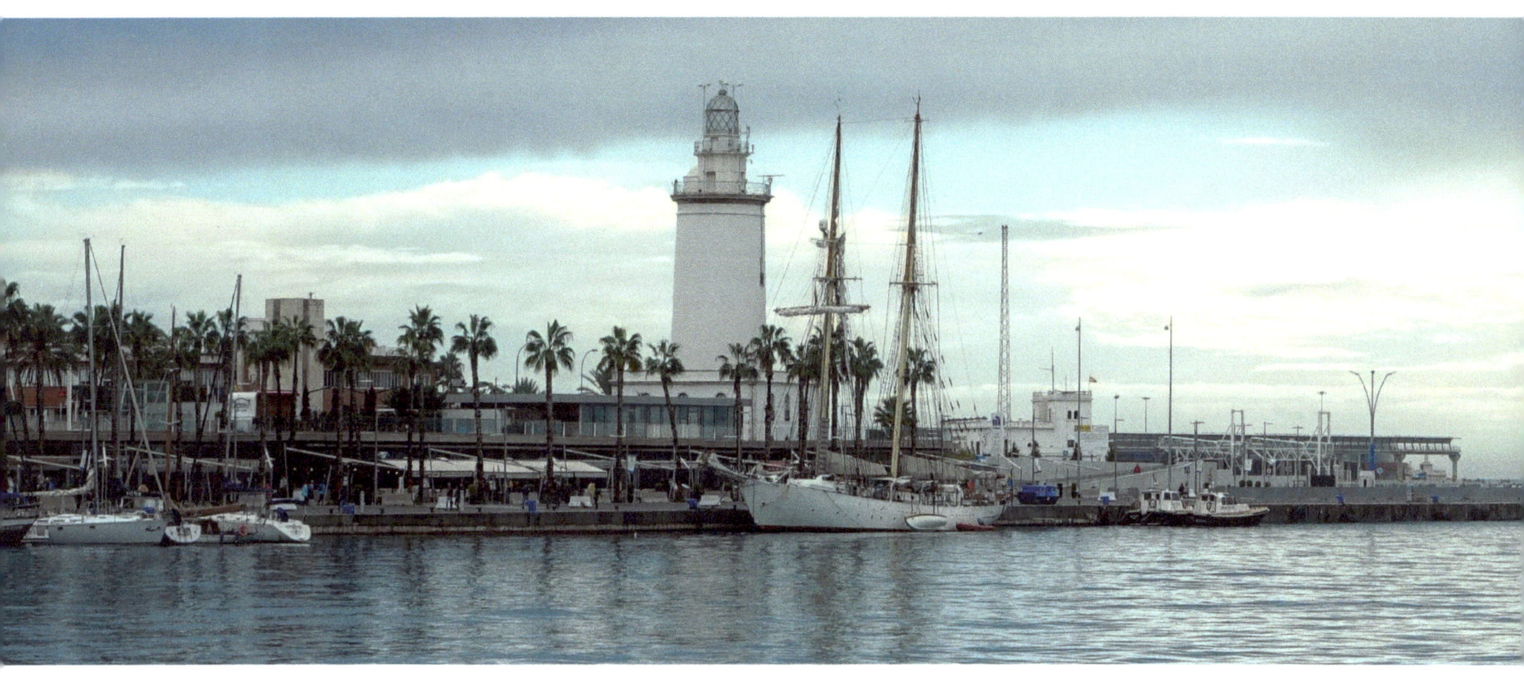

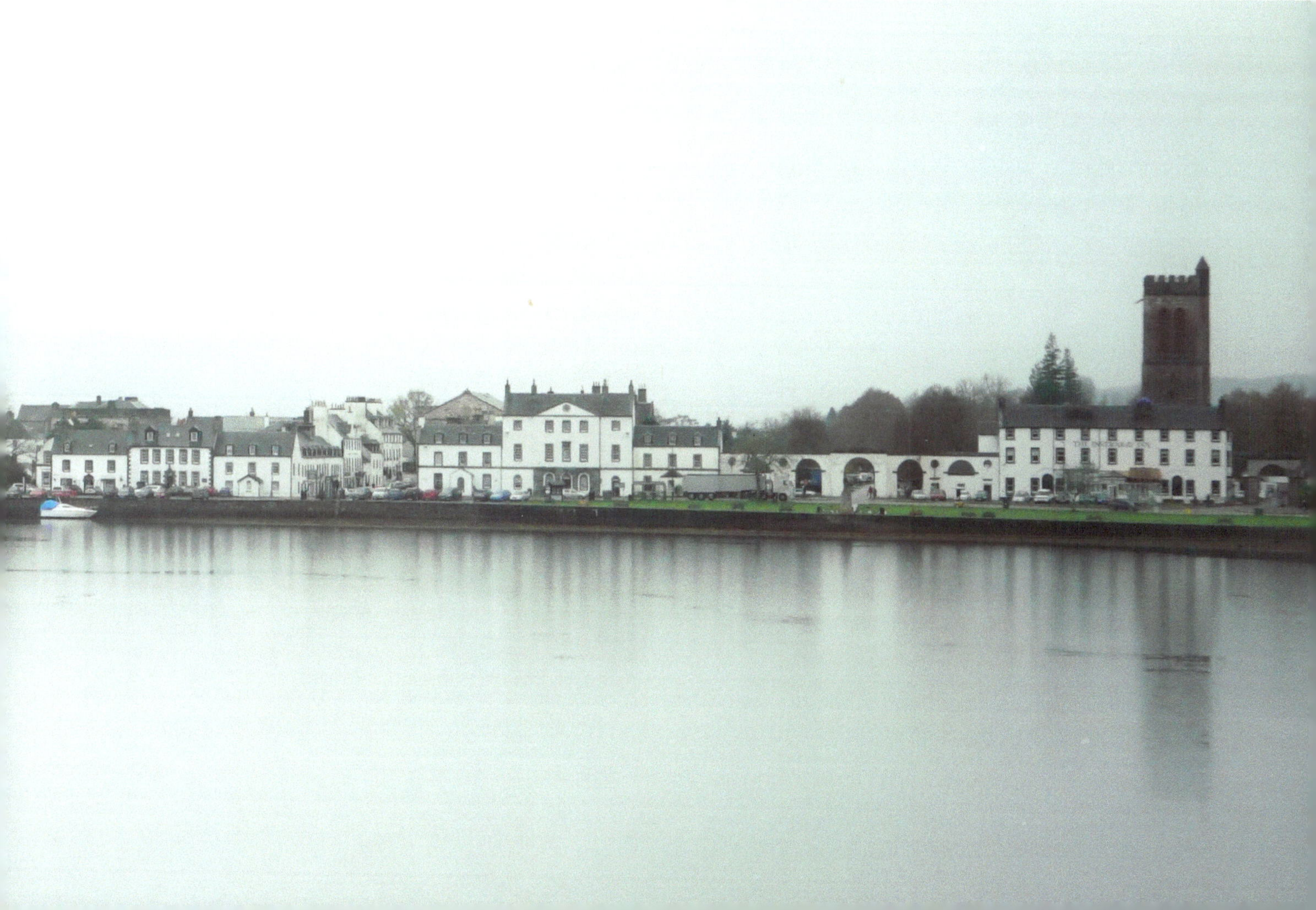

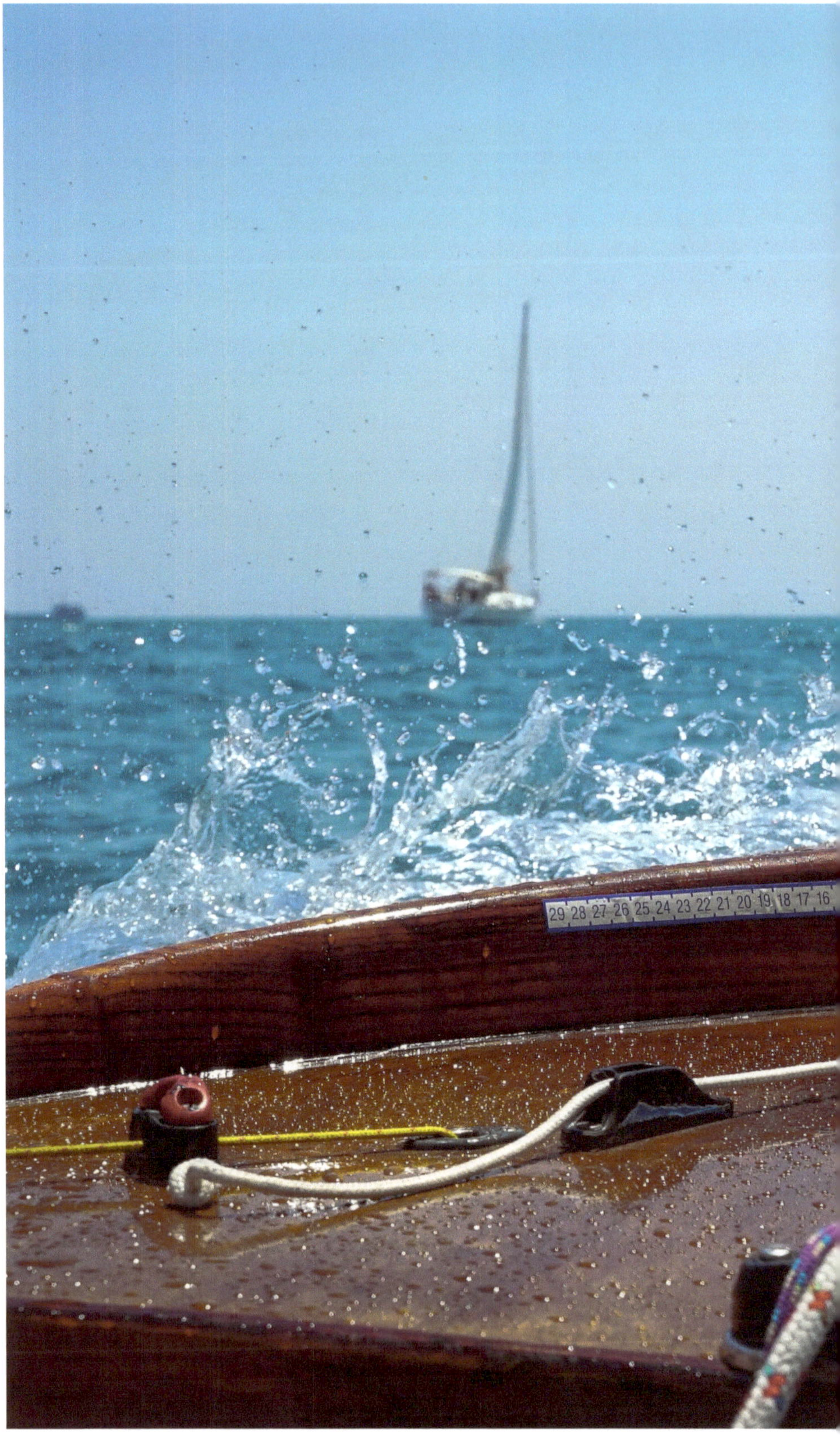

tacking
Valencia, Spain

abord the barca
de la marqués

off the coast
of the Mediterranean

*This is a snipe. A small boat with
just a jib and main sail. And yet it
took hours in preparation. Imagine a
voyage-worthy vessel, and then apply
it to every nautical metaphor.*

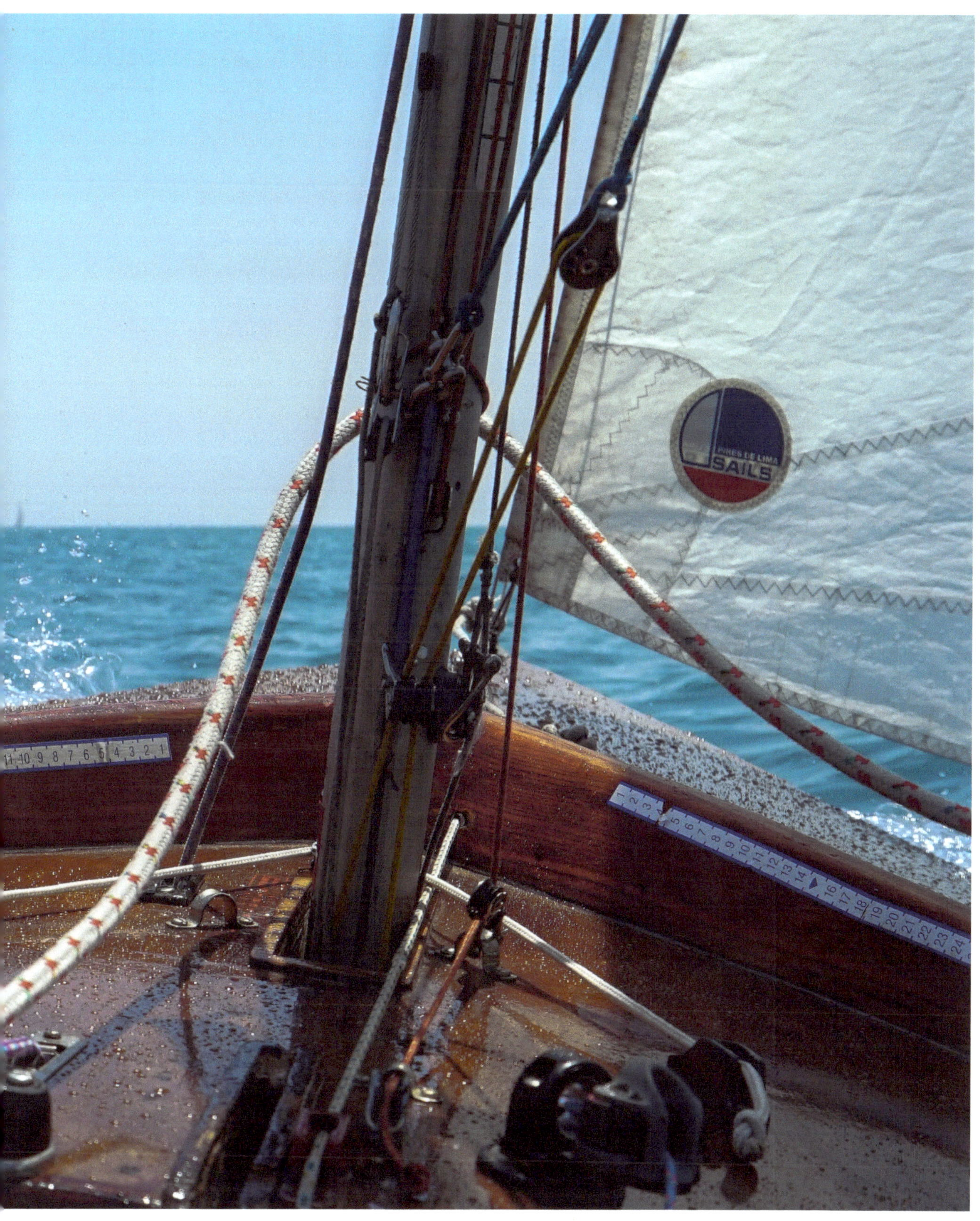

Divergent from the glocalist mantra, I chose to go to Spain purely as a holiday destination.

I was spending a lot of time in the Netherlands (not far from Spain in Texas terms) and thought it would be a nice destination for my father. For many years, we had a Thanksgiving tradition of taking a trip together.

Everyone raves about Barcelona. I threw in Valencia, Toledo, and Madrid based upon nothing else but proximity and a few pictures on the internet.

By the time the trip came along, it wasn't much of a holiday. I was a miserable companion, reeling from a broken heart and the collapse of my love life. That was just the surface. To complement my collapsing relationship was a crisis of faith. Over a year into life without a bed of my own, I found myself weary of the road and questioning the recklessness of my decisions. The novelty of nomad life had worn off, and now the most valuable thing it had brought me was slipping from my grip.

Though I found some solace in the unusual beauty of Park Güell, Barcelona reflected my suffering—a city simmering with the animosity of over-tourism.

travel el camino de mi corazón
living like hope's a letter from home
Everybody diga mi that nadas gratis
Well peace, man
I'm on a Vaqueroll...
The head says no
The heart says go
No stopung this stone

You can say, hombre, hay yippie kay yay
Go west jóvenes unpressed to experience
Dance it up, get your hands up
If the music drops
Keep your soul pointed al sol

If the spirit está buena
You en la montaña can stand
lluviosa or not
Get on your vaqeroll

are you high on something
Say los soñadors of nothing
No our doors are open
Podemos mirar el cielo

Lets get high on something
Nadar la mar of star light
Dame nos manos it alright

Nativist propaganda pours from the streets. The scowls of disgruntled locals penetrated the sensitivity that sat on my skin. Maybe it was just the anvil in my chest, but I felt unwelcome.

Next up: Valencia. All it had, as far as I could tell, was a name I recognized and a location on the Mediterranean. After a long walk with our luggage to a cafe location in one of those yellow commercial areas on Google maps, I held my head up long enough to see all the gorgeous women. Okay, Spain. Let's do this.

The pick-me-up didn't last. I quickly tumbled back down my pit of self-pity, but, contrary to the Barcelona experience, there was something warm and welcoming about Valencia. The cab driver from our ride to the hotel made us feel like special guests. I left thinking, *I'll be back here.*

Toledo, a city predating the Romans, lit me up with old world wonder that stretches to antiquity. The ancient part of the city was almost entirely intact. Unlike the skeletal ruins of Rome or the country castles all across Europe that serve as little more than tourist destinations, Toledo is an active city center set in a medieval movie.

I think I'll move to España
And spend all my money on girls
The ones you find in Valencia
On the Costa del Sol, I'm sure
I left behind Amsterdam Nederland
And my love of that European
But the puerto es muerto
And I'm rocking solo again

When I get to España
I be wearing that moda mola
Y flaquitas in summer dresses
Will besa mi, caress me down
I may be knocked down
But I'm not down and out
Just a gringo in doubt
And I'll work it out

Maybe you would believe
Cuando hablo que todo (es roto en mi)
loco con
You with me
Maybe there an in between
Where I can be
Where I can abre mi corazon
Canta el cancion della fantasia
Maybe you wouldn't see
I'm just riding a wave
Crawling my way back home
Now that I'm en España
Tengo nada, es la verdad
I guess I lied to fool myself
Into sailing on, not drowning in
My pity, in this shitty side of a wandering life
Lonly beauty that's only mine
I'll share, is there anyone there?
Maybe You Would Believe...

Sprawling walls of stone where archers once shot from parapets encircle buzzing markets and local apartments set among a maze of cobbled pathways and structures reminiscent of a fairytale.

My state of mind was more like the bitter truth: these streets have seen Celts, Romans, Visagoths, Moors, Christians, and Jews all slaughter each other for thousands of years. This ain't a nursery rhyme. *I feel like shit.*

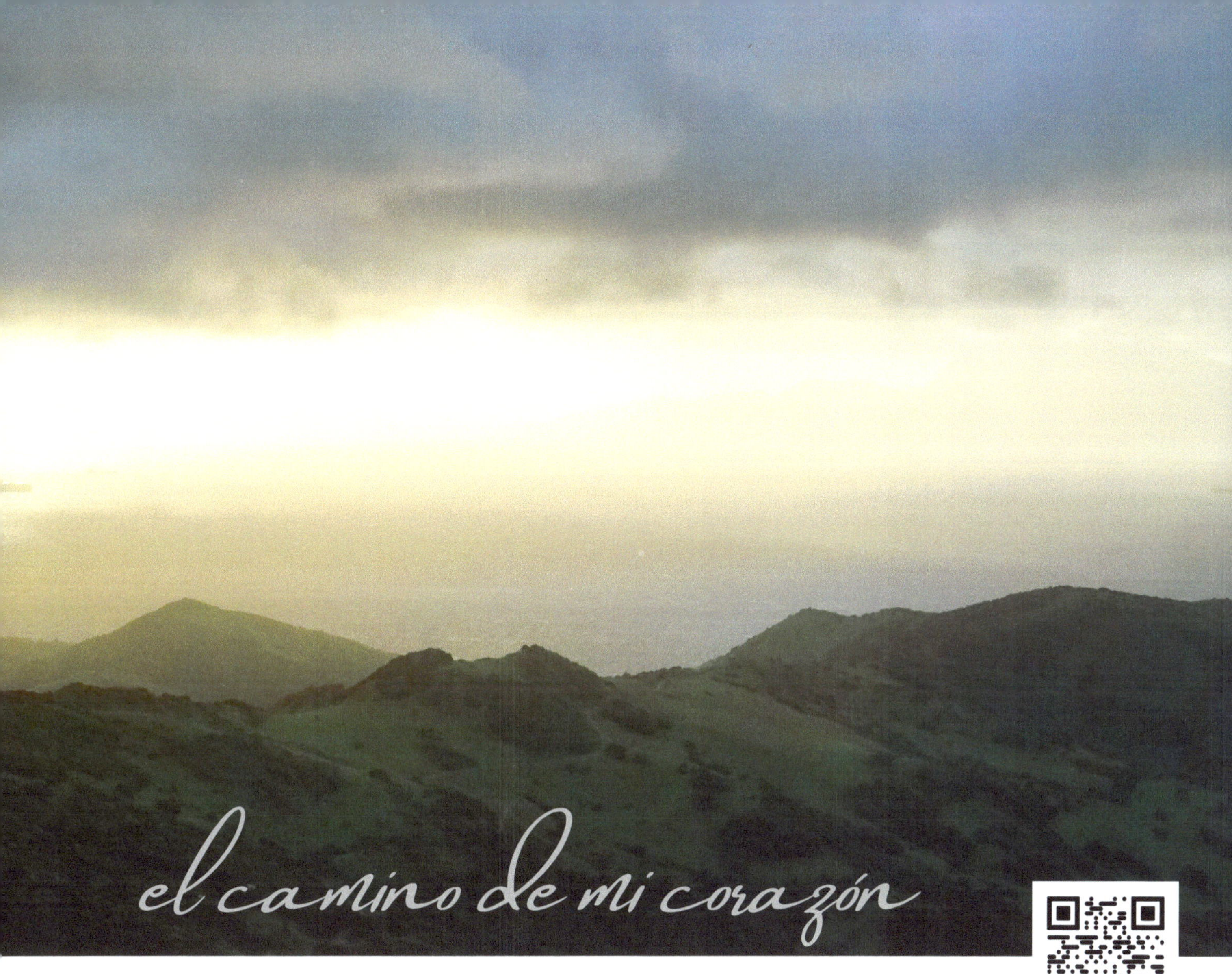

Head's been in the clouds
Heart like a balloon
Bursting as it touches the ground
Where my feet are searching for room

Thought the world was mine
Ego made of gold
Tarnish shows in the light
Of this lie that I've always told

But I don't sing the blues
Maybe I'll find something better to do
Here at these crossroads

No more fantasy
It's pointless to pretend
I never became a king
Dear Failure, can you be my friend?

At the intersection I stand
Naked and nearly broke
Rejection I leave to the wind
With its whisper I go

But I don't sing the blues
I surrender all that I thought was true
Here at these crossroads

On to Madrid. We only had one night left and showed up without a place to stay. That was a mistake.

Turns out El Clasico, perhaps the most impassioned contest in Spanish sport, was the same day. The entire city had no vacancy. We ended up staying at an outskirts hotel by the airport, watching the game from its mundane lobby, barely getting a taste of the capitol city.

That night, I couldn't sleep. I crawled out of the window and up onto the roof, where I wrote a song trying to convince myself the only lover I need is myself.

Spain would inspire many songs after that, but it would be five years before I found myself back on the Iberian Peninsula. For all the stormy sorrow that hung over me during that first foray, my intuition was right about Valencia.

This time, serendipity fulfilled my glocalist goals. I'd made a friend in India, who I'd gone to visit in Chile, but is actually from Valencia. On a trip home, he invited me to experience the city's jaw-droppingly epic festival, Las Fallas.

At the end of a relentless fireworks-filled four days the city sets hundreds of towering papier-mâché statues ablaze.

My friend and his family rolled out a welcome mat worthy of Spanish royalty. In part, that's because my boy's dad is a marqués. For real. The coat of arms hangs in his entryway. Their surname is engraved on battlements hundreds of years old. At one point in my repeated trips to Valencia, this charming family patriarch showed me official paperwork from the king that dates back before the thirteen colonies.

It's called the city with its back to the sea. The center, with its neoclassical Spanish edifices covered in white, is several miles from the place I targeted on my first Valencian voyage. That'd be the beach.

At one point, Valencia was arguably the most prominent city in Spain. Though its port has become the largest in the western Mediterranean, the rice fields (paella please) and oranges are what brings pride to the marqués. At the zenith of Valencian influence, the city produced the finest silks outside Asia.

Today, the long stretch of warm coastal waters has developed into Valencia's second city. I happened to be there twice during the summer solstice celebration of San Juan, where revelers gather all night on the beach with bonfires and plenty of party favors.

I fell in love with the heat of Spain. Through this cloud of smoke and spice, I crashed into infatuation with a daughter of Granada. For a few weeks, we exploded like a super nova of blinding passion. Let's just say I had my Danny Zuko moment. *Summer lovin'. Had me a blast.*

A few years back, *The New York Times* wrote, "Don't go to Barcelona or Madrid. Go to Valencia." At one point, consumed by my infatuation, I was convinced I needed to move there. My summer of love died, but that dream hasn't entirely. Stand by.

My Spanish conquest continued on to small towns in Castellón and Alicante, and then down through Andalucía. At the southernmost point, I stood over the Strait of Gibraltar at dawn with Africa in the distance.

I finally explored Madrid, where Catholic parades pop up in the day and squares are filled with young and old festive folks well into a Wednesday night. With each thirst-quenching glass of tinto de verano, the accent of Castilian kings infiltrated this Texas boy's Mexican Spanish.

Now, I can't say "gracias" without the world's most pleasing lisp.

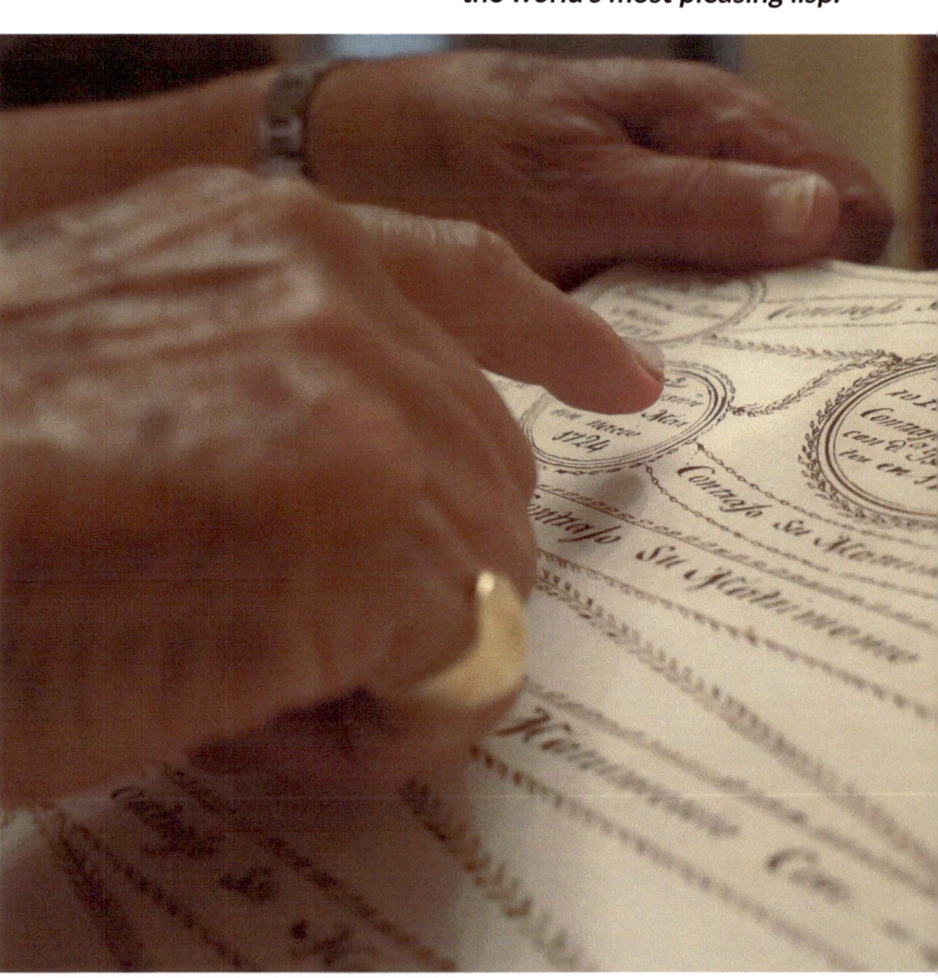

In España, the Old World hit me with the hammer of human history.

It was most viscerally felt in the arena of bullfighting. Like that person squinting through their fingers, both appalled and intrigued, caught in the uncomfortable limbo between watching and looking away, I felt connected to generations of Spaniards and even further back to gladiators of Rome.

Oh boy, here we go. What can of condemnation did I just open?

Through our 21st century lens, it's easy to berate such brutality. My Spanish teacher in Valencia said without a second thought, "I could never be friends with someone who goes to bullfights." Her self-righteous stance is understandable and valid. It is also vapid. Reality doesn't fit in the pretty, little jewelry box of idealism.

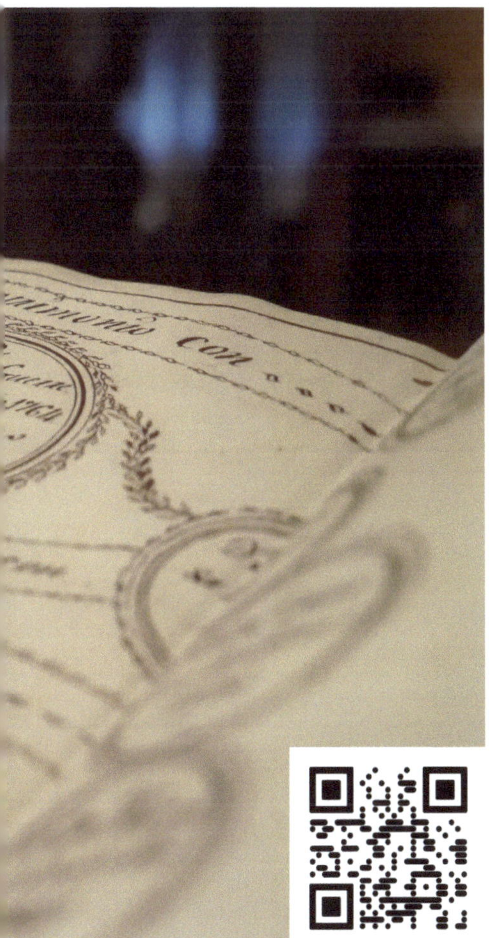

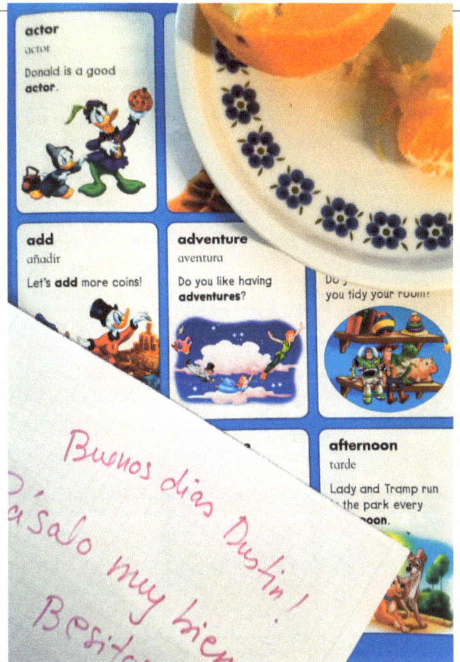

If reading this makes you start to hate me, well, you're proving my point. The ugliness of such contempt highlights my conveyed nuance.

My friend called bulls "the most revered animal in the Mediterranean" and suggested that bullfighting was a celebration of that truth.

Many toreros (Spanish for bullfighters) and conocedores (the ones who raise the bulls) live isolated lives and have a profound love of animals. Perhaps this is far more sophisticated a phenomenon to consider. While I recoil at the grotesque spectacle of watching a bull quiver, vomit blood, and then collapse after a sword has exploded his heart, spouting condemnations of cruelty while scarfing steak of unknown origin is a more monstrous practice. It's certainly hypocritical.

To be clear, if there was never another dude in a funny outfit stabbing the shit out of an animal for our viewing pleasure I wouldn't be sad. The more famous word, matador, literally translates to killer. There's no getting around the violence, and I'm innately pacifist. But while I blast Bizet, singing "toreador" (another name for a bullfighter) in my best operatic voice and cooking up flesh for lunch, I face my own contradictions.

When the weight of *the Old World* hurls its tribulation upon your back, you can thoughtlessly cast off the past, protecting your spotless ideology, or you can let it sink beneath your skin. We can tear down statues and institutions, but does that do anything to assuage the human demons so simple to chide, but difficult to exorcise?

Spain is still reeling from the legacy of its most prominent 20th century politician, Franco, the longtime dictator who came to power during the civil war that happened while the rest of Europe was dealing with Hitler. On the world stage, the two men are often placed in the same fascist basket.

Go to Spain and you'll find a much more intricate debate.

In 2019, Franco's remains were exhumed from the monumental Valle de los Caídos (Valley of the Fallen). This was executed by a democratically elected left-wing government far more sympathetic to Franco's defeated adversaries, the Republicans (ironic, I know), for the political and practical reasons of combating the right-wing. Though his new resting place is a fancy mausoleum worthy of Pére Lachaise, I question if the removal from such a visible, famous location serves their purpose, defeating the scourge of fascism. I prefer my villains in the open. This only pushes extremism underground.

In the very least, I hope you can appreciate the pun. If I'm being honest with myself, I'm torn, too. Maybe I'm better embracing my man of La Mancha.

"Too much sanity may be madness—and maddest of all: to see life as it is, and not as it should be!"

Enough with this heady diatribe. You'd prefer to be at the beach. Me, too. Spain has lots of those. I may just retire there someday. Turns out Spain has this fabulous thing called the golden visa. It's very different from a golden shower. Google it.

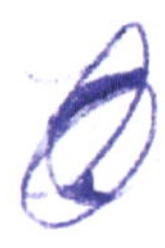

MELIÃ
HOTELS & RESORTS

How did I get here?
Lost somewhere on a rooftop outside of Madrid
No, I know where I am
Just not really sure who
Everything that I'd planned never came, just went
I thought that I had found love
But what I found is it's not like the poets said
No, there's no Juliette
But still we get the tragedy
I'm down & I'm out but somehow I can see clearly

Let it all go, I'm alone now and thats how it will be
Company will come & will go, but this road never leaves
All these reasons I have, they're just a passing fad
Let it all go, I'm the only lover I need

Don't get me wrong
I am confused and little more than an overgrown kid
Yes, the doubt it is strong
My stomach it turns
    I am an open wound

But this weak and frail me
That's being human & maybe it's all in my head
Really I am strong
I've learned how to get along
Life it dies, life it grows, ebb & flow like this happy/sad song

But I don't want to be alone
Growing old with empty home
With no lover there to hold me in the dark
Courage come against the fear
When I feel I'm not enough
May I ~~find within myself the love~~
May I find the love within myself to help

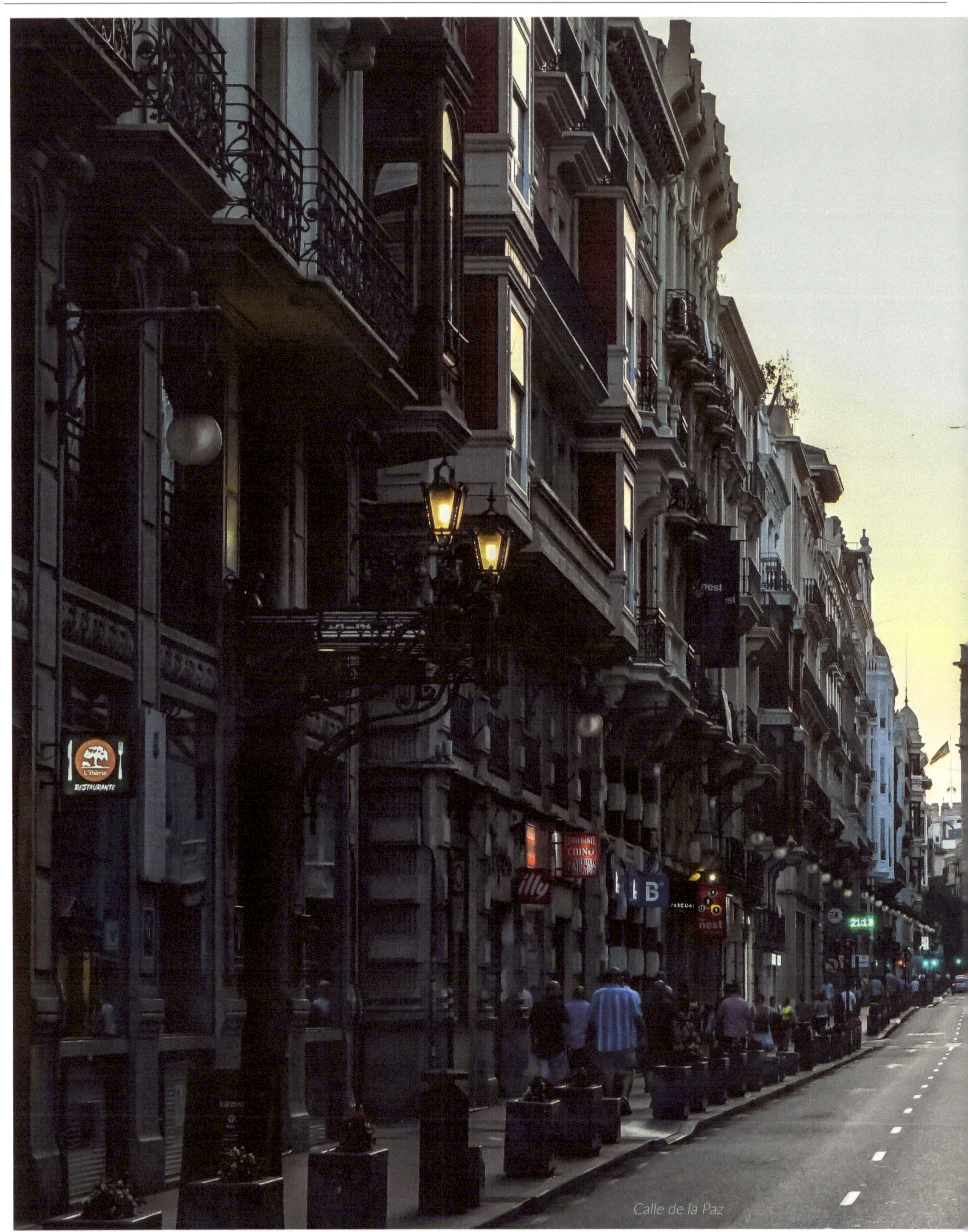

Calle de la Paz

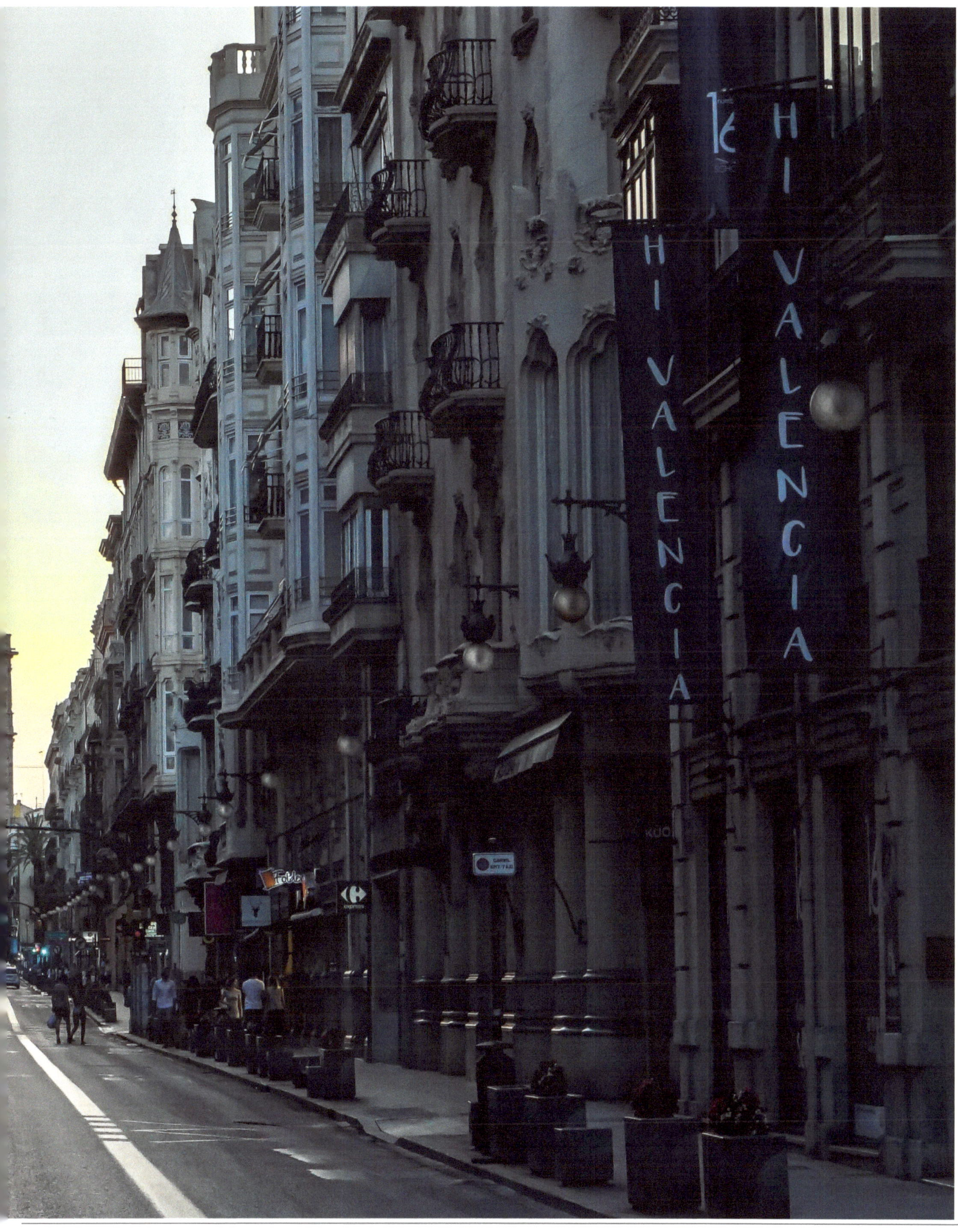
HI VALENCIA
HI VALENCIA

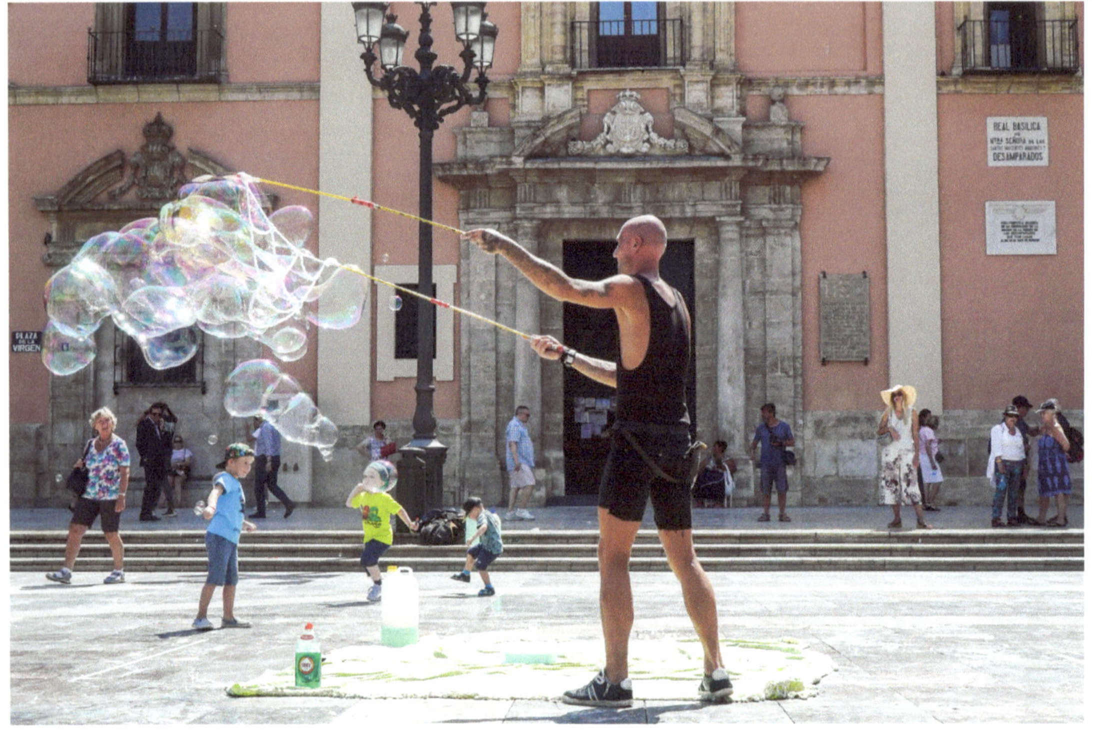

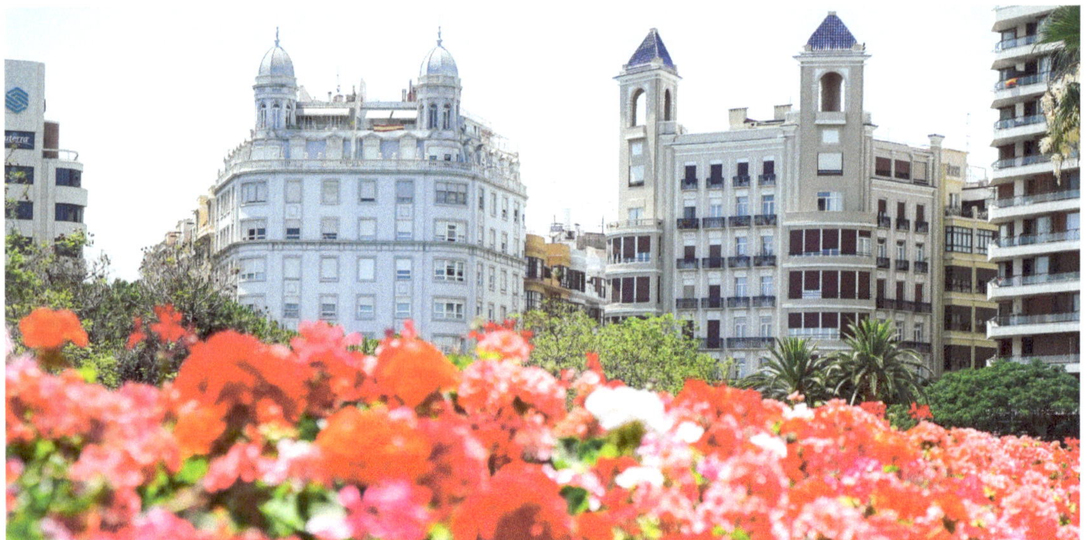

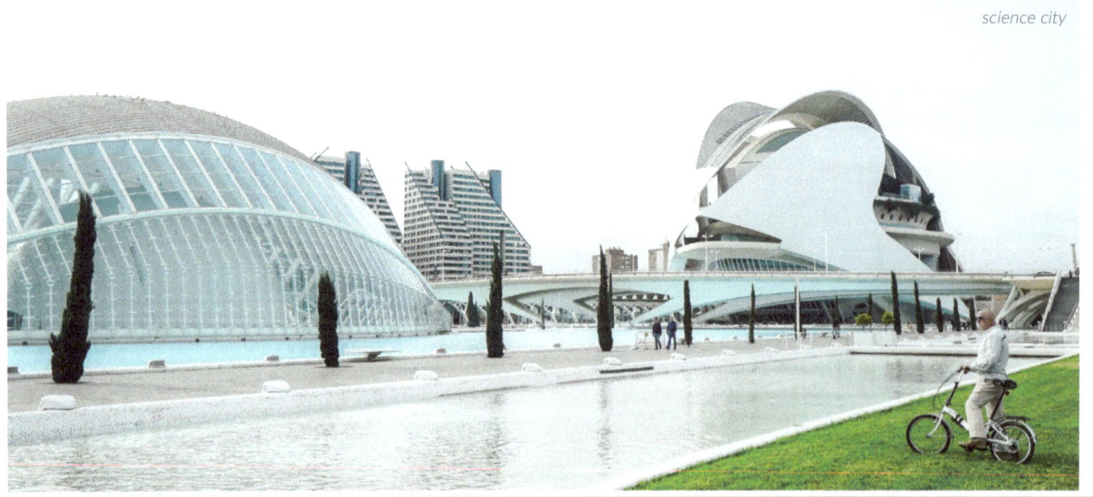

science city

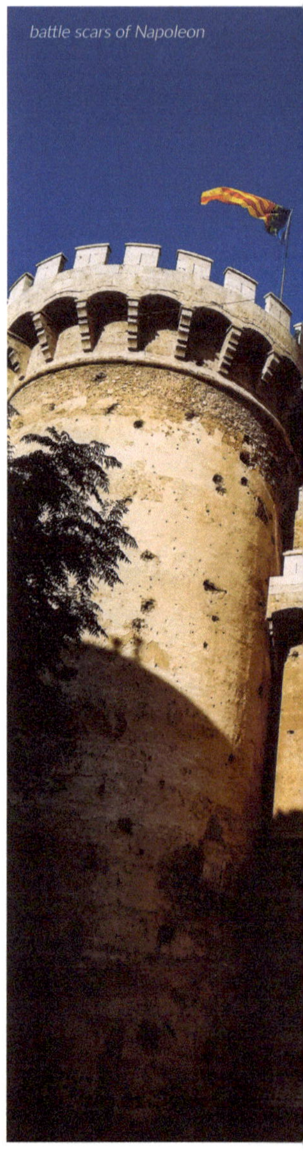

battle scars of Napoleon

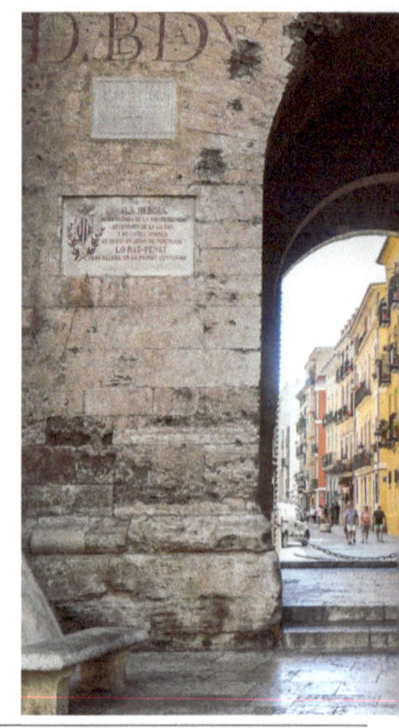

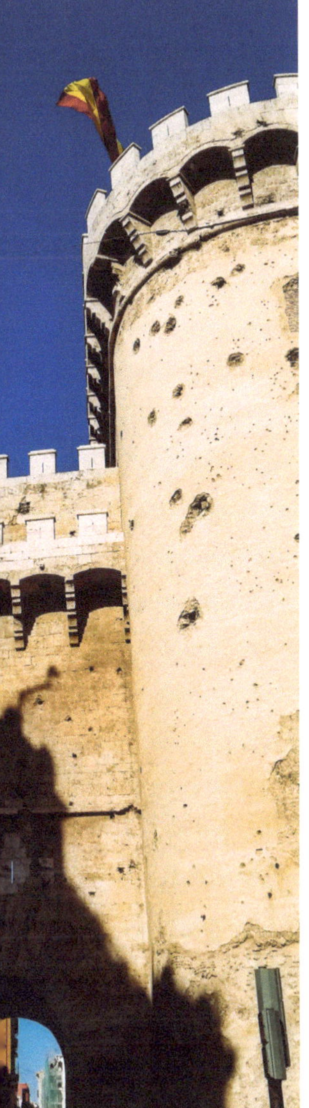

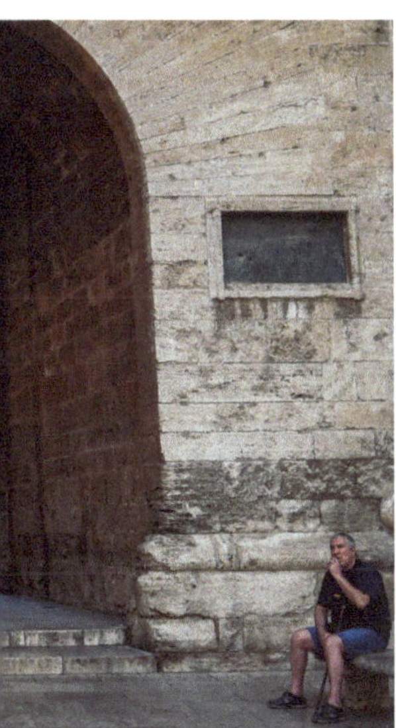

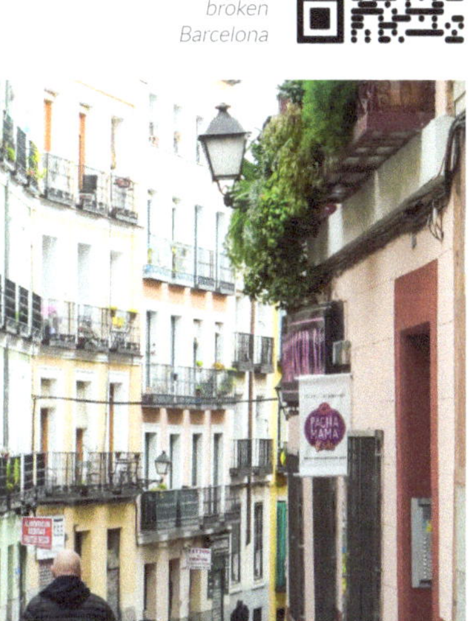

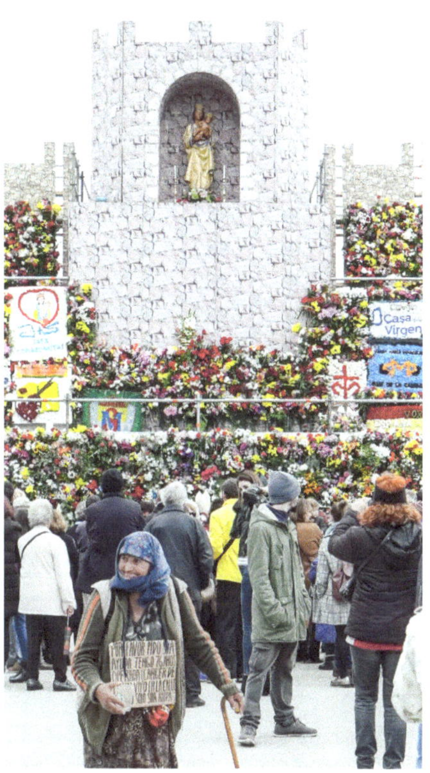

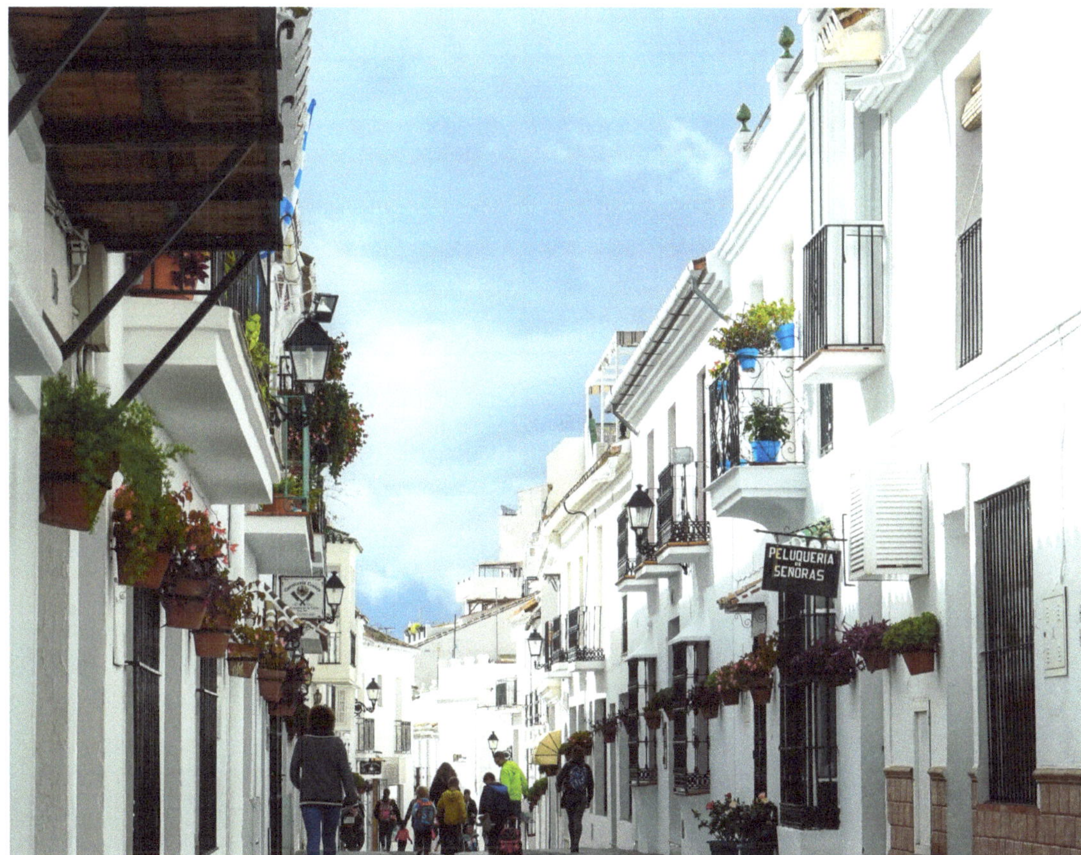

*the white cities
of Southern Spain*

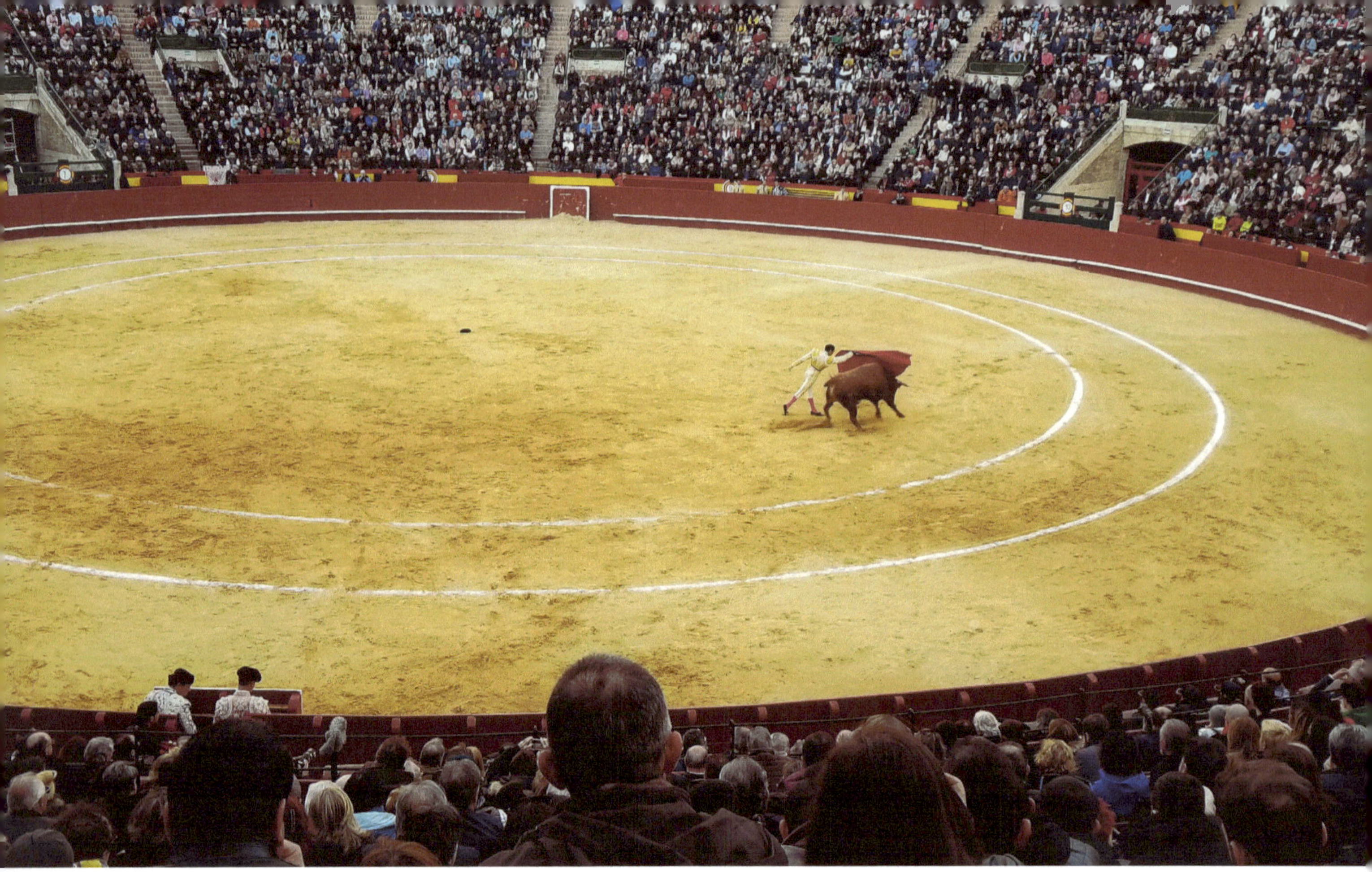

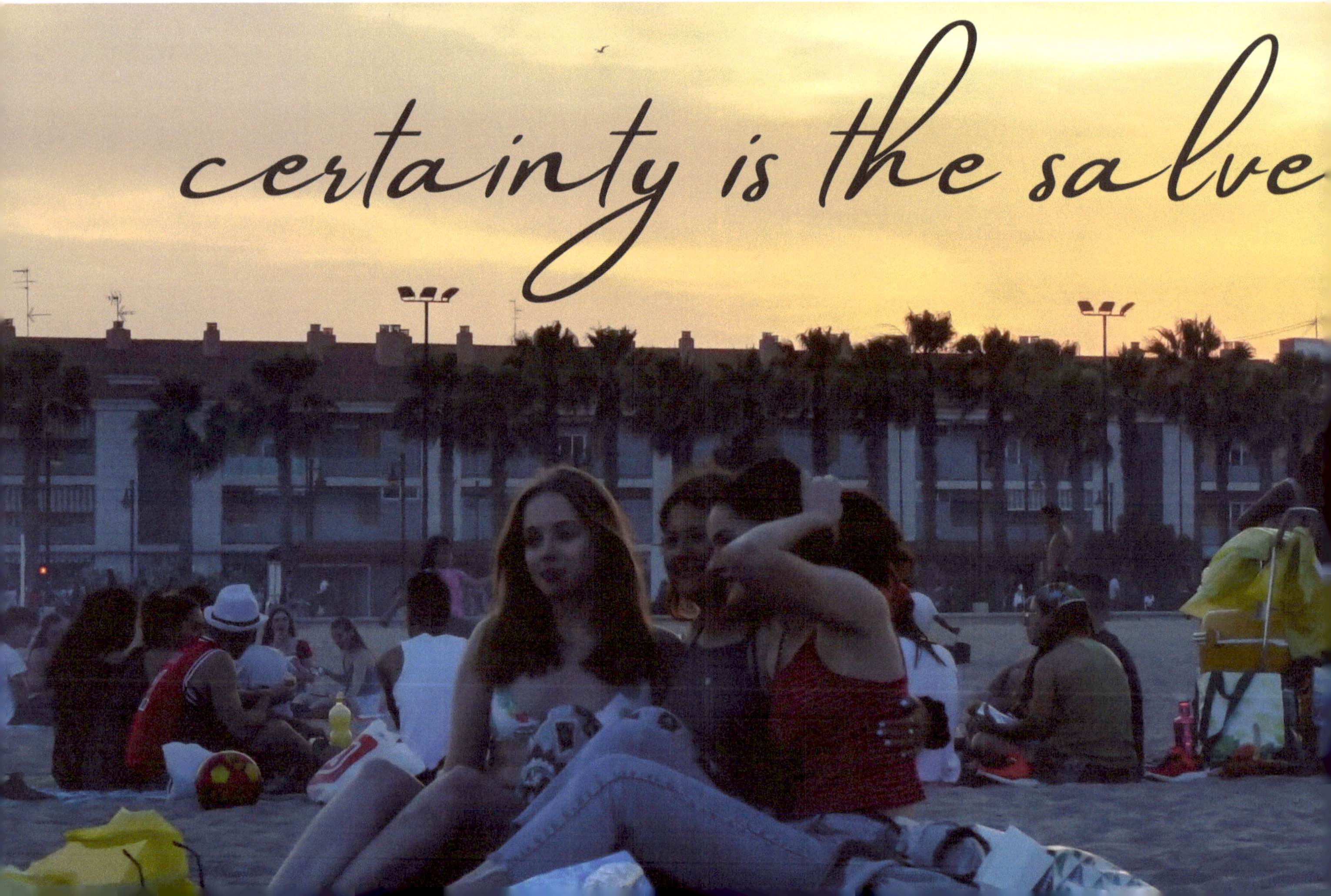

certainty is the salve

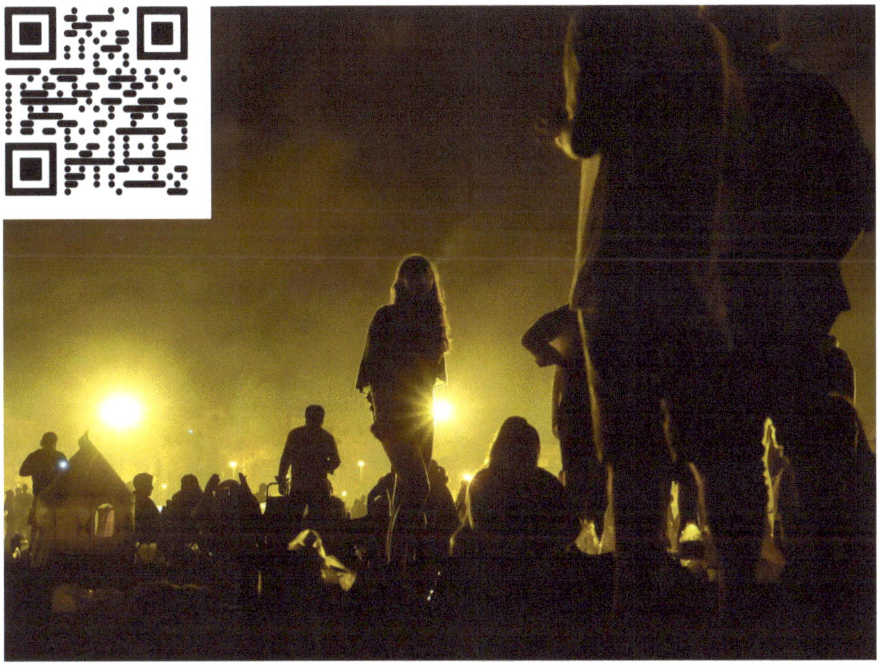

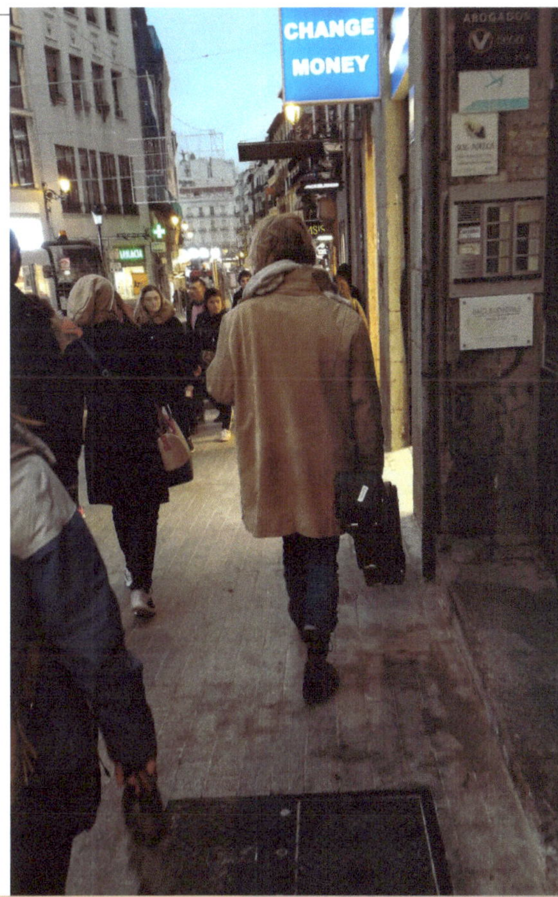

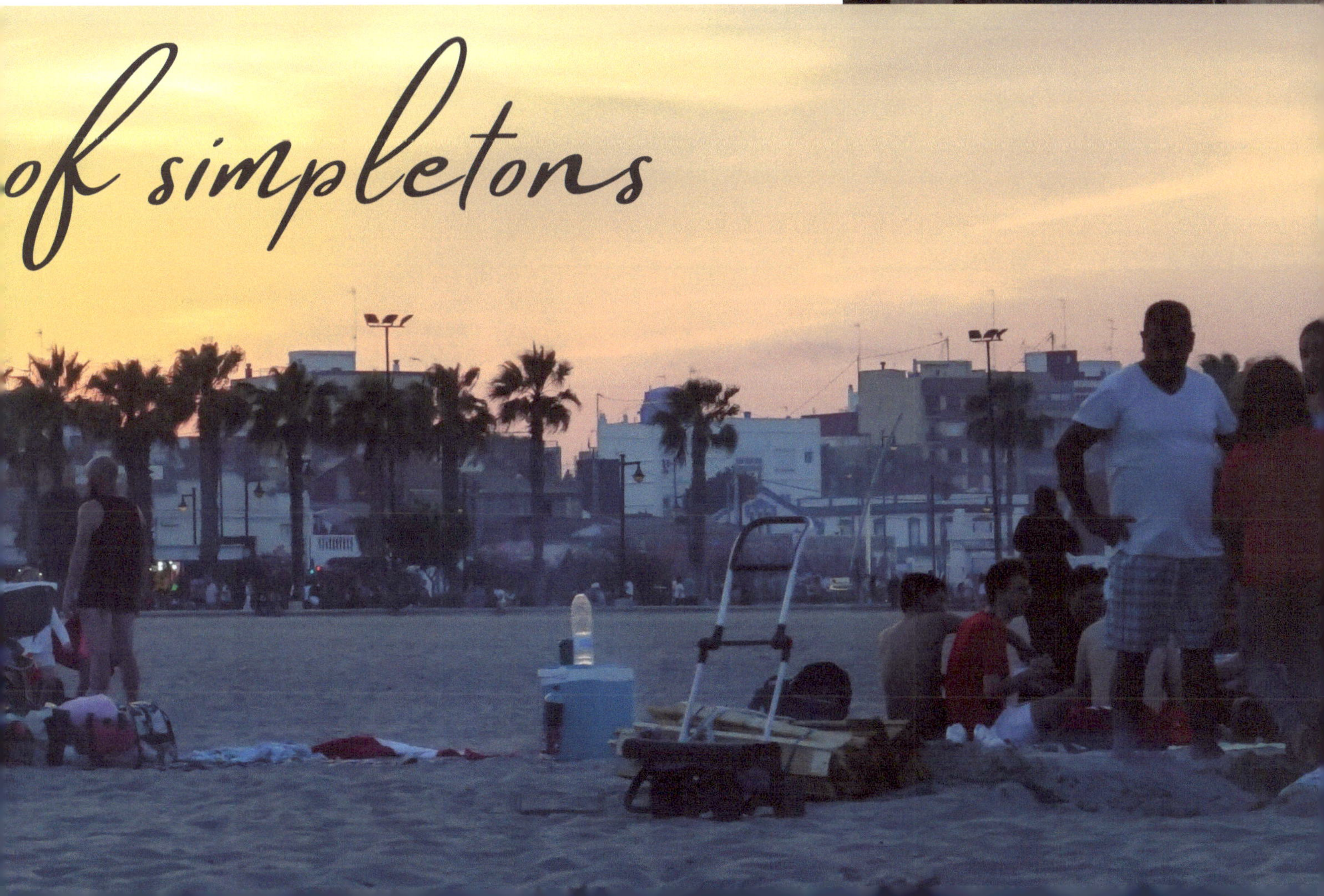

of simpletons

On the Night of San Juan all the people parade to the sands of the Mediterranean
Reinas and Reyes of the warm Spanish days make their pits and their pleasures of fire

On the Night of San Juan through the smoke I was drawn to the lips of Andalucian love
An angel sang tunes as we tumbled into the divine

On the Night of San Juan we jumped o'er the sun and we swam in a midnight moon
We burned what is gone and embraced the moment in the heat of our bodies' perfume

On the Night of San Juan to her bed we would come, spark and the bliss of a summer's romance
We danced with the dawn incarnations of life so sublime

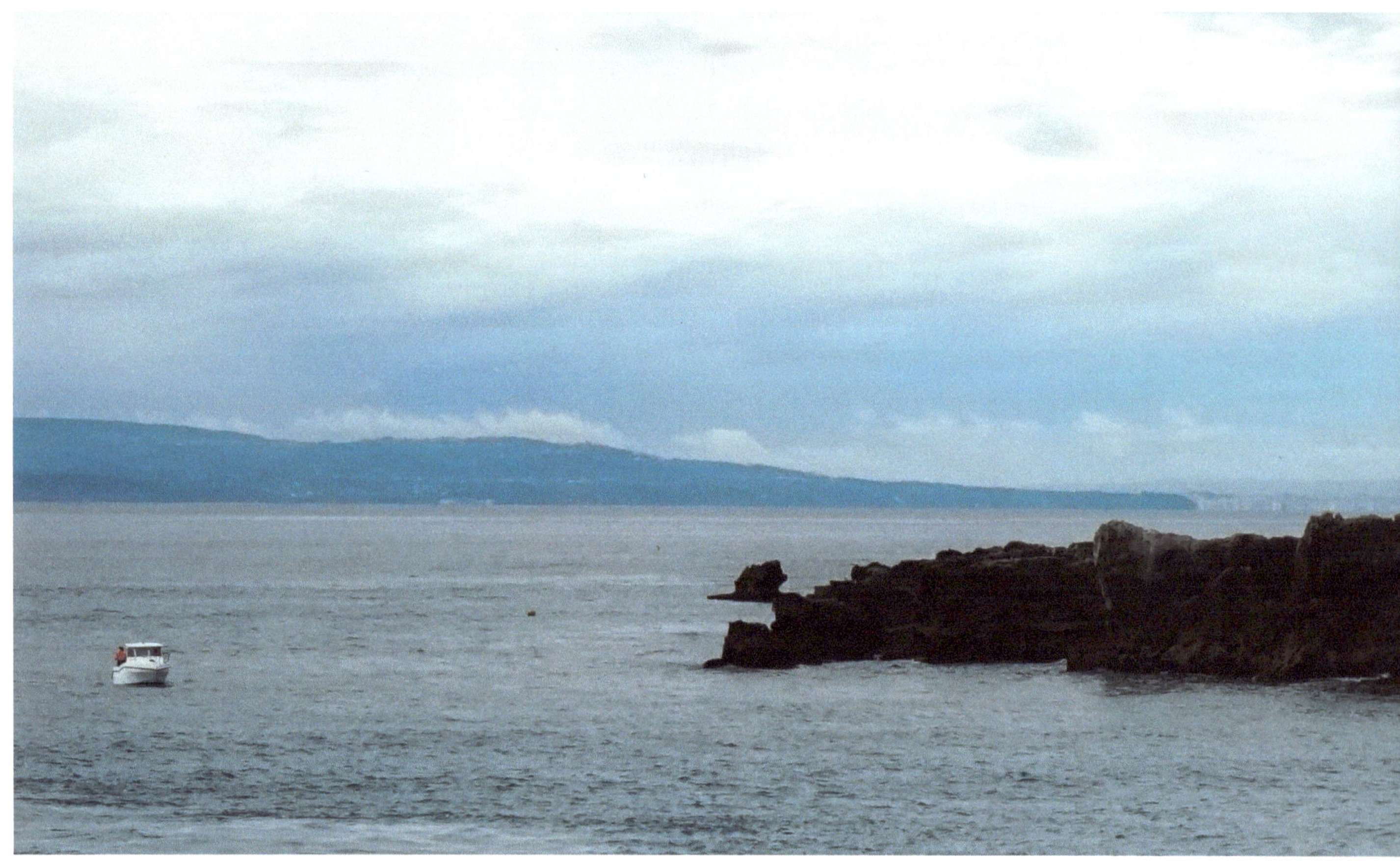

To the Night of San Juan my heart still belongs, though autumn has come to collect
The sea it turns cold, all the travelers go home, yet my soul still longs to connect

Oh, Night of San Juan I will never forget you, your memory's always with me
But I will write down her name and throw it into the flame of San Juan

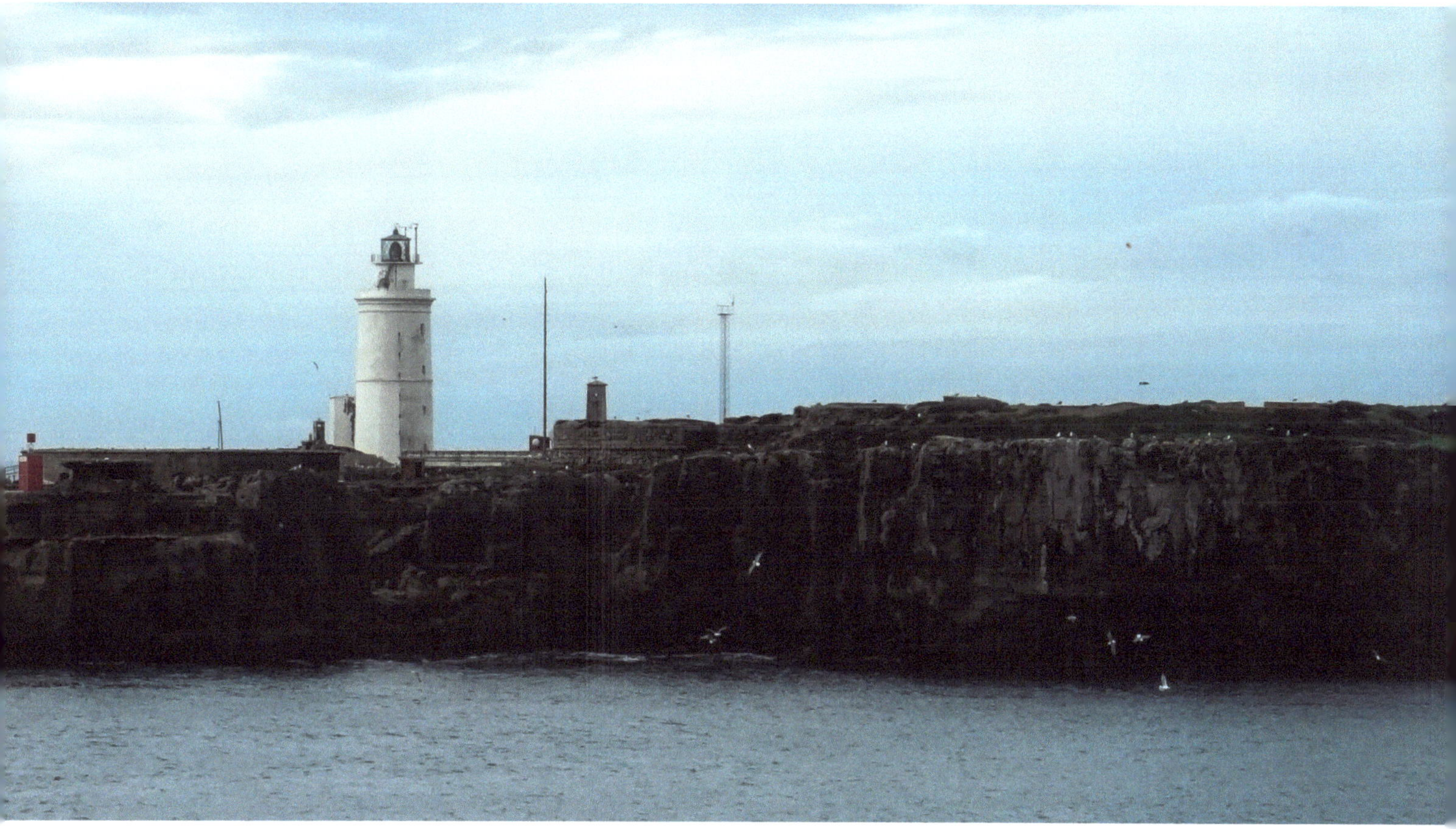

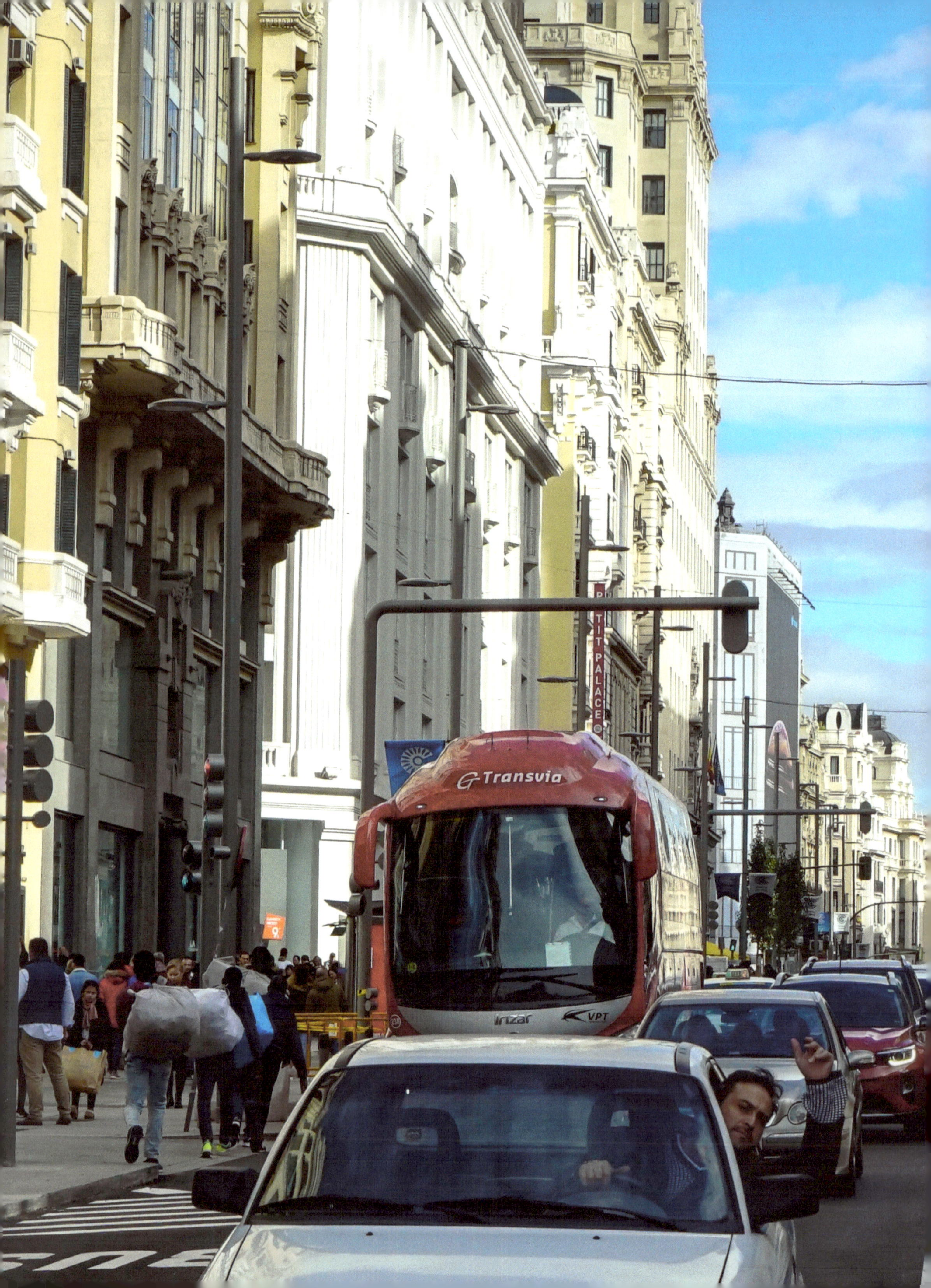
G·Transvia
Irizar
VPT
TIT PALACE

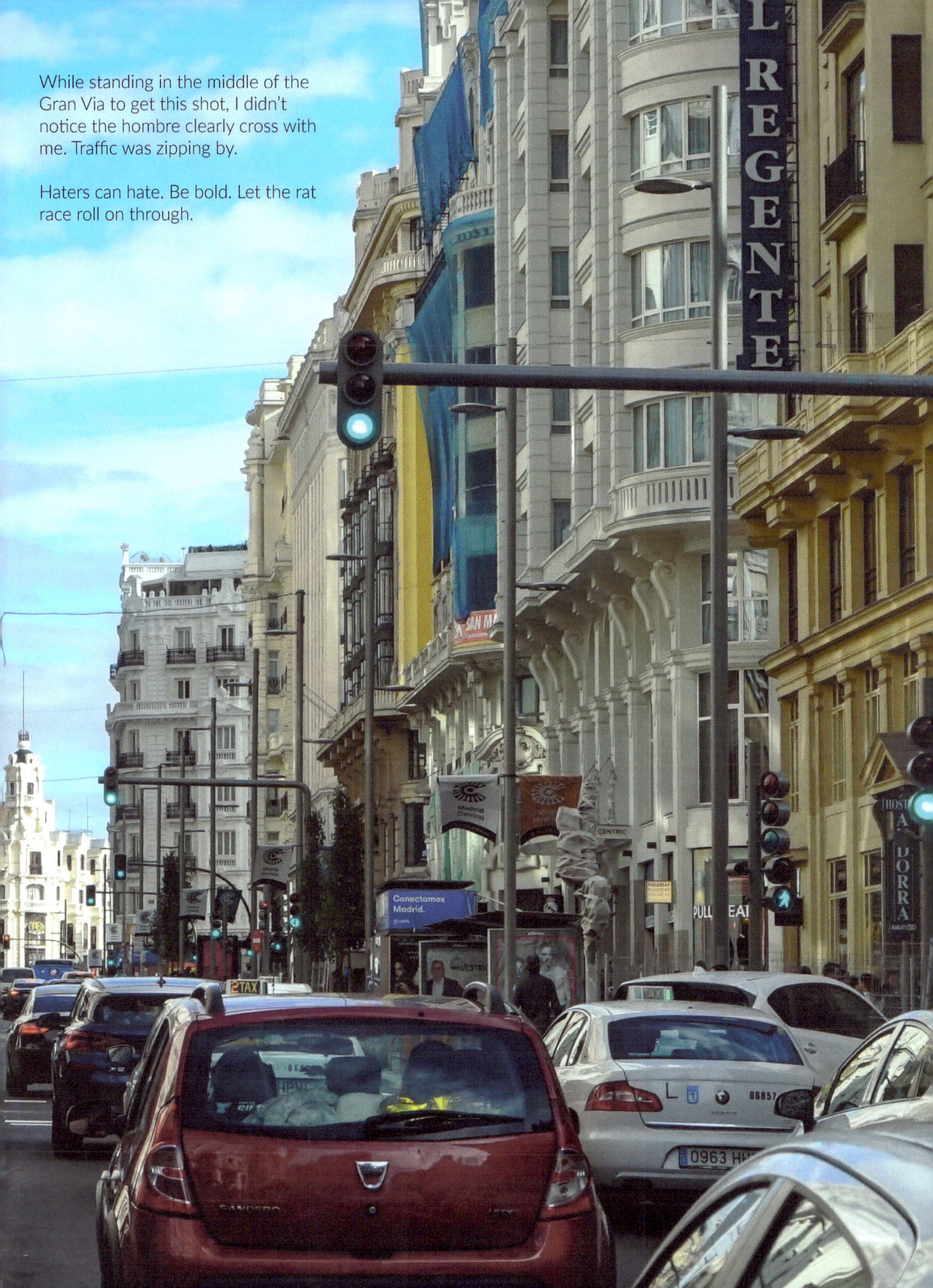

While standing in the middle of the Gran Via to get this shot, I didn't notice the hombre clearly cross with me. Traffic was zipping by.

Haters can hate. Be bold. Let the rat race roll on through.

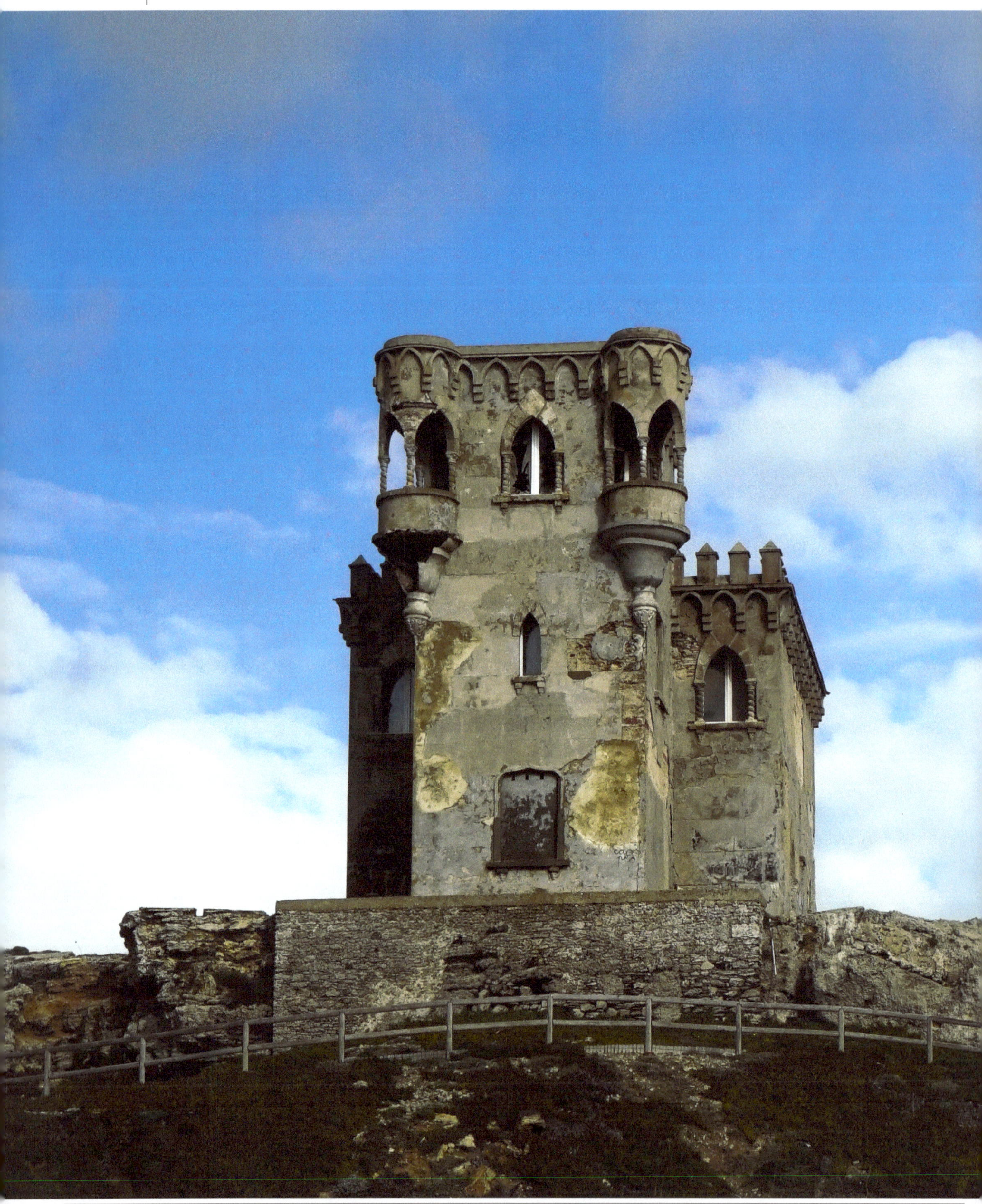

"Don Quijote soy, y mi profesión la de andante caballería. Son mis leyes, el deshacer entuertos, prodigar el bien y evitar el mal. Huyo de la vida regalada, de la ambición y la hipocresía, y busco para mi propia gloria la senda más angosta y difícil. ¿Es eso, de tonto y mentecato?"

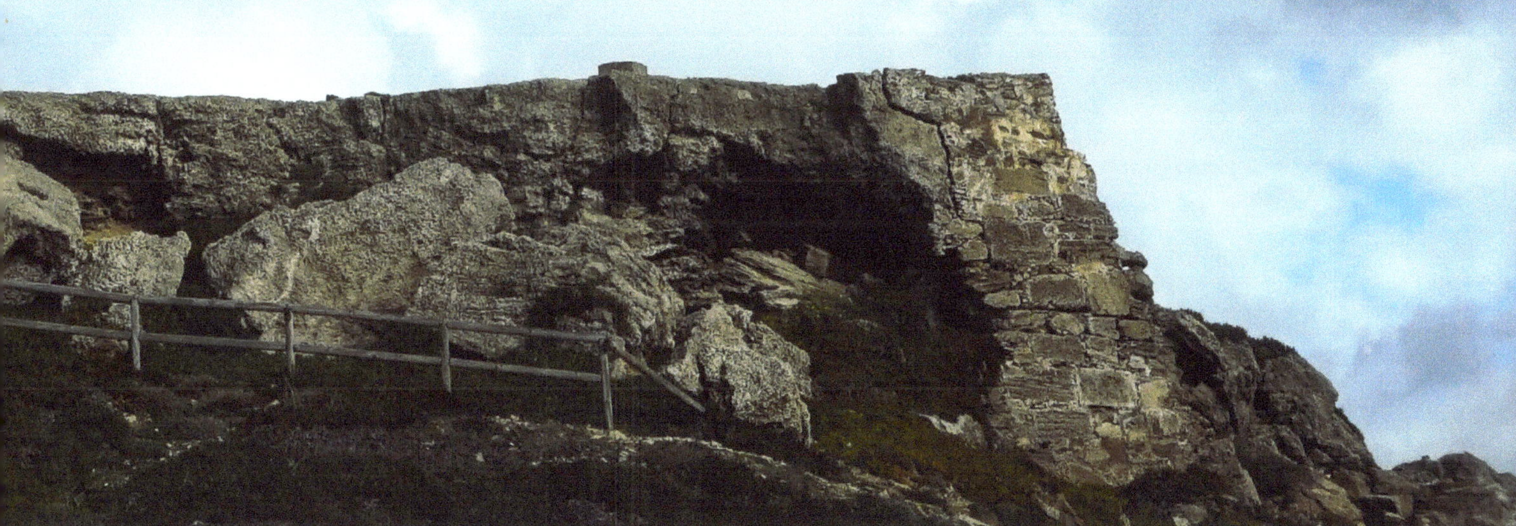

56

Back on the couch of an Amsterdam friend my finger hovers over ~~the~~ computer trigger, the quiver of my confidence in the uncommon choices ~~I make~~. Voices in my head saying a sofa for a bed is stupid. When does it end? Click send. Payment made. Bound for Spain ~~again~~. ~~The thought crosses my mind~~ this might be the last time. ~~Hustling out to make~~ It ~~seems~~ ~~It~~ unsustainable ~~and never amounts~~ ~~to punch in my bank~~ I'm GC ~~account~~ ~~I have~~ ~~just enough to cover the cost of a ticket~~ I book it because a Vaquero must go. ~~Six years on the road without failure~~ I guess. Six years on the road and I'm closer to Valhalla than home. But honestly, there's no turning back. My back's against the wall to make it all make sense. ~~I said~~ I wanted to change the world, but istead the world has made me strange. I take off the buffalo nickle dangling round my neck and set it yet again by my bags, ~~waiting for a Dutch dawn when~~ ~~I dawn it on~~. I contemplate the value of ~~such~~ small change. ~~I wait for close~~ ~~my eyes~~ and wait for the Dutch dawn to help me move on.

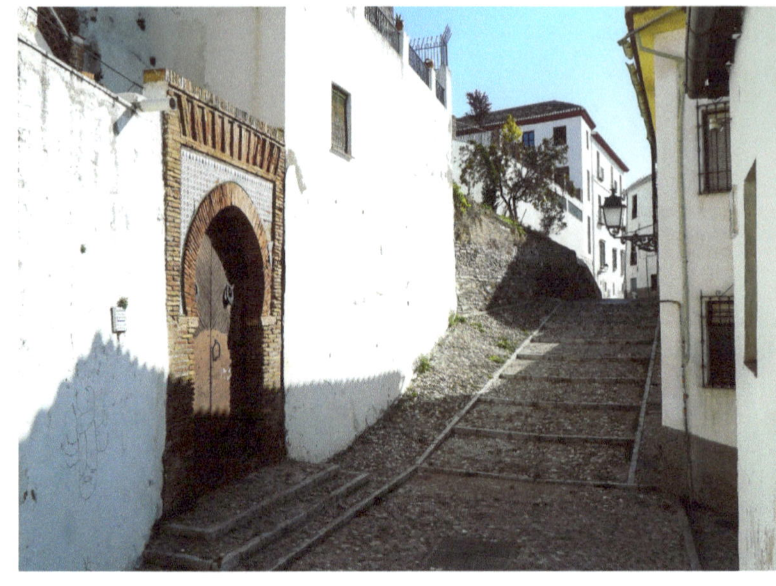

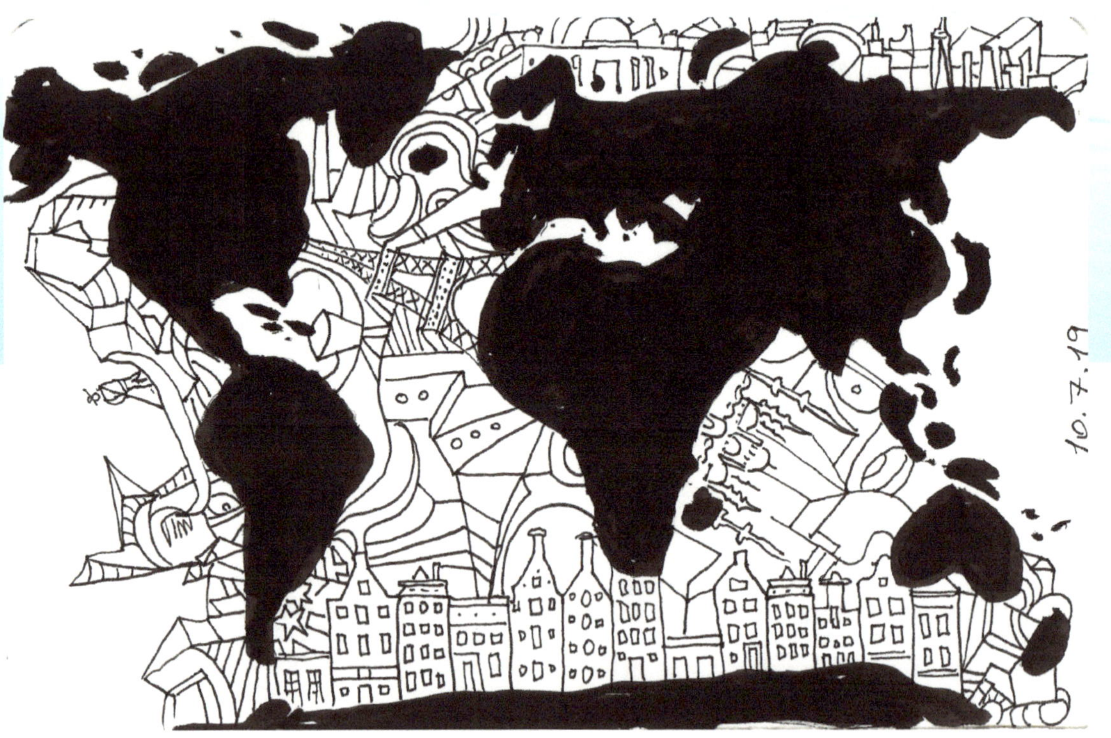

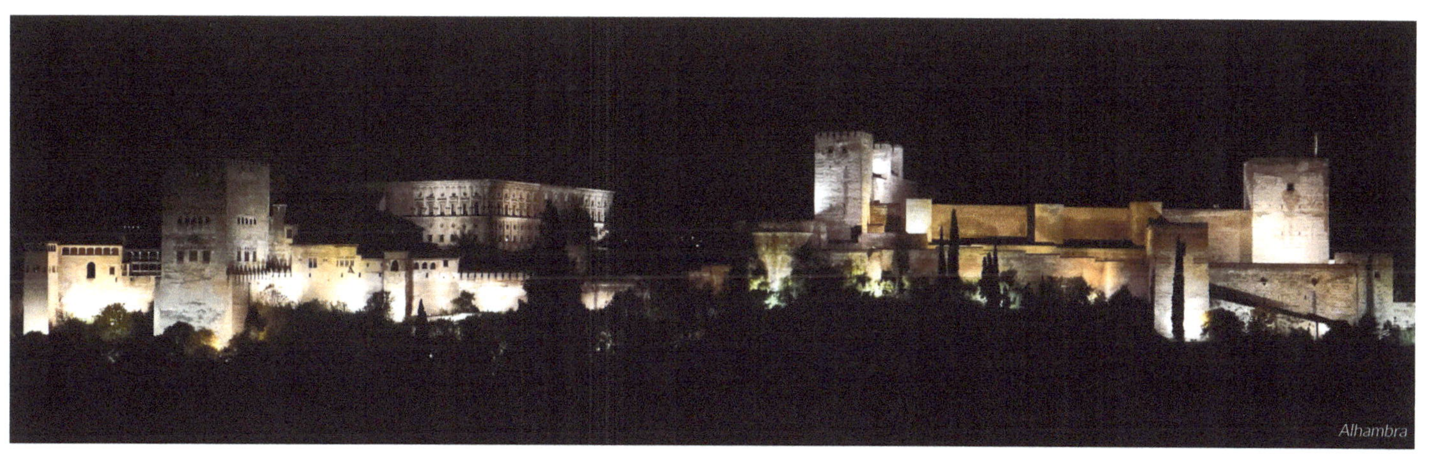

"Do you want to be free, or do you just want to feel good?" - Ram Dass

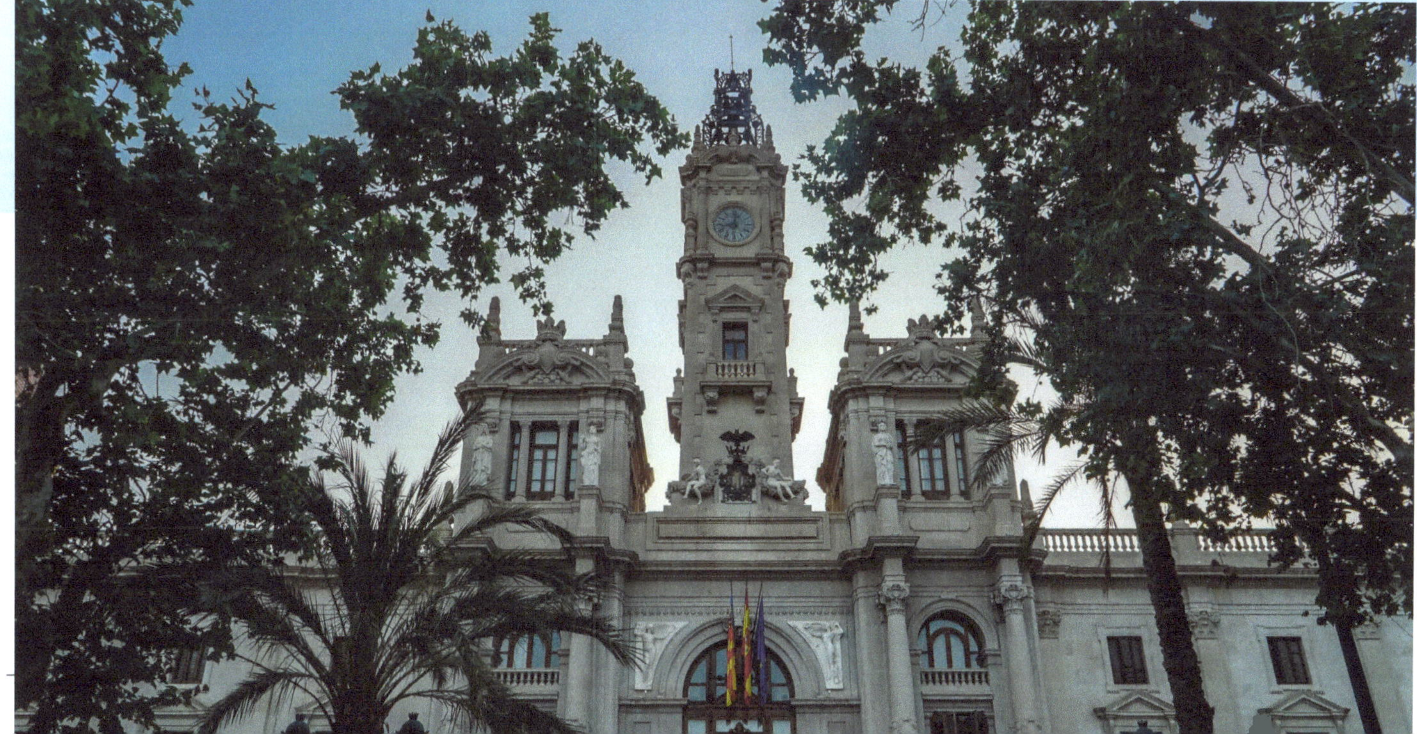

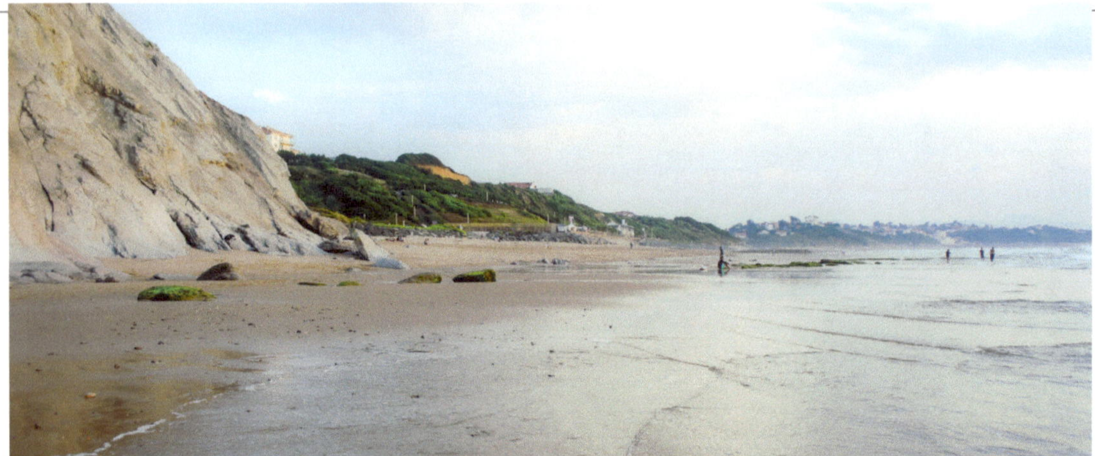

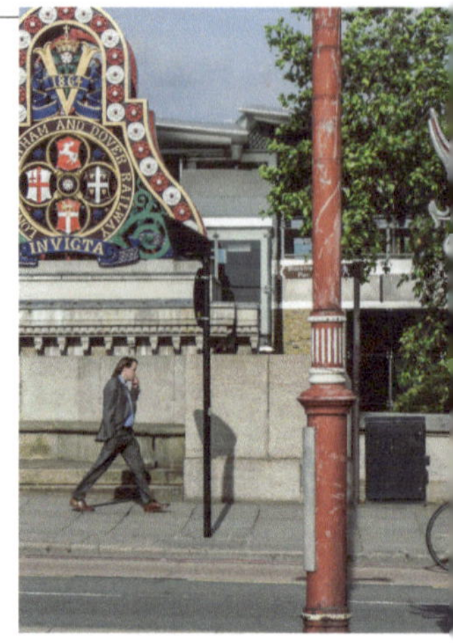

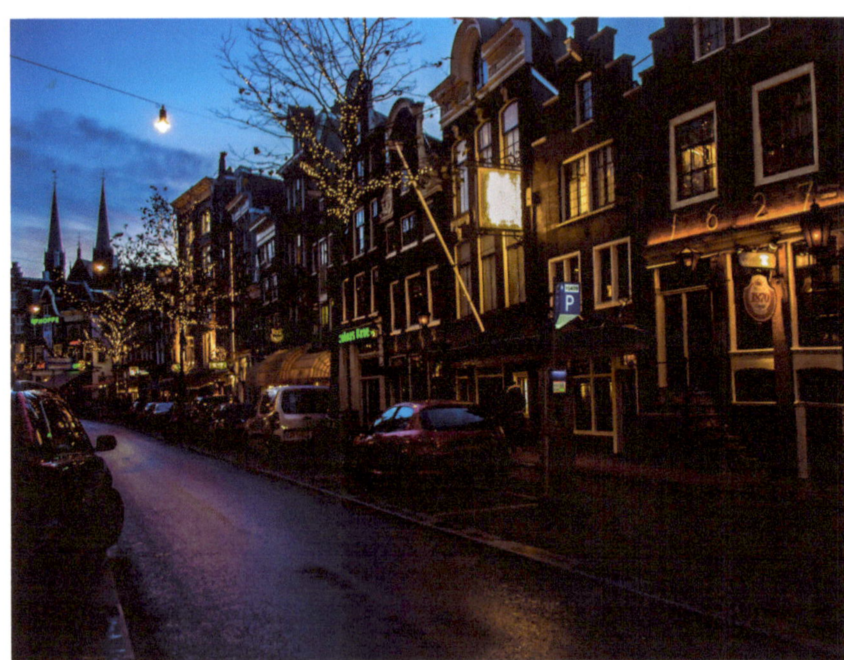

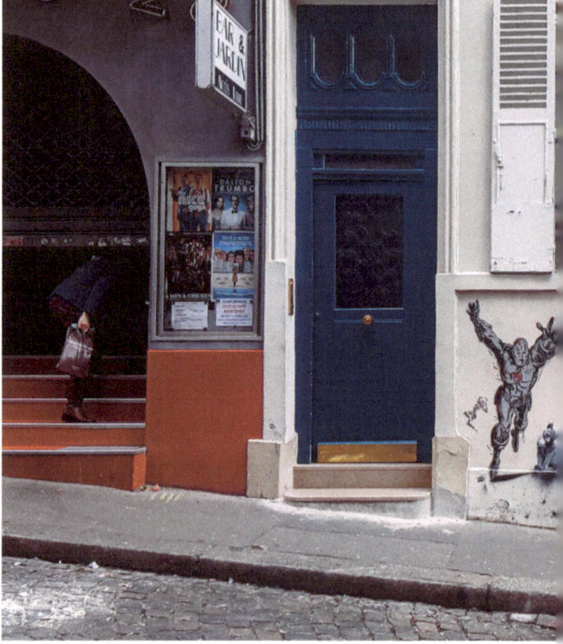

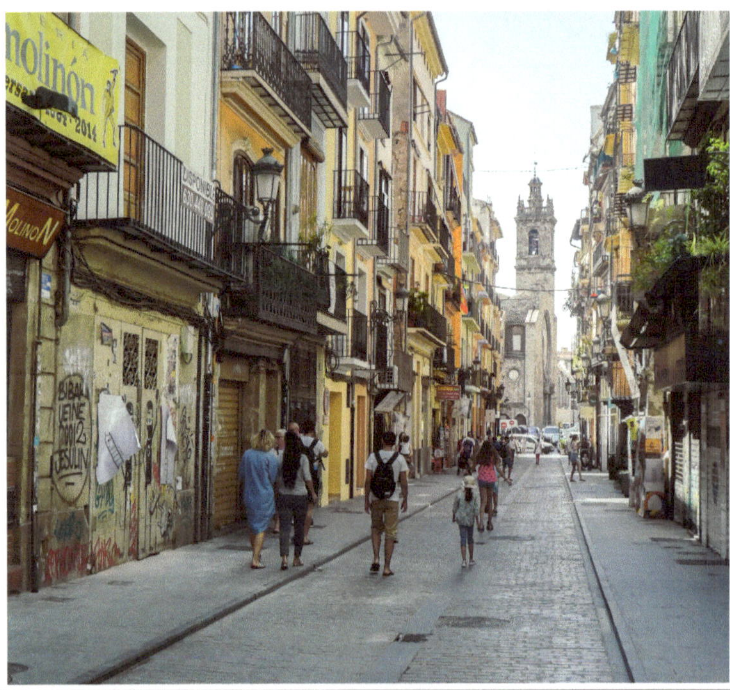

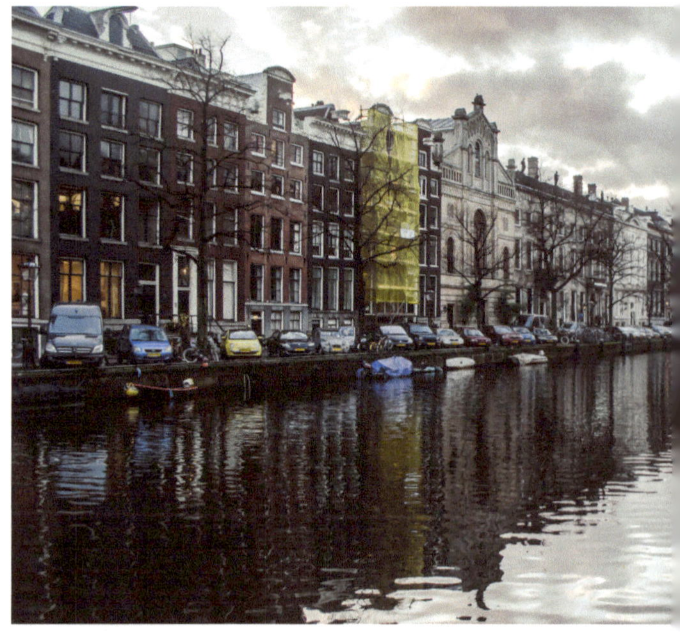

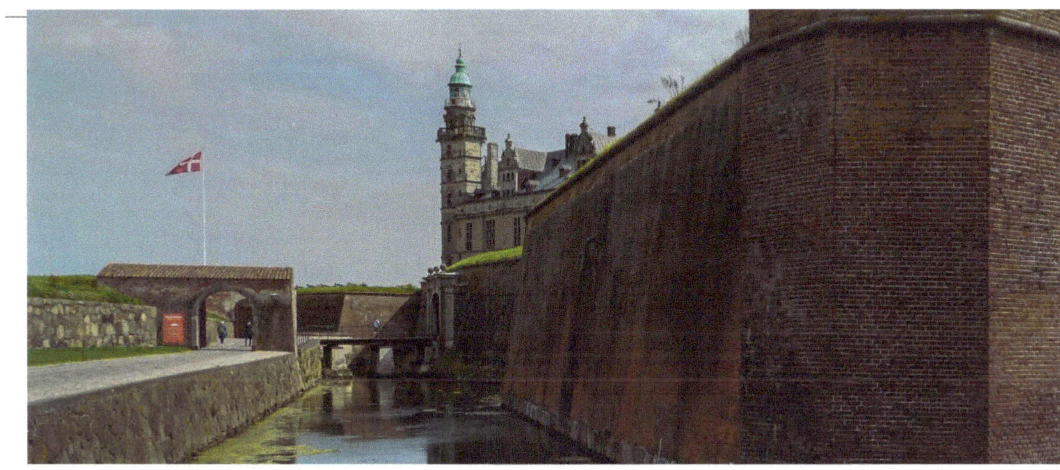

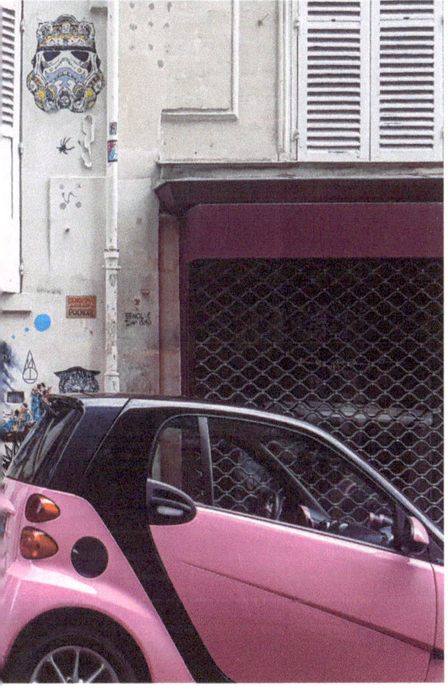

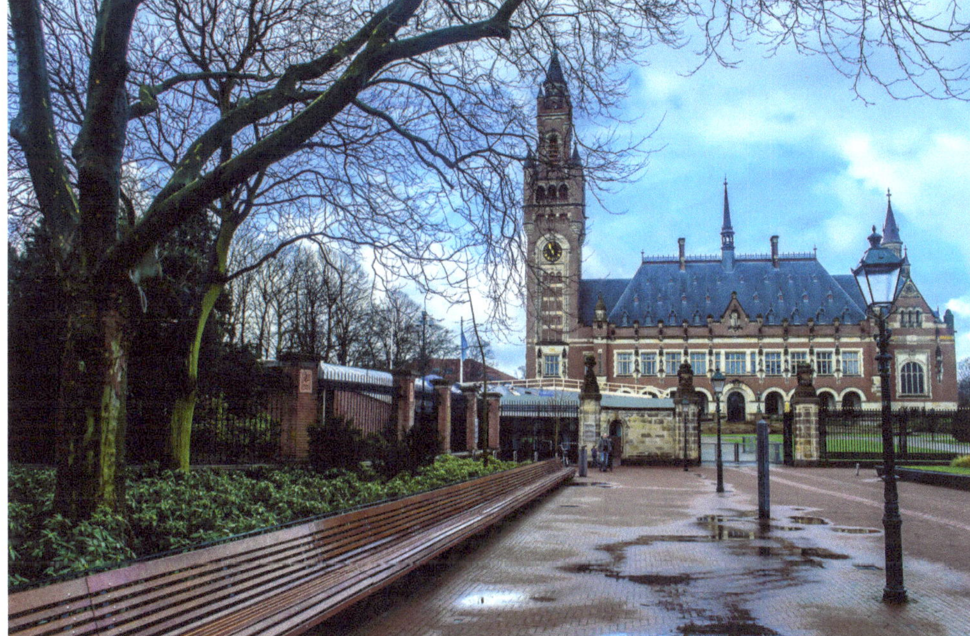

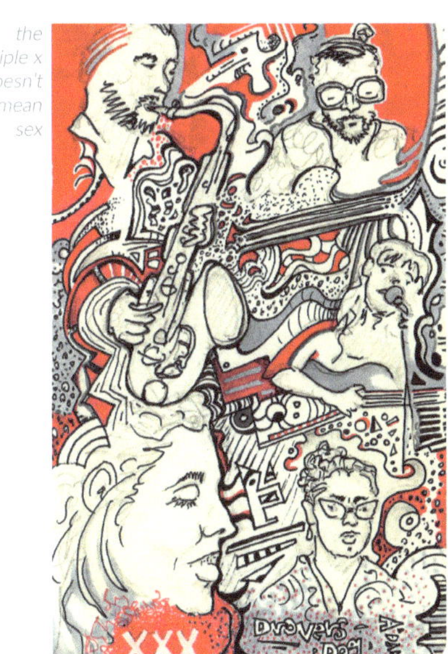
the
triple x
doesn't
mean
sex
XXX

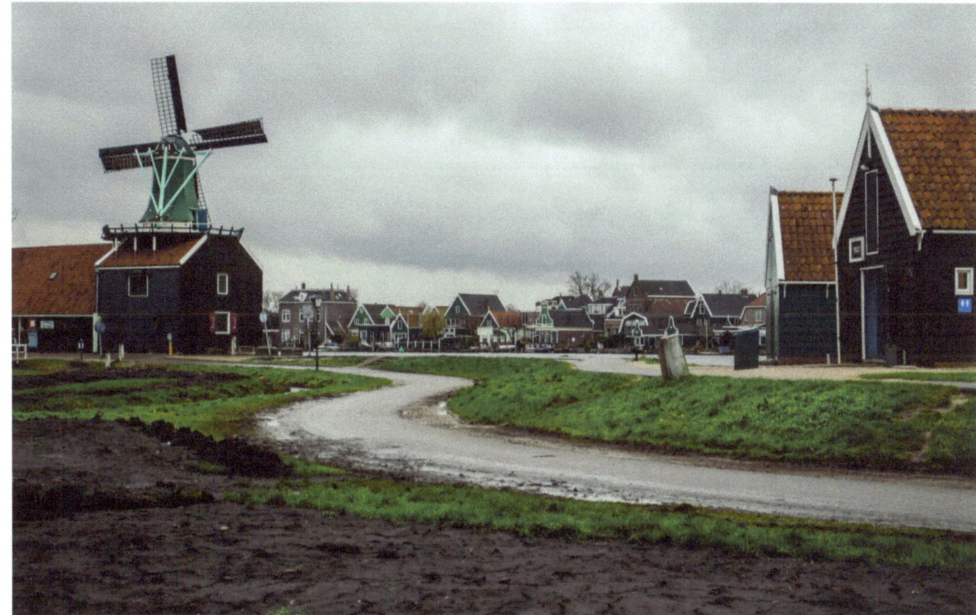

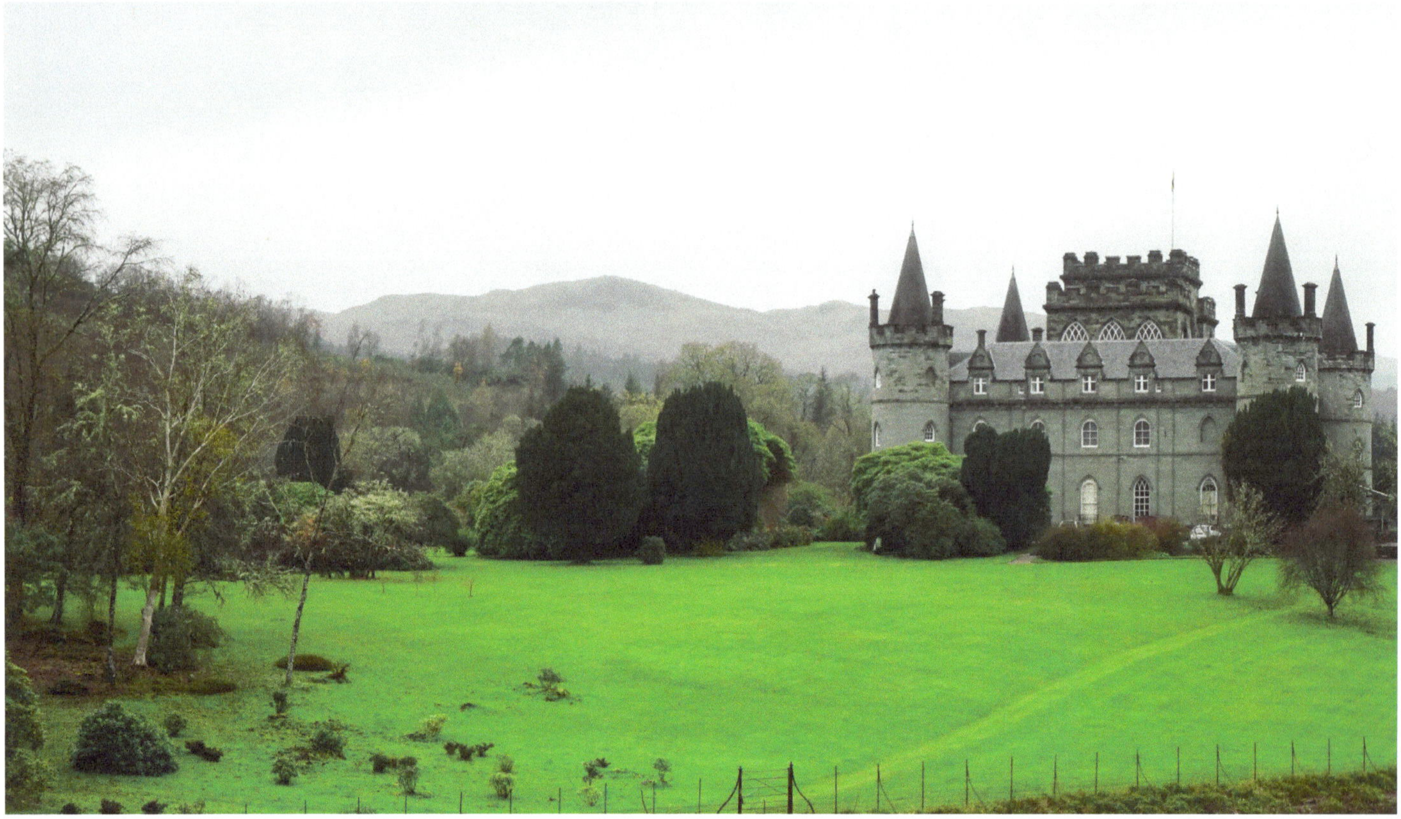

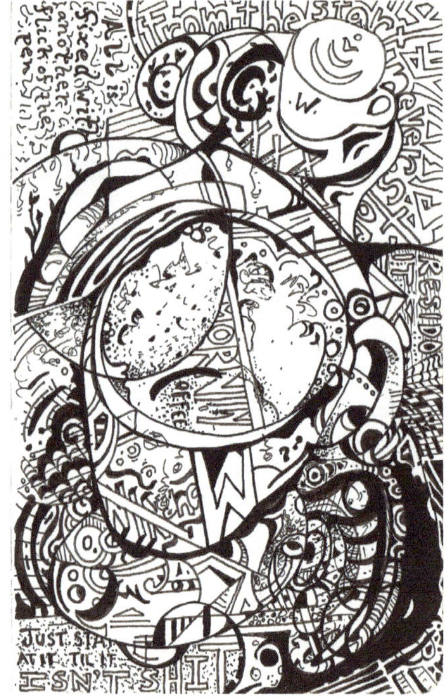

I'm gonna tell you something you may not want to hear.

Being a traveler (and even more so a nomad) comes with curses. It's Pandora's box. Once you've opened it, there's no turning back. It's like that time your best friend shattered his arm on the homemade halfpipe. You can't unsee that mangled appendage with the bones sticking out. The imprint is on your brain.

What does this have to do with travel?

Let's just say it leaves a mark and sometimes that's a scar. It's the dark side that comes with the mind expanding coin flip of stepping beyond your borders.

At first, it's like, "oh wow!" and then it becomes "hmmm..."

You'll find yourself lost. That's when you know you're in the right place.

Tearing down the walls of preconceived notions is a joyous battering ram of liberation, but now that you're in the wide open, you have to make sense of it. The more you see the world, the more difficult it is to put perspectives in a tidy, little box. Pandora might actually be Mary Poppins' cousin. It's not a box at all. Turns out the mixed bag is vast and bottomless.

Back in your shitty town (the Street Musician of Amsterdam said it, not me), it might have been easy to think things are the way they are, filing beliefs away into your routine.

Travel thrusts you into the endless desert dunes where binary thinking becomes a mirage.

Lines become harder to draw. Suddenly, nothing is what you thought it was, and as you traipse across the Sahara of your mind, you find any attempt to define ideas is like a fistful of sand sifting through your fingers.

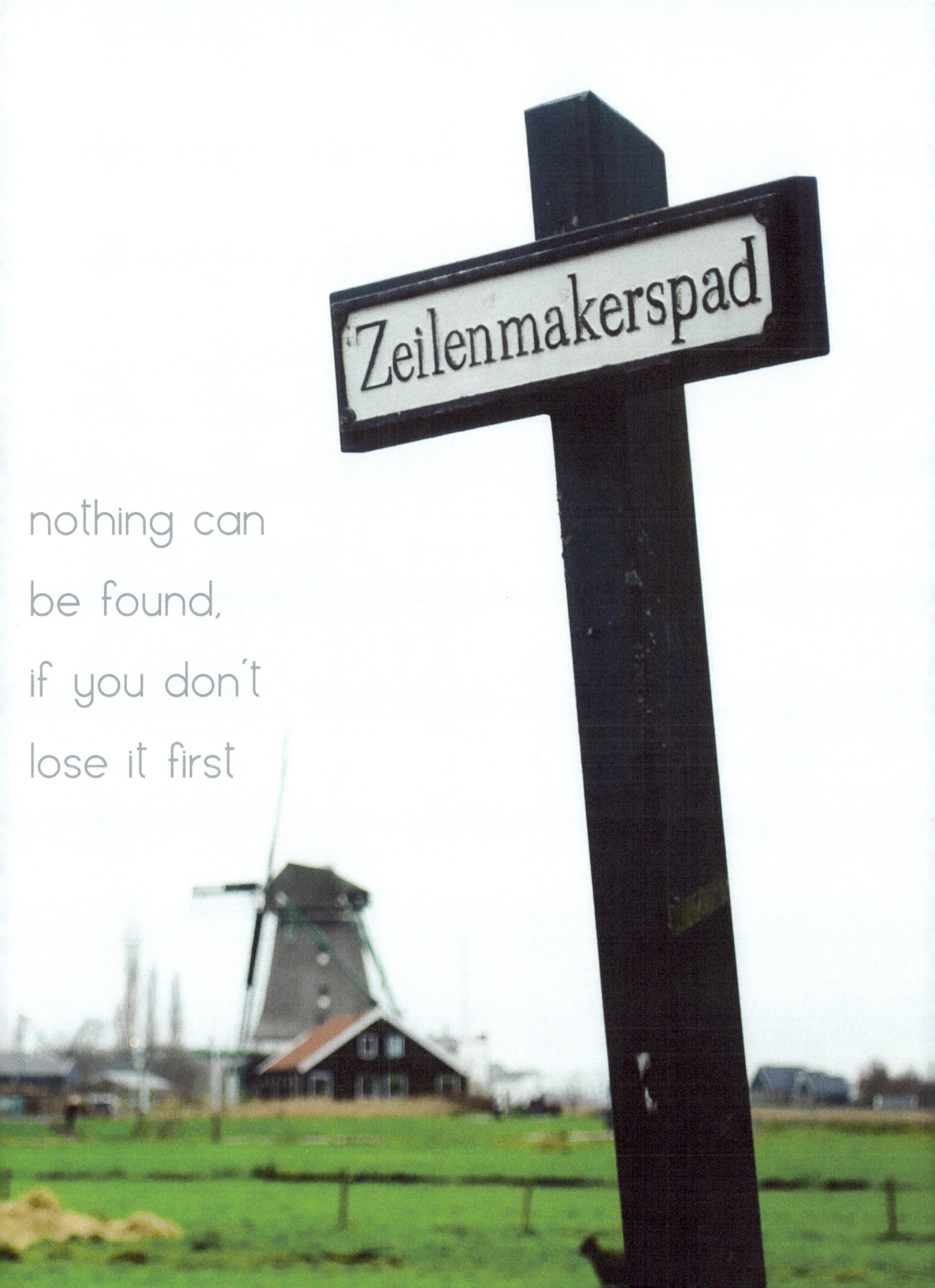

Zeilenmakerspad
nothing can
be found,
if you don't
lose it first

De molen gaat niet

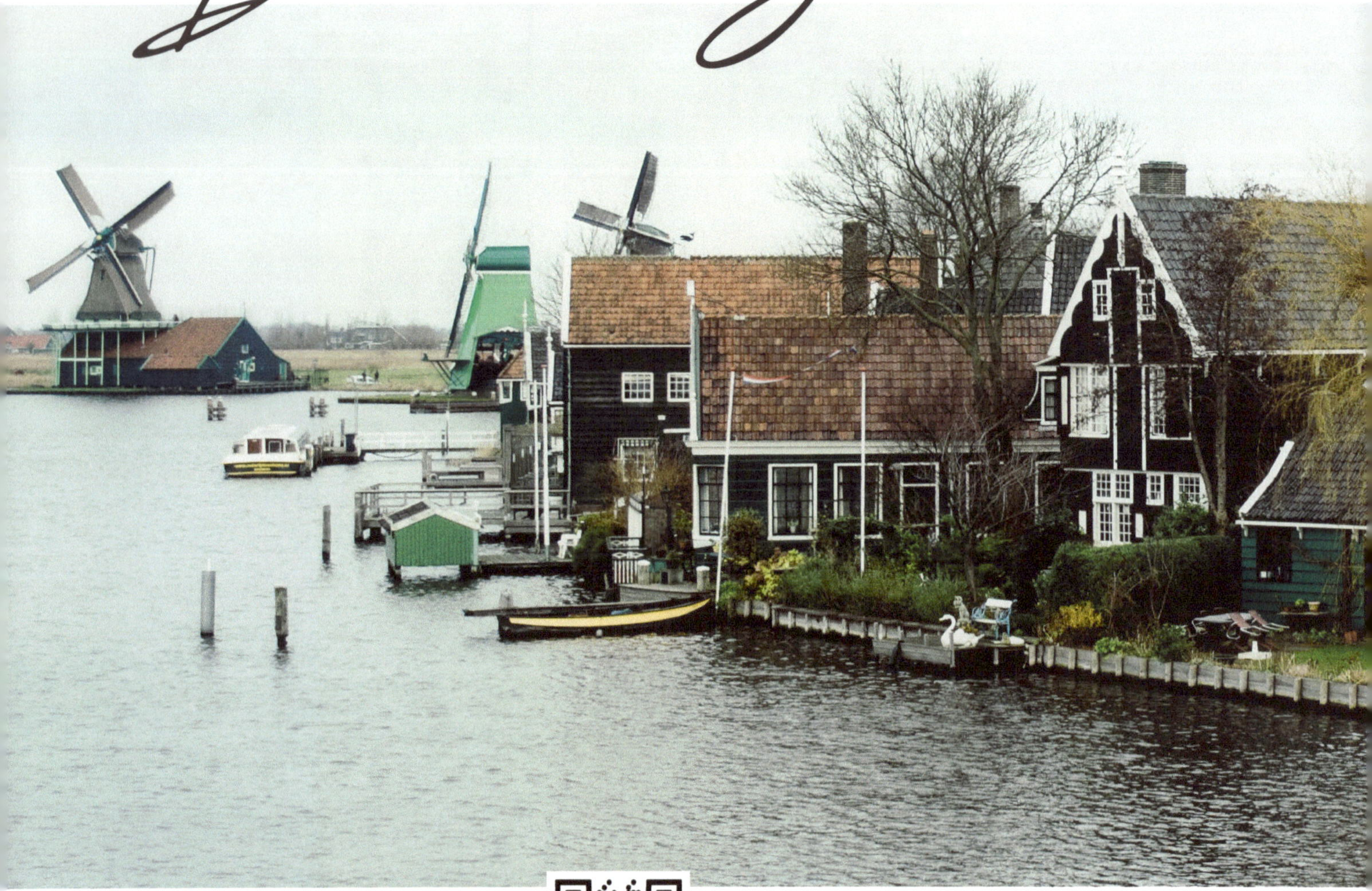

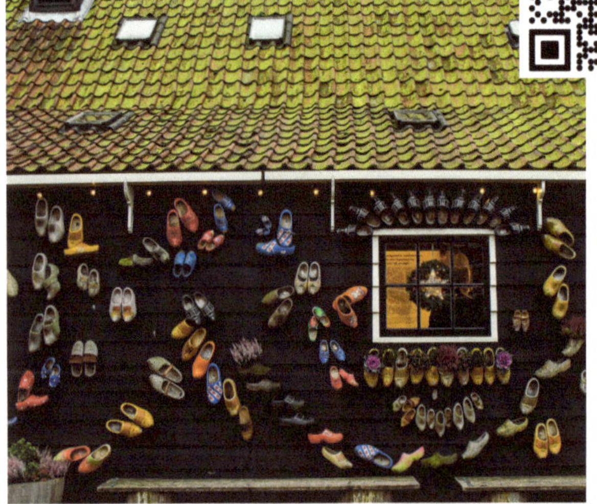

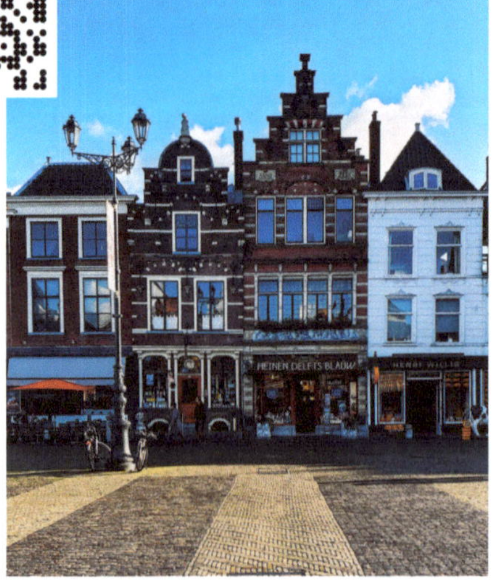

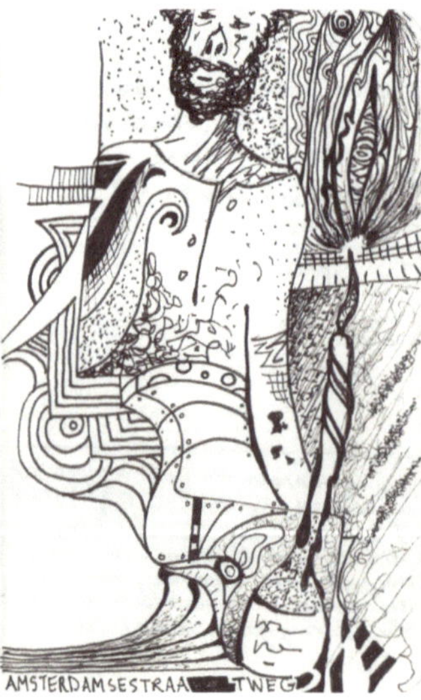

om met wind die voorbij is

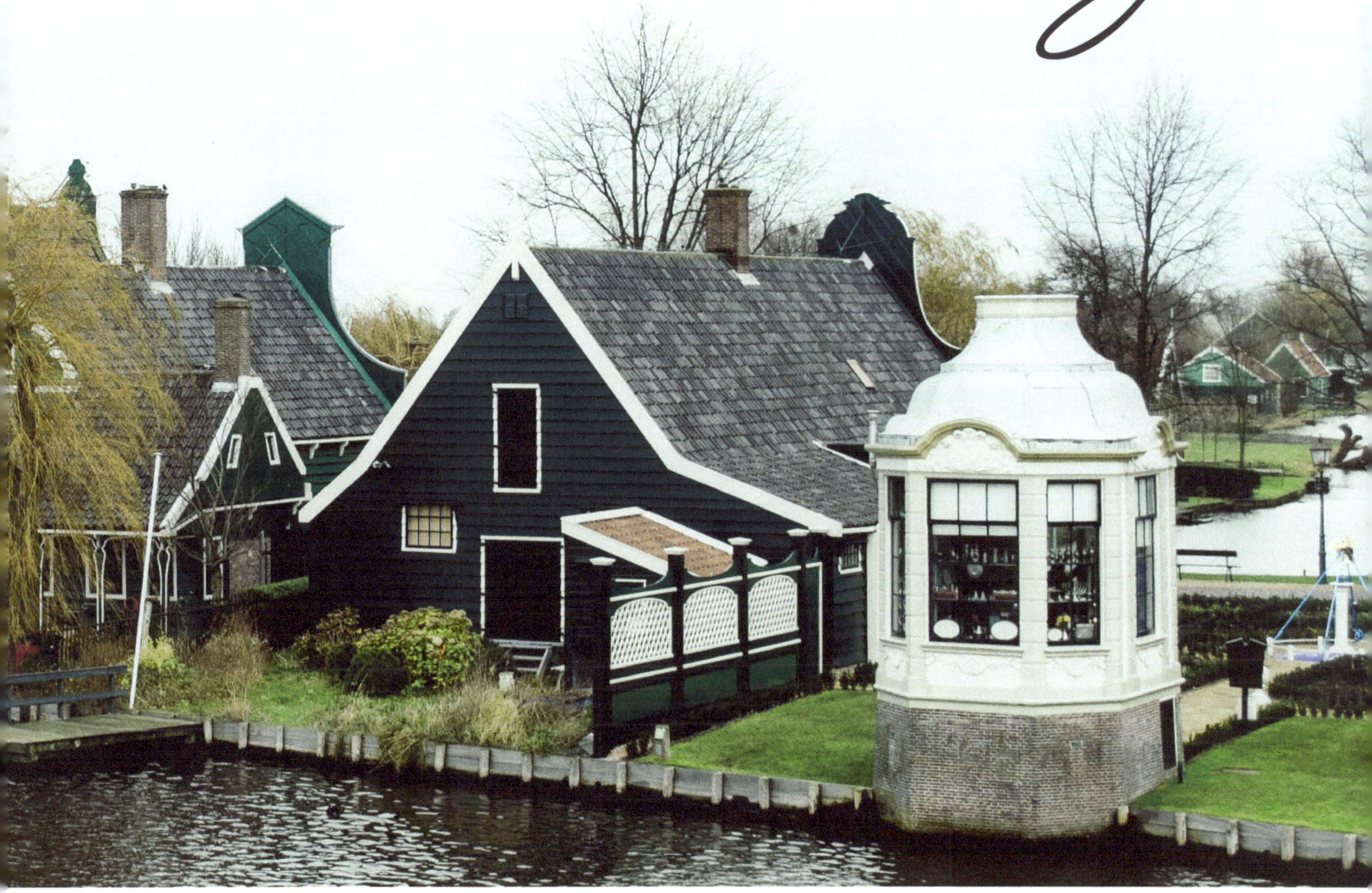

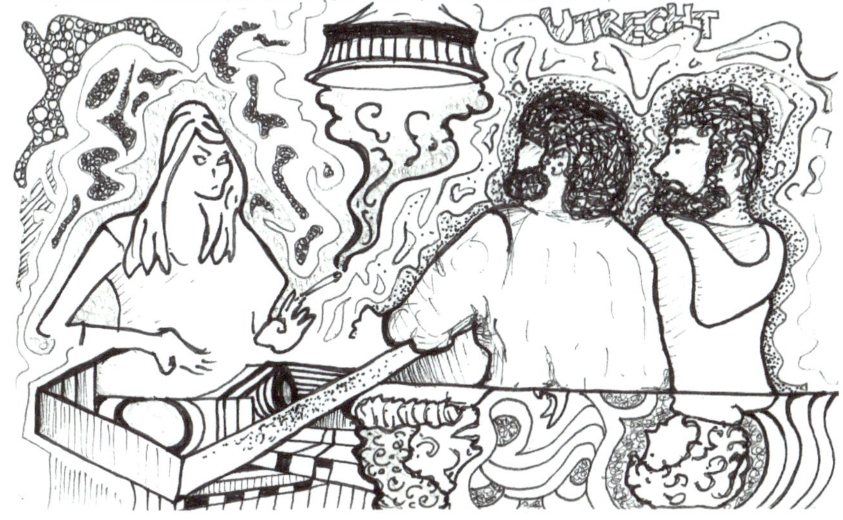

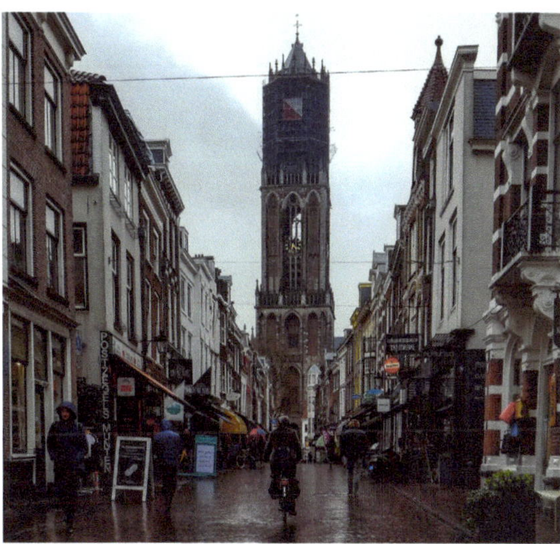

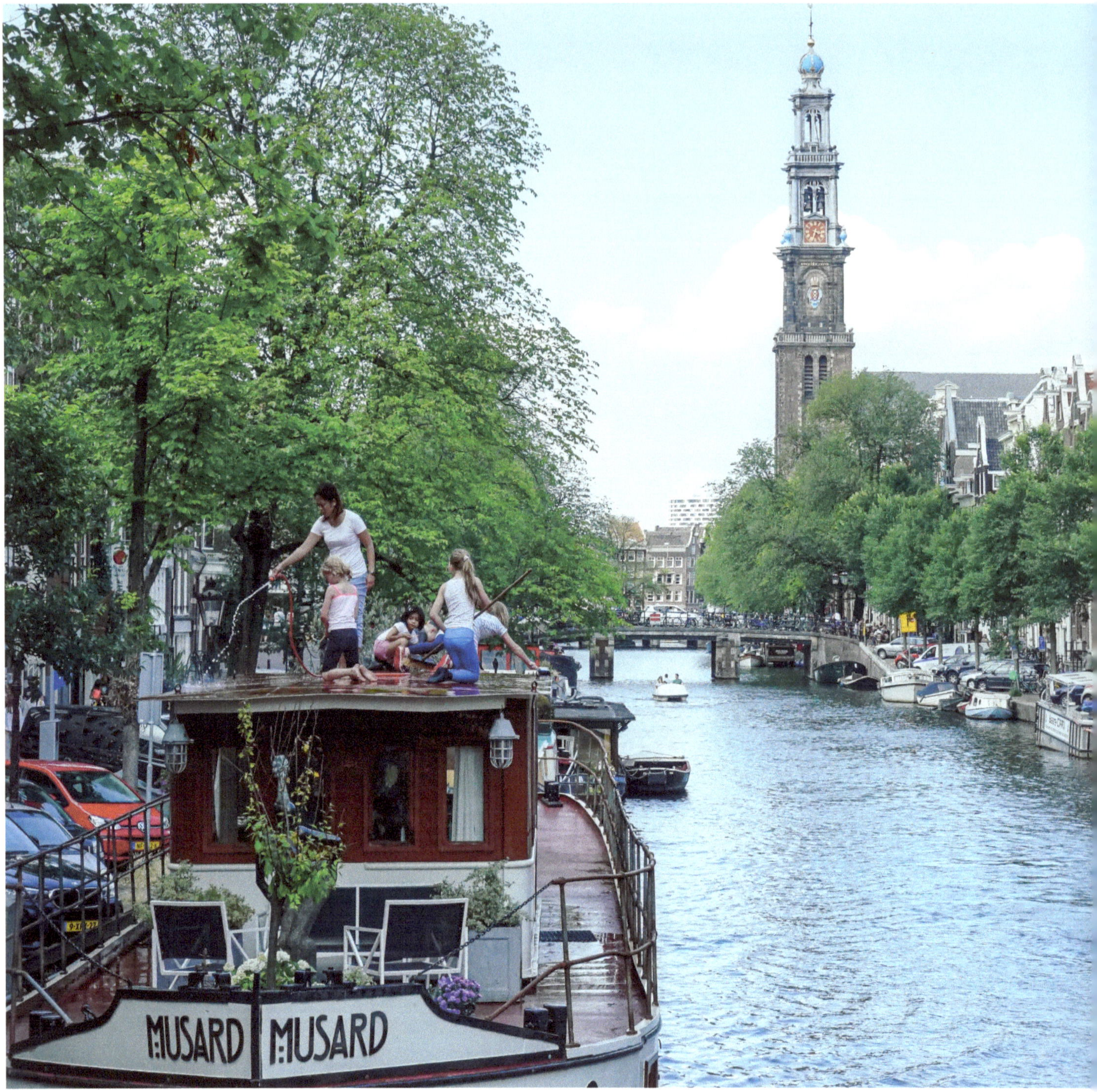

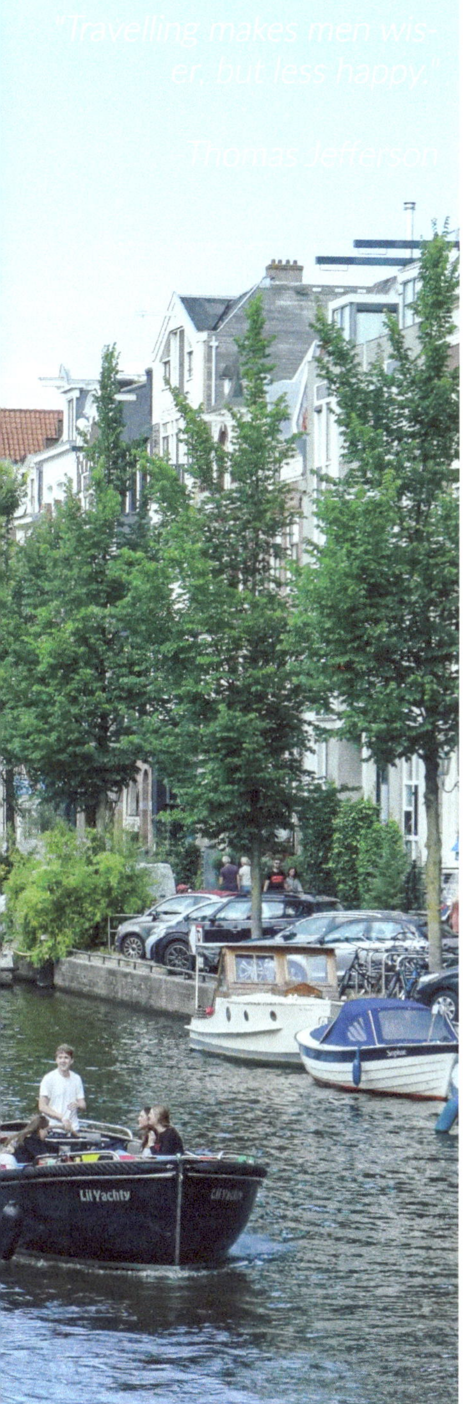

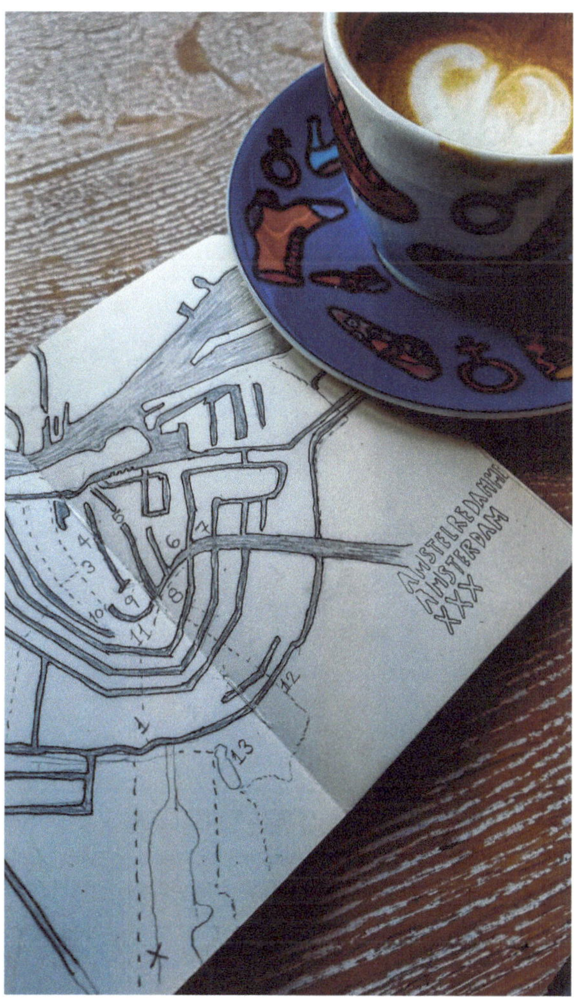

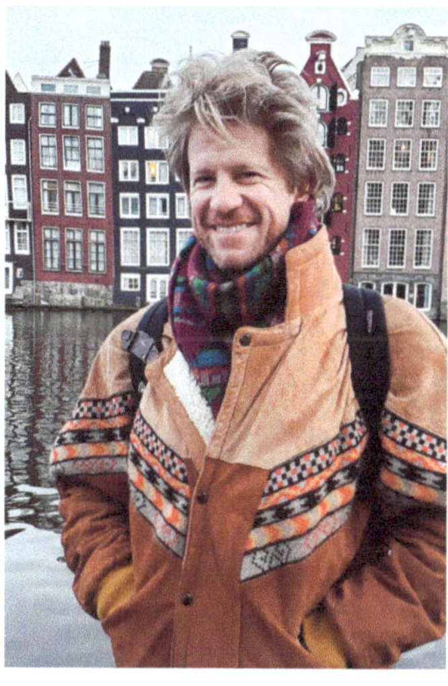

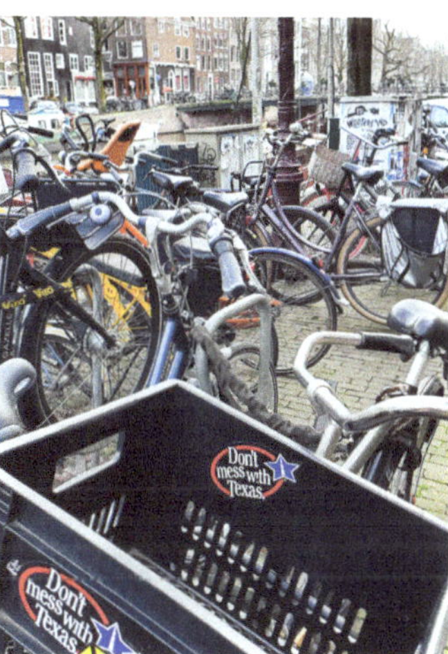

I find it interesting Thomas Jefferson, the guy accredited with penning those wise inalienable rights that includes the pursuit of happiness, would come to suggest wisdom and happiness don't jive. I may be adding some personal context, but I see the truth in it.

Happiness is often associated with comfort and assuredness. Travel will rip that right away from you.

Perhaps this hazy, grey conundrum is revealed in the beloved founding father himself, former French ambassador and American president responsible for the Declaration of Independence, the Louisiana Purchase, and a profound well of intellectual sociology, while at the same time a slave owner capable of despicable human behaviors.

If you're bold enough, it'll make your head spin and your stomach turn.

The good news is, this breakdown and transformation is part of the path to a more elevated form of happiness: enlightenment.

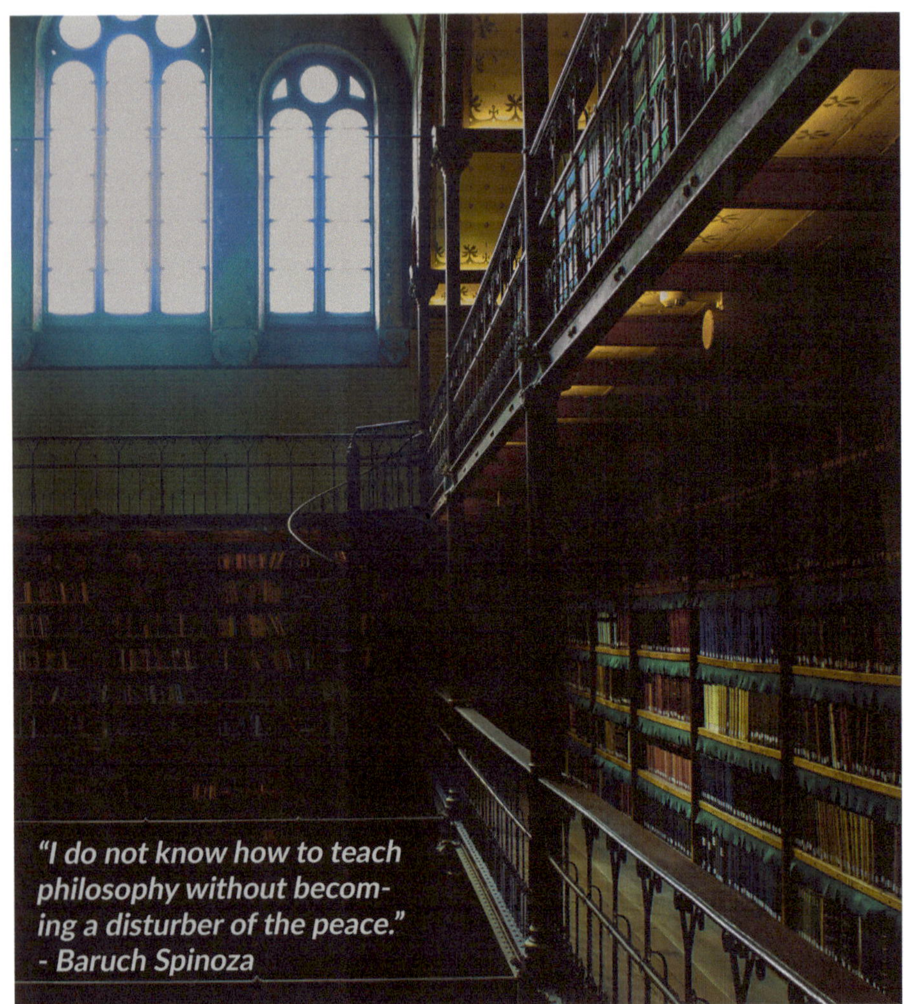

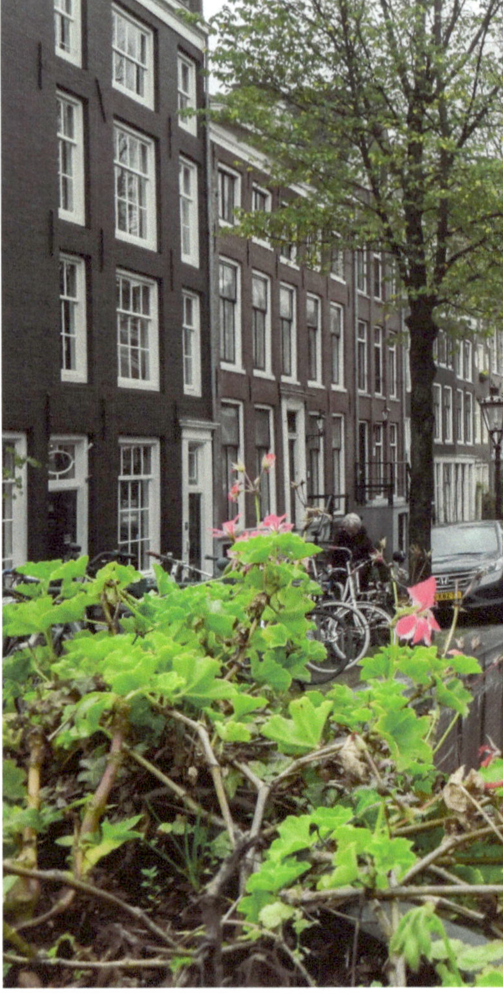

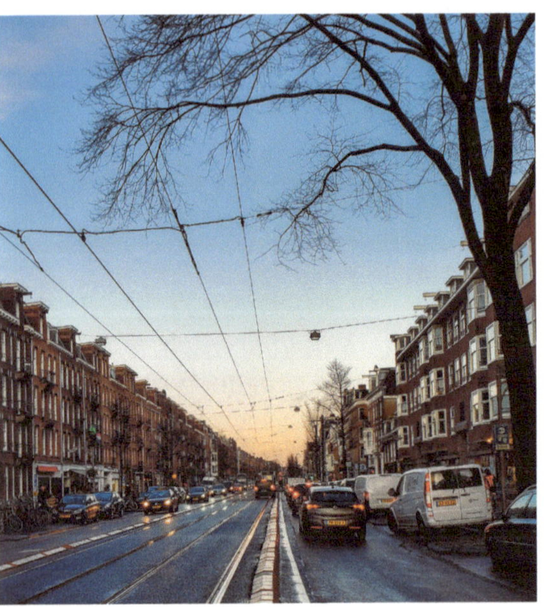

the Overtoom
and the
gauntlet
of Amsterdam

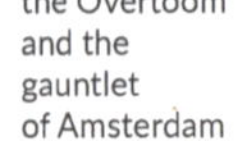

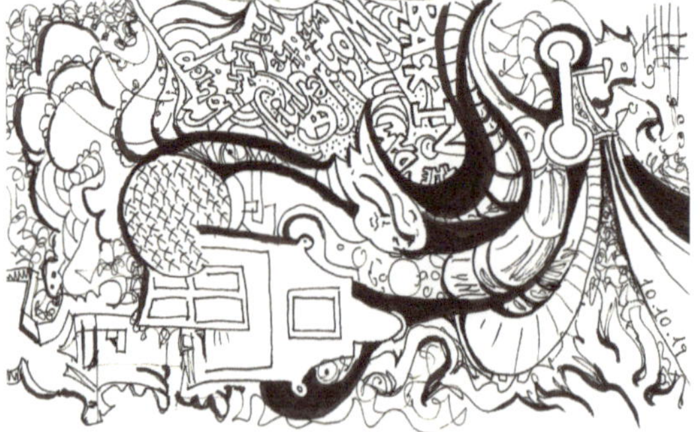

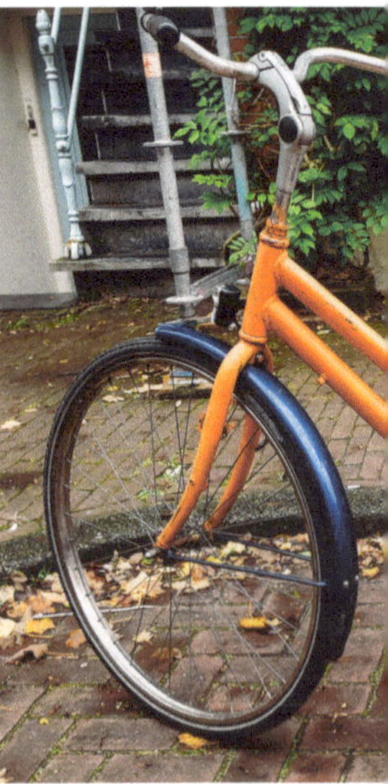

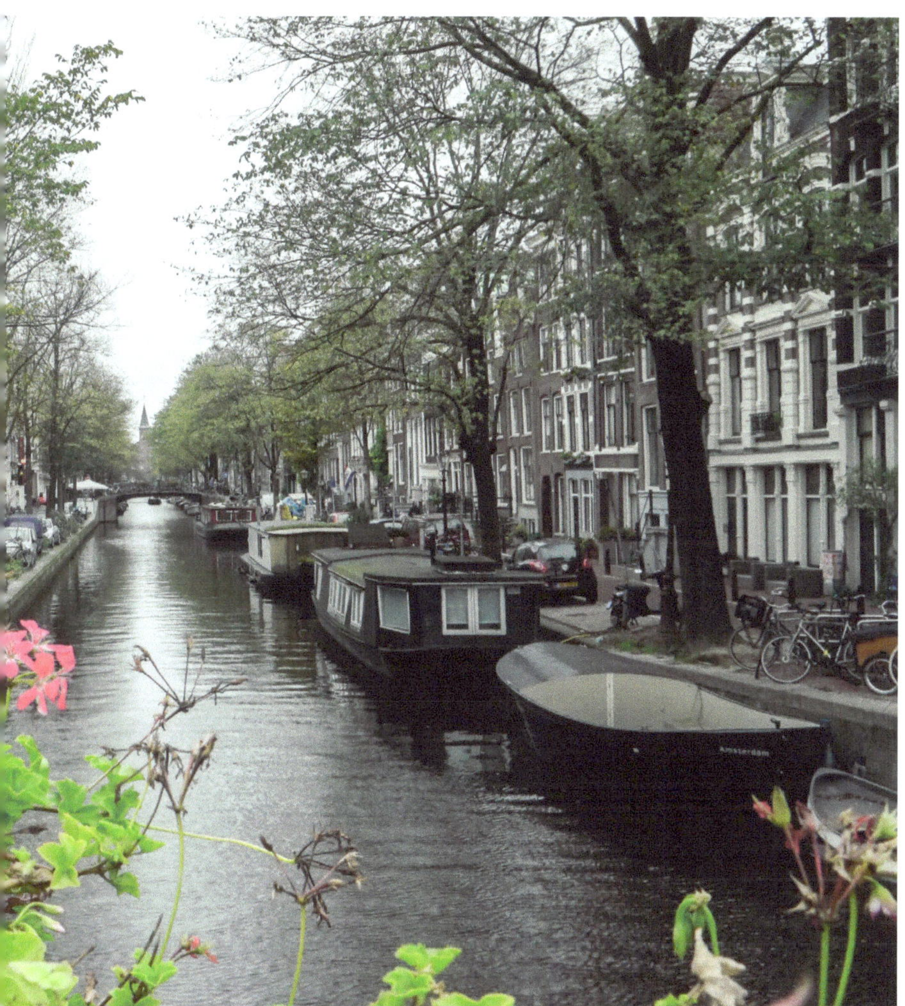

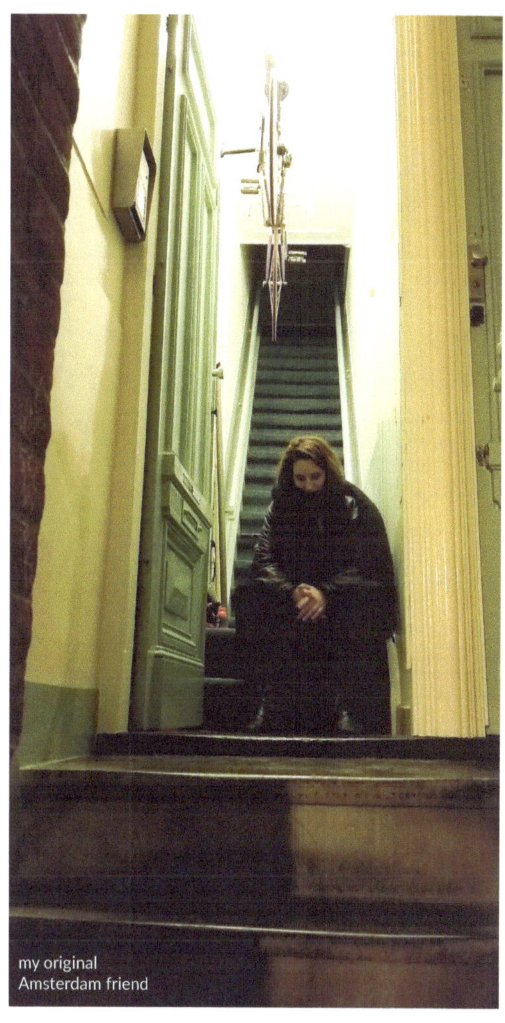

my original
Amsterdam friend

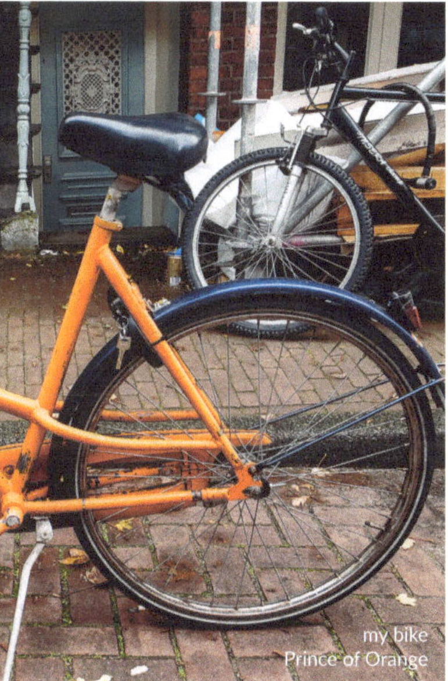

my bike
Prince of Orange

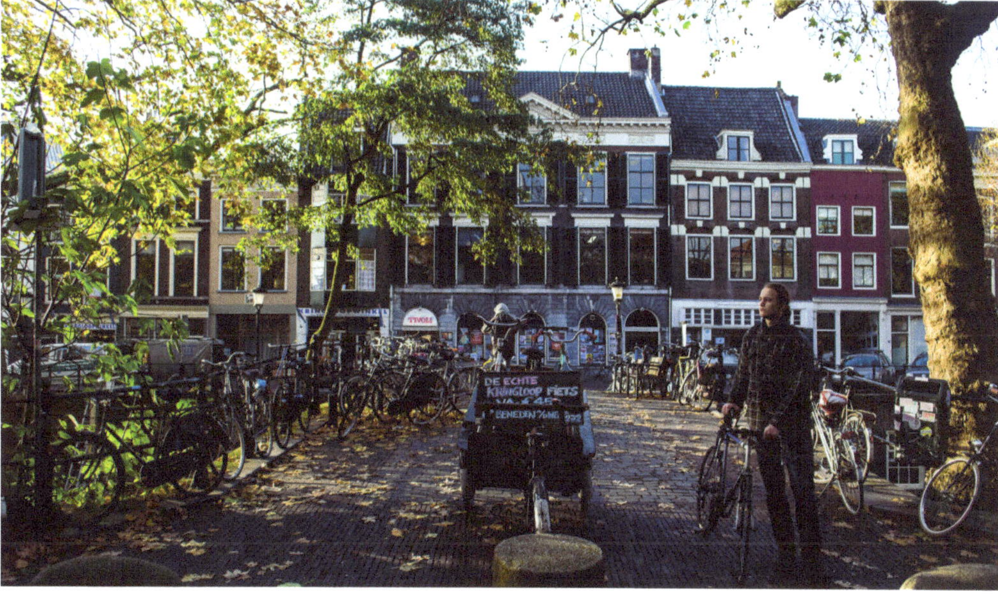

Barely a man when I met you at the Dam
Wandering red windows and cafes of green
Over bridges, through the fog where the world comes to walk
In Starry Night daydreams you whispered to me

This is your song of Amsterdam
Come cowboy and castaway
This is your story
This is your song of Amsterdam
Gezellig, you get it free

Fell in love with a girl from the lowlands
Again I would come to a city beneath that swallows the sea
At the Cafe de Koe and out in the Oud West
Friends opened their homes when the girl wouldn't

This is your song of Amsterdam
Come cowboy and castaway
This is your story
This is your song of Amsterdam
It's gedoog, light your smoke and sing

Je pense donc je suis
I am Amsterdam

A western wind blows and I'm going home
But a new Amsterdam I am
And you're always here

I think therefore I Amsterdam

On a glorious summer day, I was hanging out with the Street Musician of Amsterdam at Museumplein, a large, grassy square surrounded by the city's most famous museums. Out in front of the enormous, renaissance-styled national gallery that houses priceless works of Dutch masters, stood a playful structure more social media famous than any of the paintings inside the Rijksmuseum.

If you've ever been to Amsterdam or dreamed of going there, you probably know the red and white Instagram magnet that draws every selfie-loving tourist on the planet.

My buddy scoffed, voicing his distaste for the kind of mindless tourism climbing all over the art installation's huge letters, absentminded to the real works of art housed in the monumental building serving as their backdrop. He went on to tell me that the "I Amsterdam" brand was created by the tourism board in the 20th century twilight as a marketing ploy. Things weren't so good then. I guess it worked.

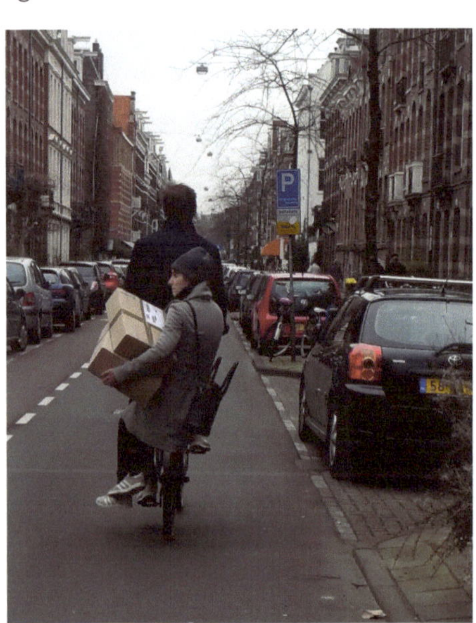

Fast forward twenty years and Amsterdam is such an international hot spot the same board is trying to backpedal on their success. During the summer months, hordes of inebriated idiots and basic bitches flood the smallest big city in Europe, the effect of which has generated the ire of locals like my buddy (albeit he makes a living from the music lovers who have enough wit to tip such a talented street performer).

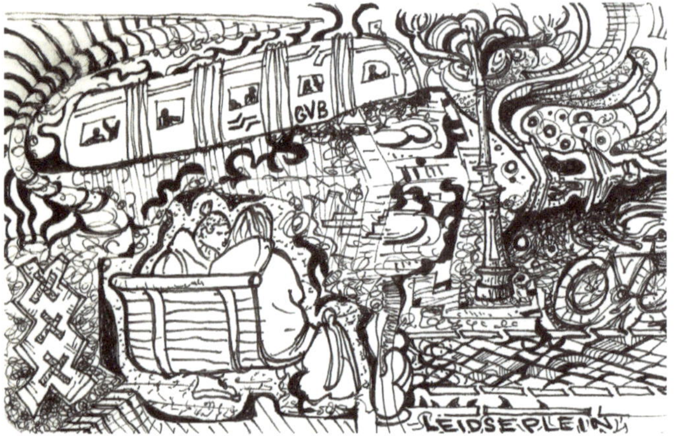

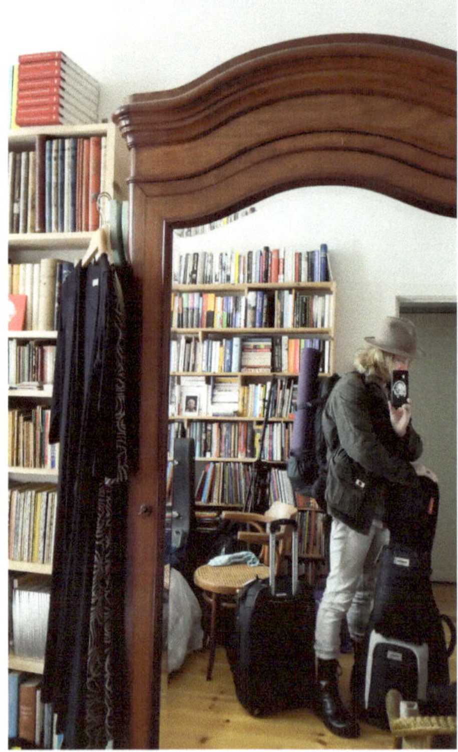

You can't blame them. I'm familiar with this phenomenon. Hell's Kitchen, where I used to live, is next door to Times Square in New York City. If you want to have a look at people lost in their own personal experience, oblivious to what's around them, mouth hanging open like a lobotomized nuthouse patient as they stare into the lights, then the number one most photographed place in the world is your spot. That'd be Times Square.

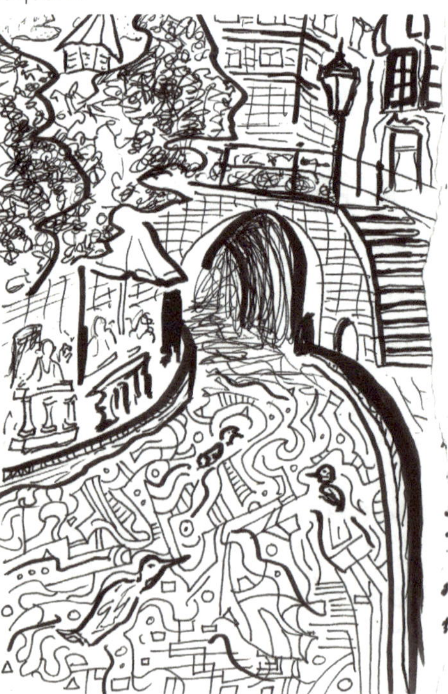

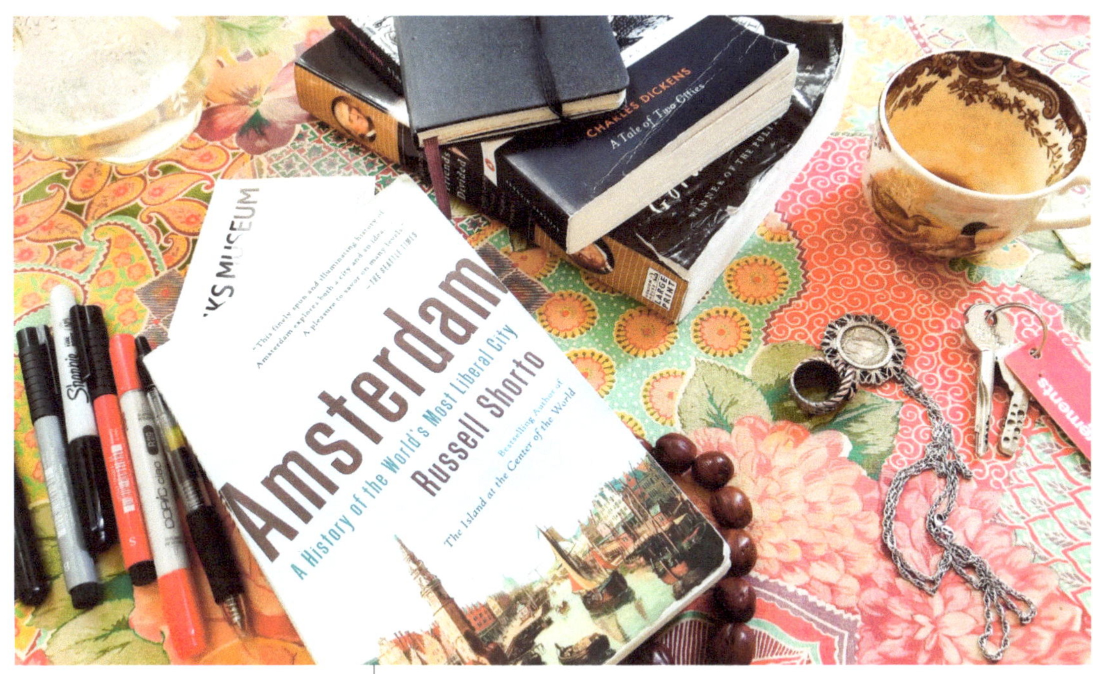

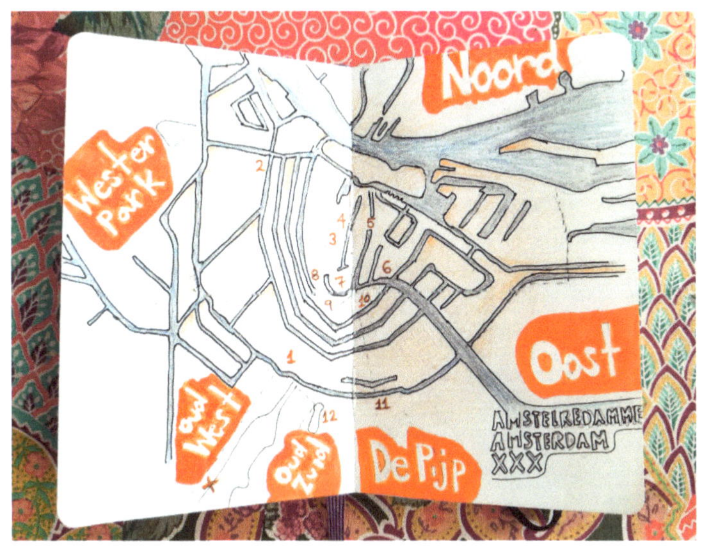

dizzy doodles
Leidseplein

waterways &
neighborhoods

the home of my soul
Oud West

The balancing act Dutch cyclists pull off is like a circus lives in their genetics. I once tried something like what you see on the left and it almost cost me my relationship, and my gf her temper.

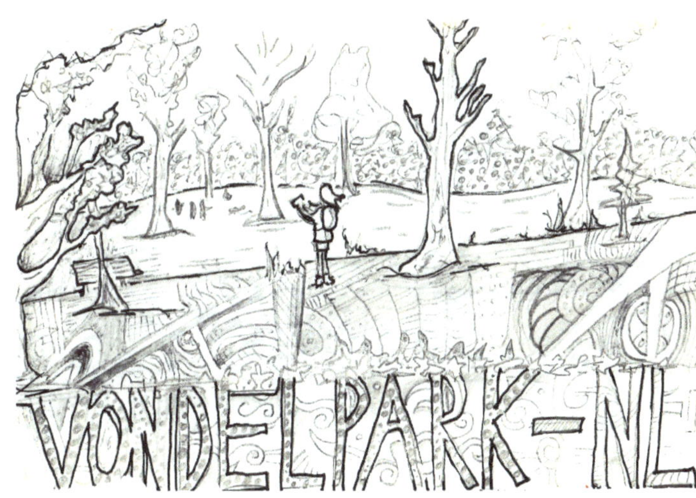

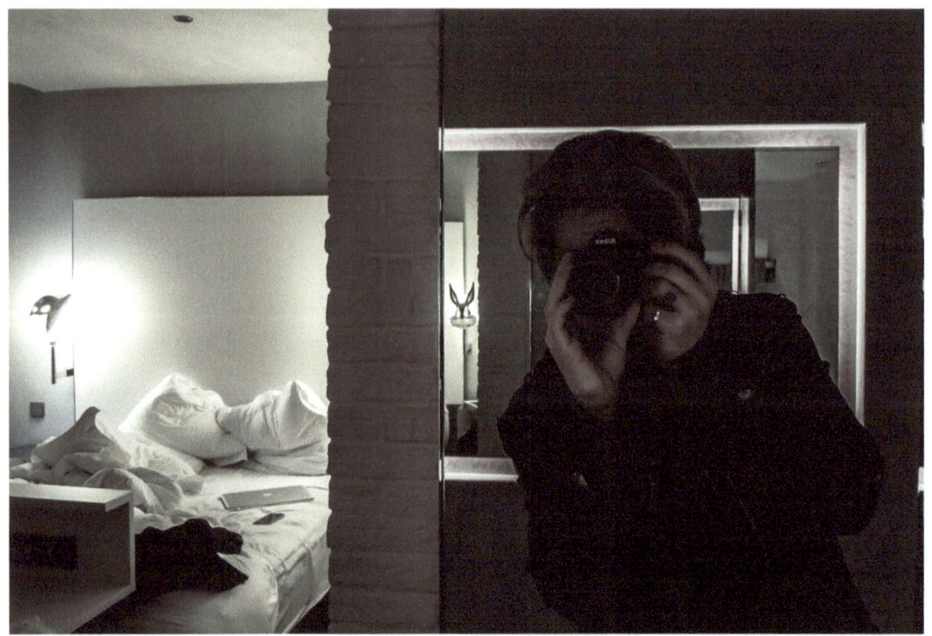

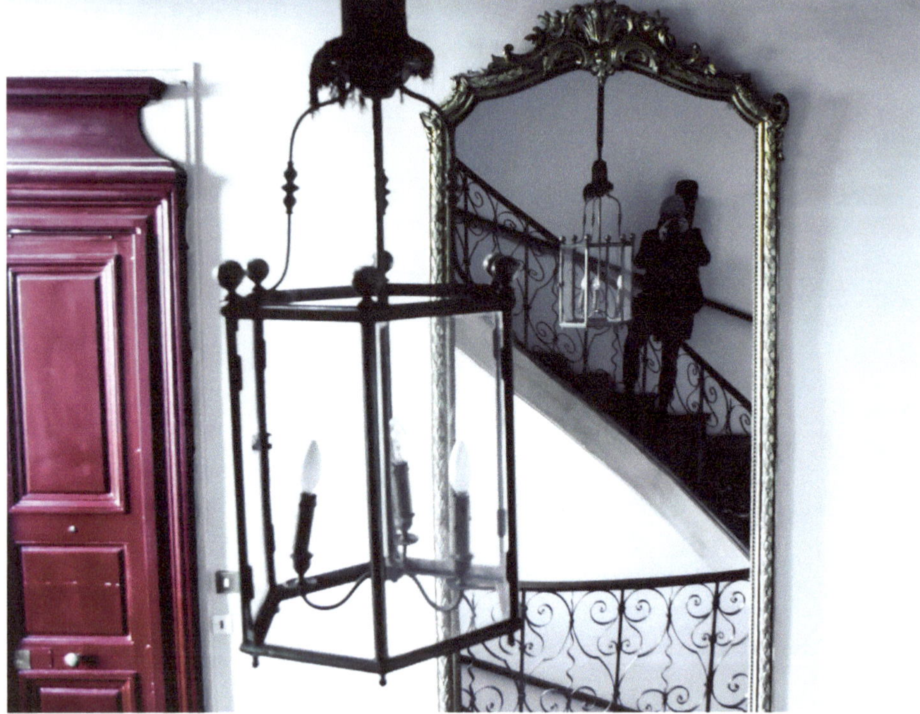

*Bugs, Batman and Narcissus
in a Taksim hotel
I didn't pay for*

*in Paris
even the stairs are like whoa*

*Londinium
via doorways of the 21st century*

Given this experience and my glocalist mentality, you might think I'd be with my buddy, scornful of the clueless teenagers in "I heart NY" shirts and the small town, fatass families clogging the sidewalk. It's annoying. I get the frustration, but my take is different.

We all have to start somewhere. I was once that gawking tourist who knew no better than to loiter around the locations found in a top ten list online. My first time in Amsterdam, I was that cliché with a head full of mushrooms wandering from coffee shop to coffee shop, snickering at the windows of the red light district.

Truth is, if it weren't for these moments that might embarrass my pedantic, well-traveled sophistication today, I wouldn't be the nomad I've become. There are very few shortcuts in life. We all have to start at step one.

It comes full circle realizing the best kind of traveler and human being is always going new places and learning new things, which means step one is like the hair on your head. You can shave it off, but there's no getting rid of it (no offense bald people, sorry that analogy doesn't work for you).

Sure, experience makes me more clever and aware when I find myself in a freshly foreign locale, but I've come to crave that fish-out-of-water sensation that may appear idiotic and basic to a local passerby. At one point in my nomadic education, I would hide my lost confusion or dumbfounded ogling in an attempt to conceal this touristy behavior. I later figured out the douchiest thing I did was thinking myself too good for step one.

I'm not giving carte blanche to that jackass in a MAGA hat complaining that the restaurant doesn't serve ranch or the pampered princess who thinks the Anne Frank House is her personal film set, but we should all give way to the playful childishness of selfie seekers and ignorant idlers.

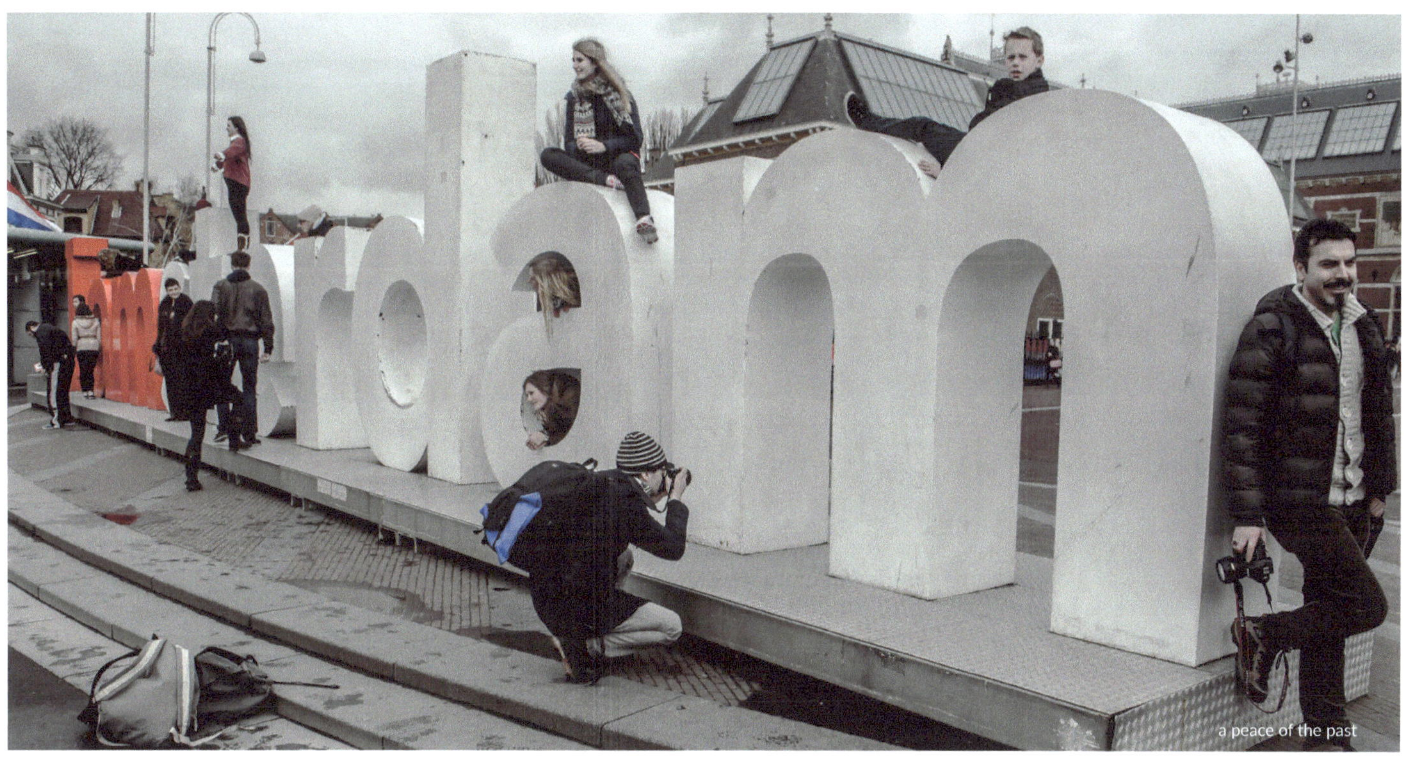

There's no shame in being a novice. If you haven't been there, you either live in isolation or you're lying to yourself.

Back in Amsterdam, the tourist trap at Museumplein has been moved. The official reason was that it was too individualistic. Okay. That's a bit odd coming from the city that rose to power based upon concepts of personal liberty and gave birth to the famous philosophy "I think therefore I am." I'm calling bullshit. This was more of a "you kids get off my lawn."

I'm not ripping on Amsterdam (or my talented homie). If I had to choose, it's actually my favorite place on the plant. There is nowhere else in the world I have felt more welcomed. Making friends in Amsterdam is like getting out of bed in the morning. With a little effort, it'll happen. To contradict myself, the tourism board's reasoning does make some sense. Amsterdam is the sum of its parts, and community happens easy.

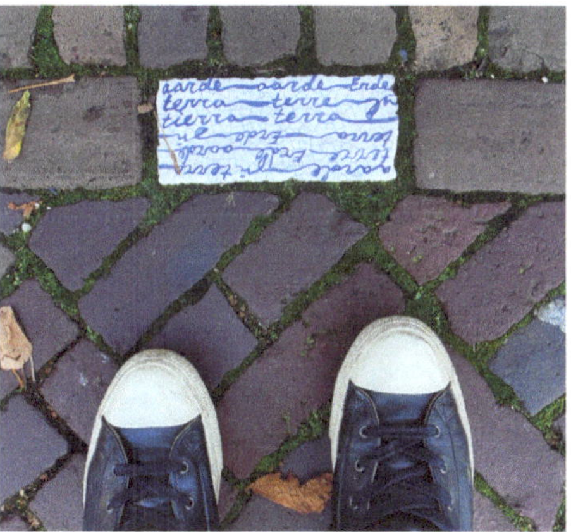

Over the course of my time there, I've collected a few Delfts blauw houses that represent architectural landmarks across the Netherlands. It's a trend started in the 1950s by Royal Dutch Airlines as a gift to first class passengers and filled with Jenever (Dutch gin). When I mentioned my admiration of these fragile collectors items to my original Amsterdam friend and native daughter of the city that swallows the sea, she said, "Oh, those cheesy things that tourists buy?"

And there you have it.

From the Texas plain where it all began
To Rocky Mountains where I ran away
In the Broadway lights I became a man
Found the sun in Hawaiian sands
Chased the dream out in LA
New England's autumn leaves taught me how to dance

I'm the traveler, I am
All I have is on my back
In my hand a guitar to tell the tale
I'm the trubador, I am
the aint no turning back
My heart's a sail

To London town I crossed the sea
I long to see the Old World
In Amsterdam there is a girl gave love to me
Oh the melancholy Paris streets
Inspiring spires of Istanbul
Peddled my songs in Italy.

No, I really don't know where
this road goes in a month or so
I maybe I fall flat on my face

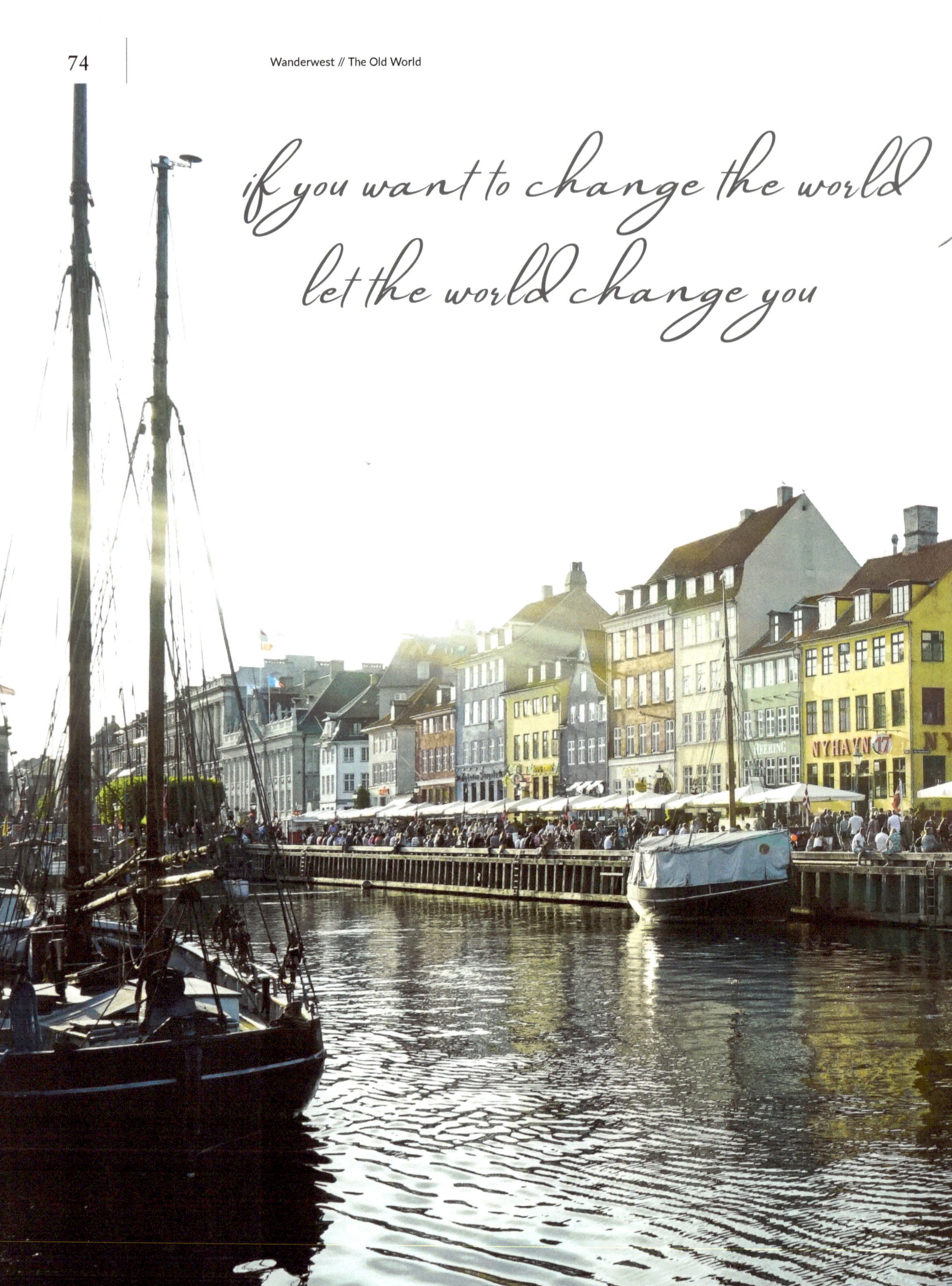

if you want to change the world
let the world change you

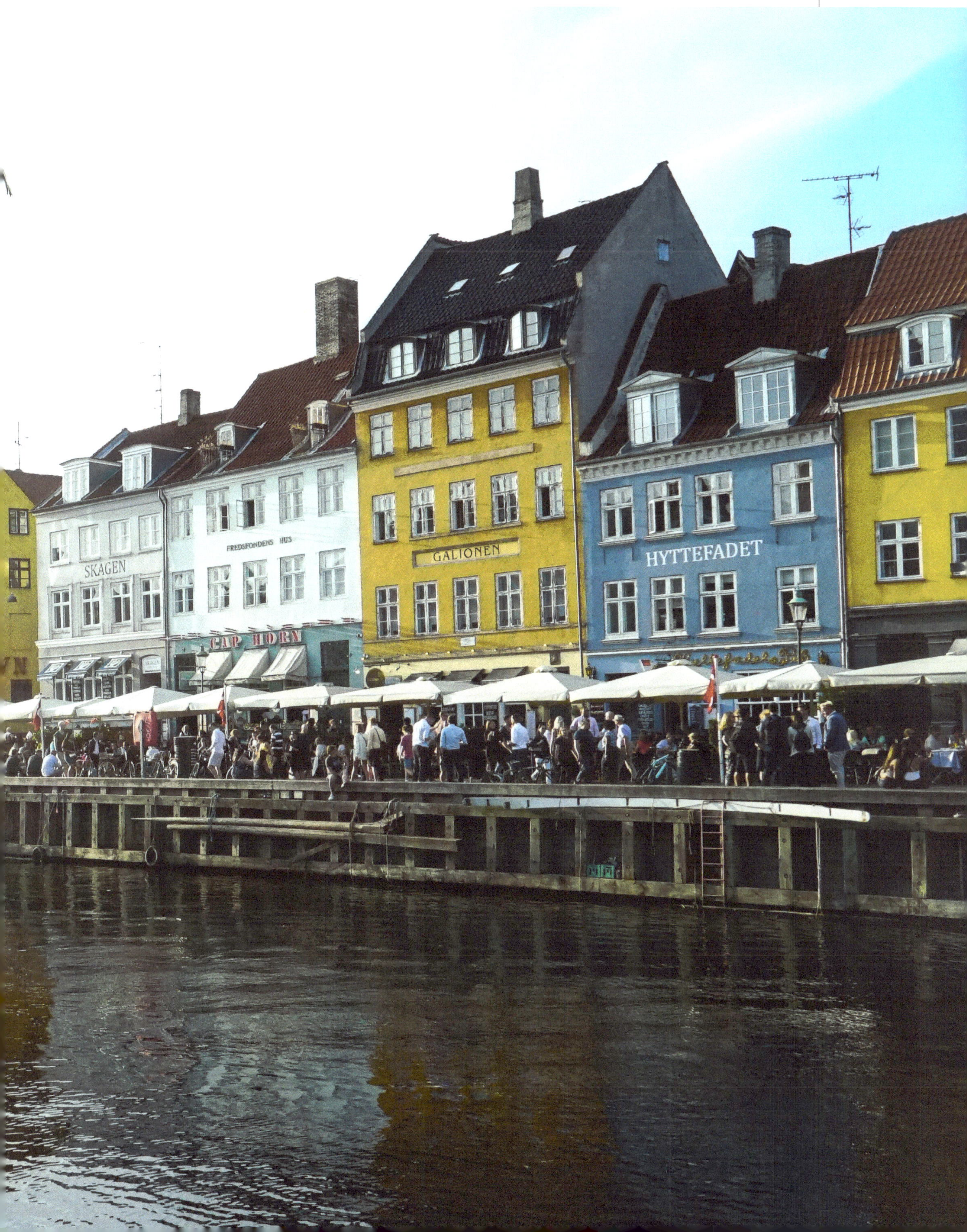
SKAGEN
FREDSFONDENS HUS
GALIONEN
HYTTEFADET
CAP HORN
SKAGEN

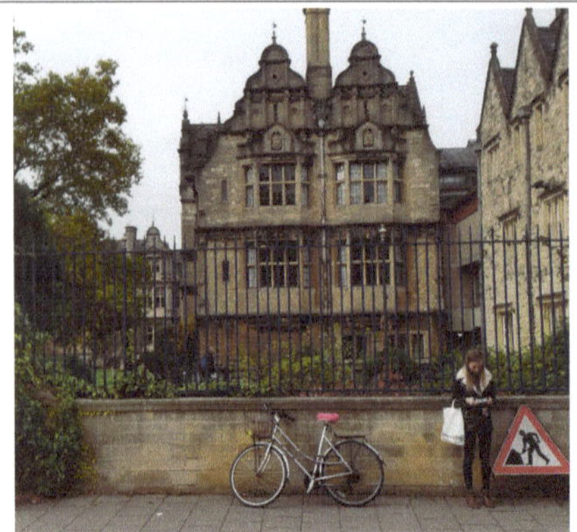
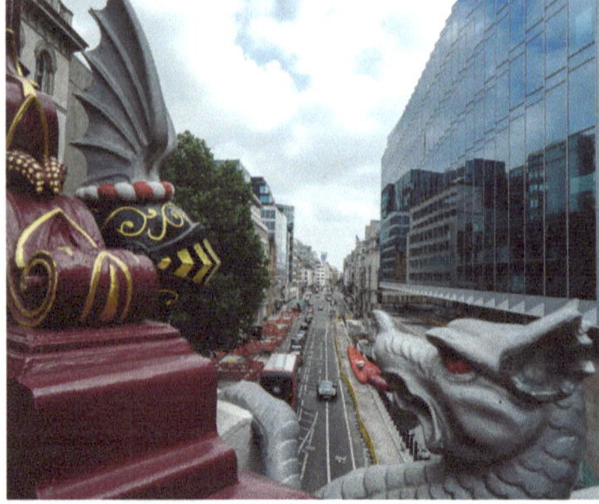
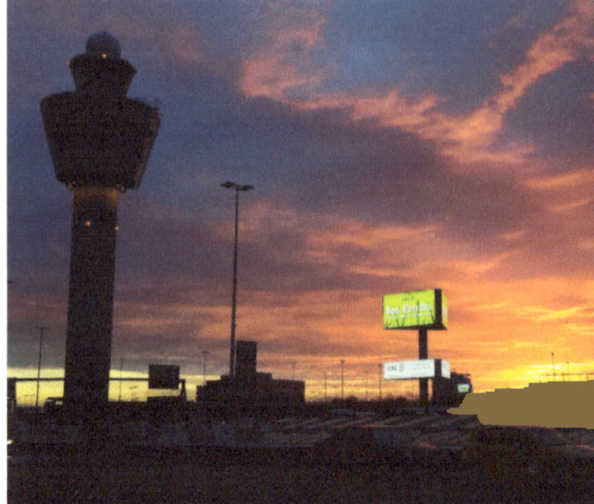
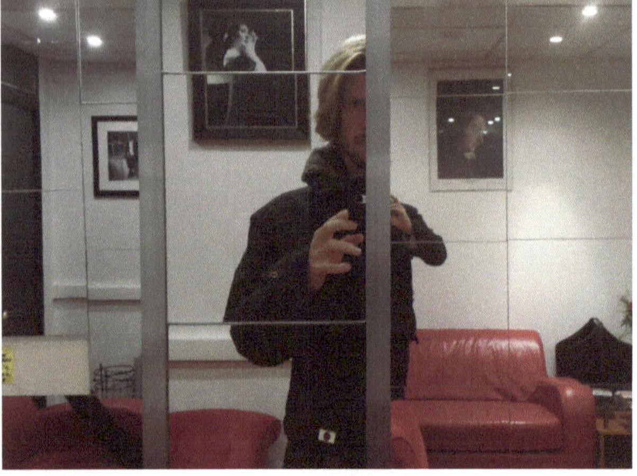
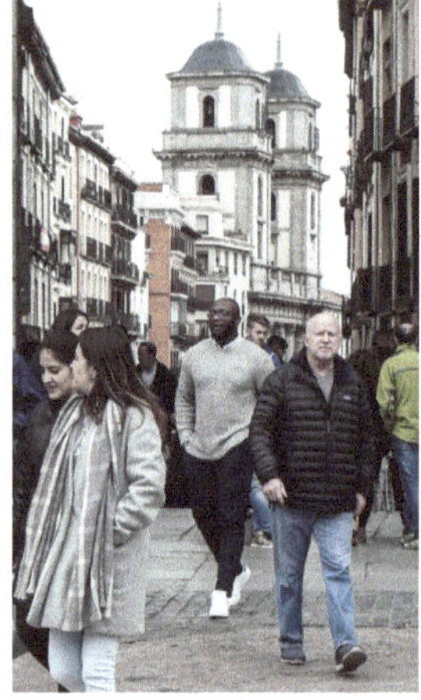
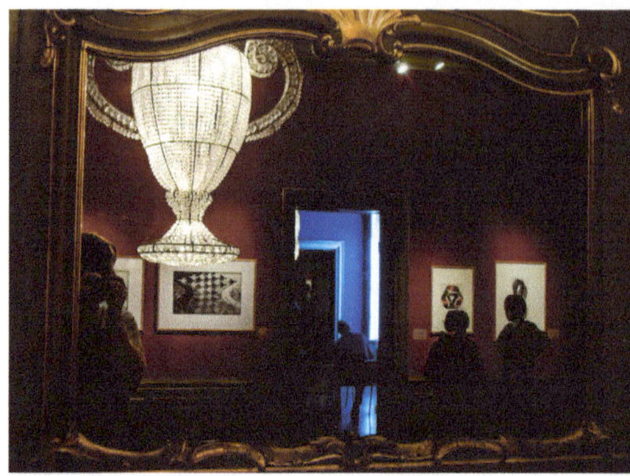

WHAT IF
ART
RULED
THE WORLD?
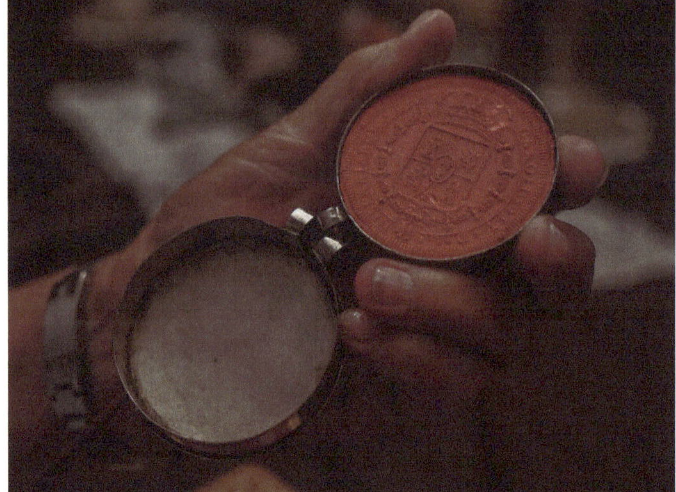
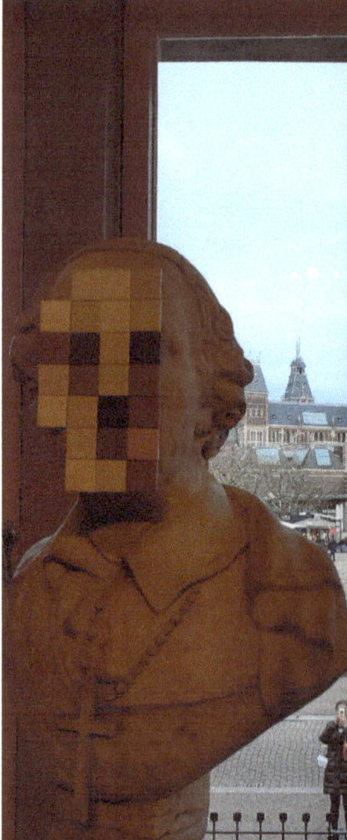
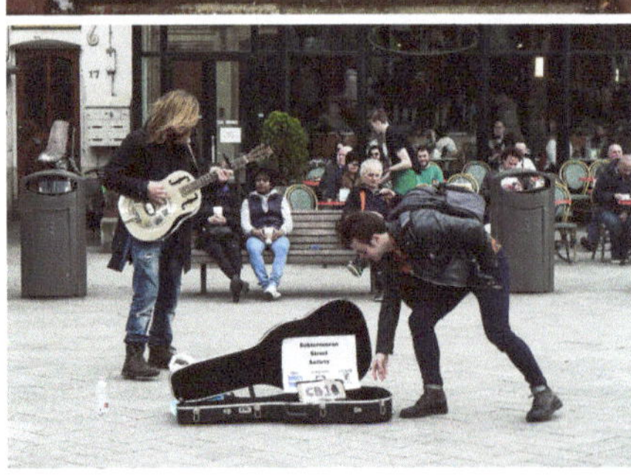
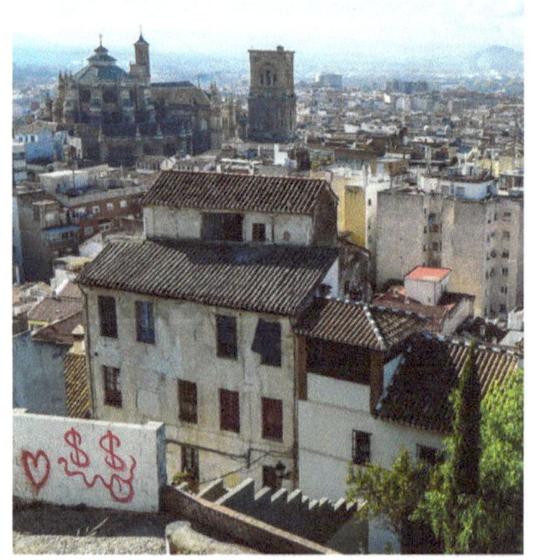
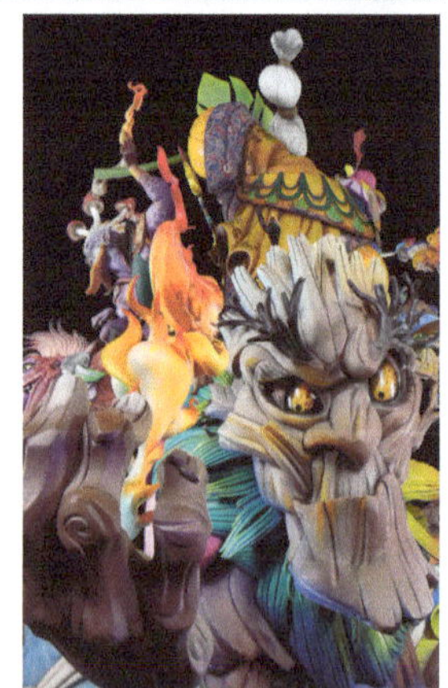
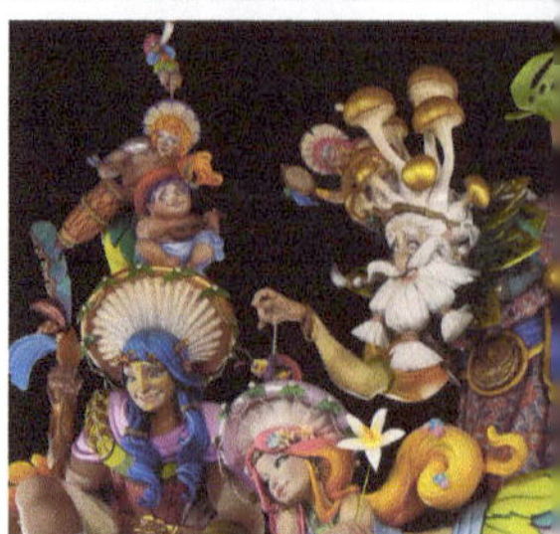

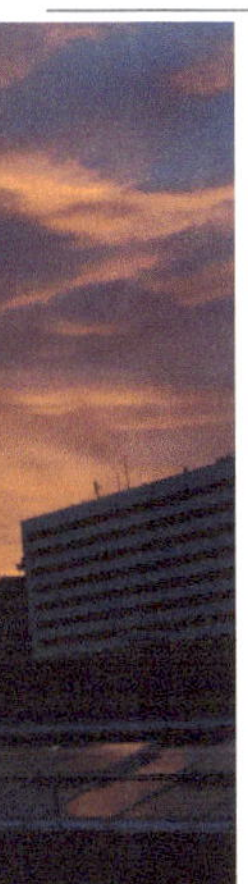
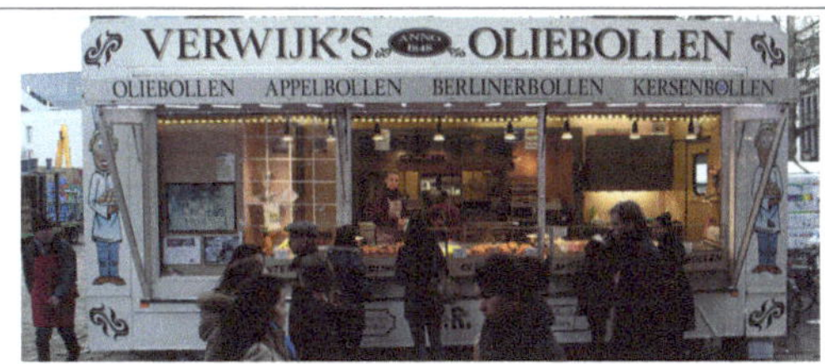
VERWIJK'S OLIEBOLLEN
OLIEBOLLEN   APPELBOLLEN   BERLINERBOLLEN   KERSENBOLLEN
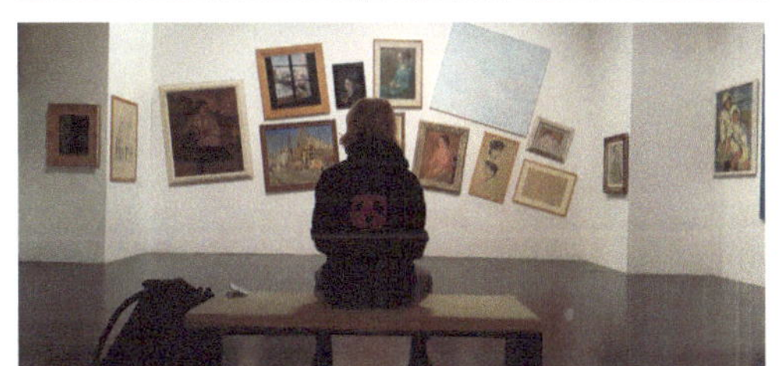
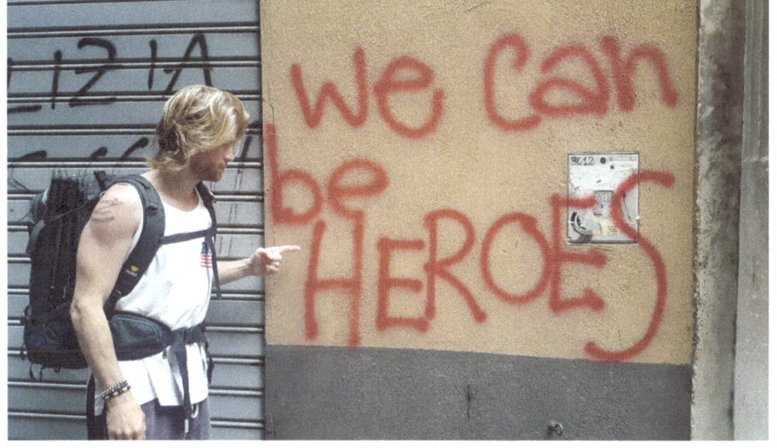
121A
we can
be
HEROES
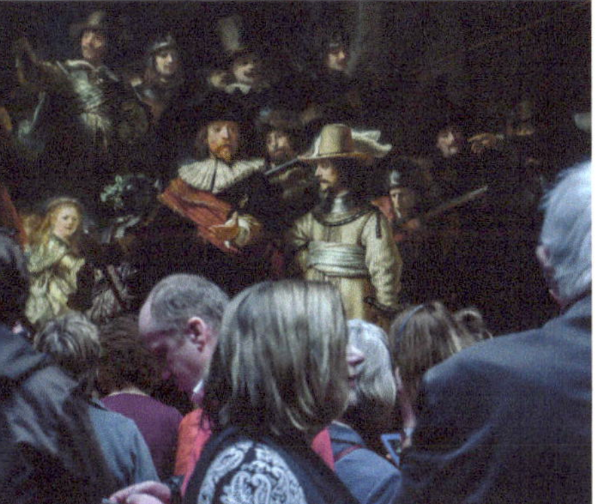
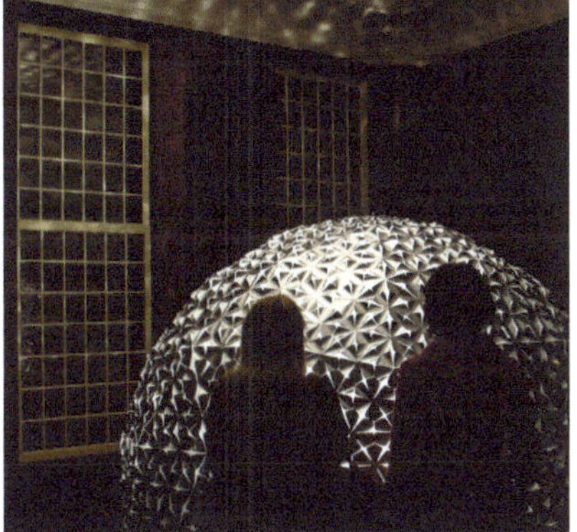
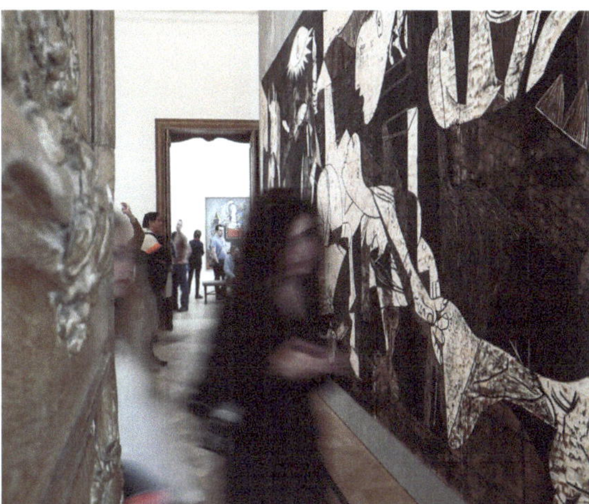
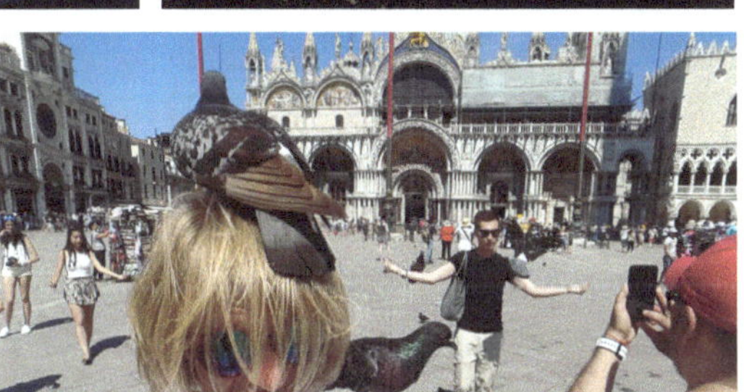
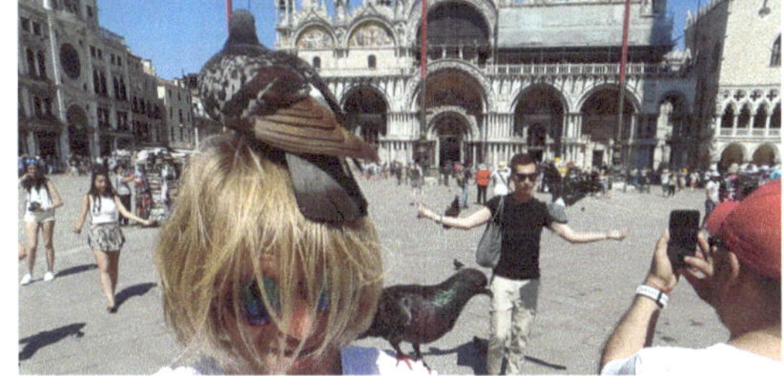
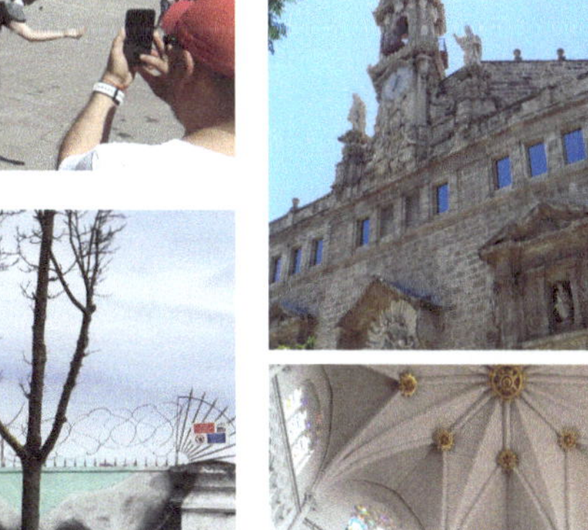
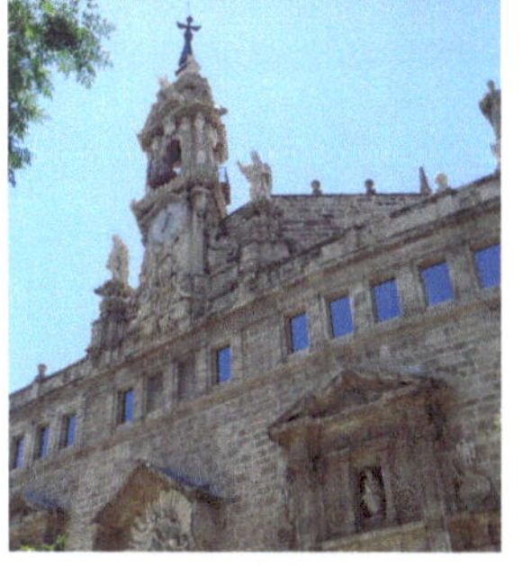
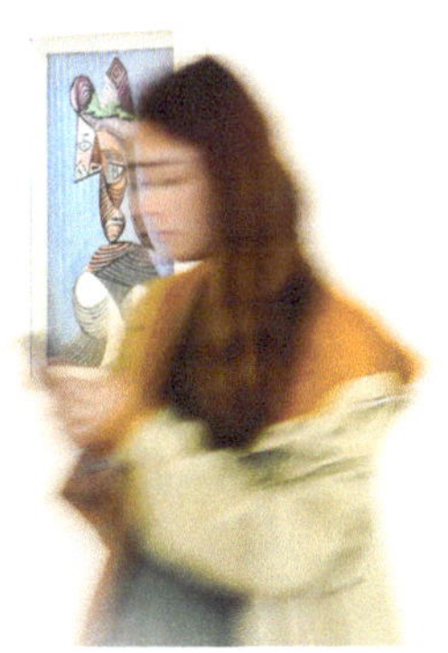
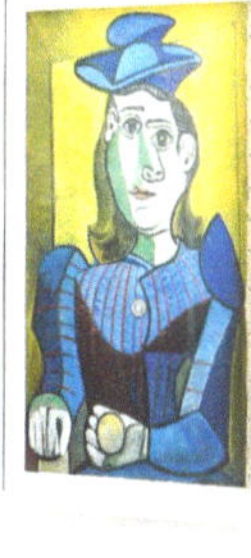
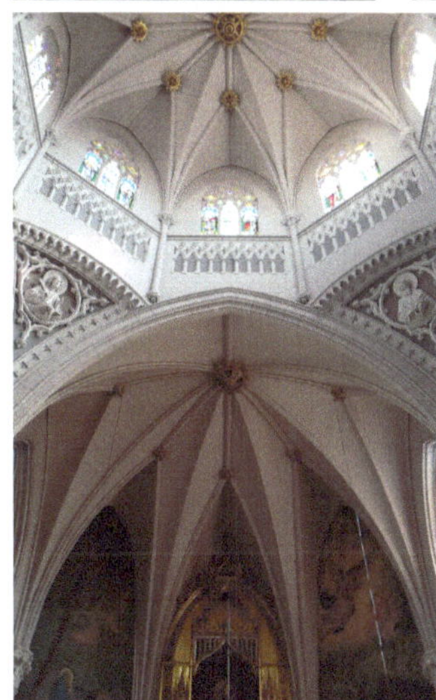
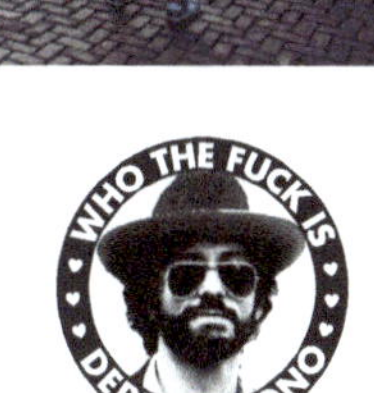
WHO THE FUCK IS
DEREK DEBONO
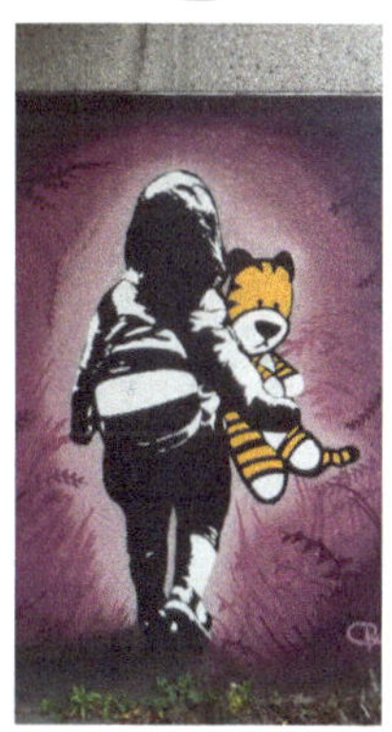
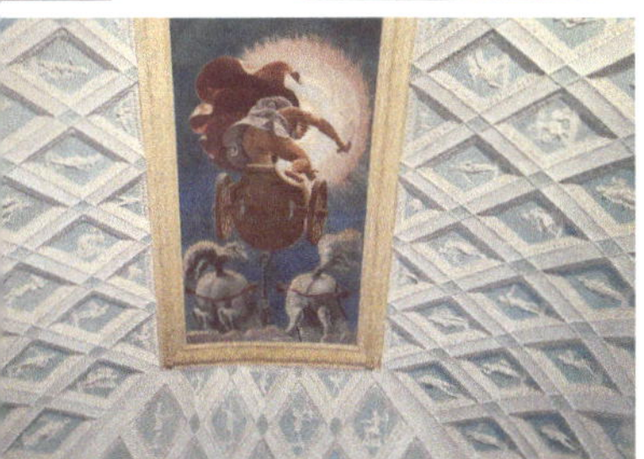
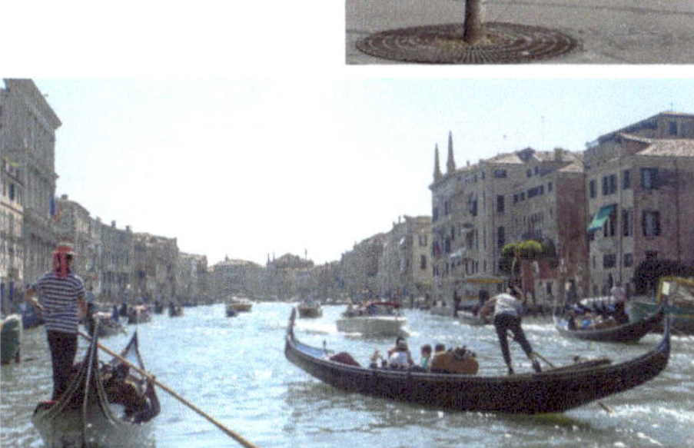
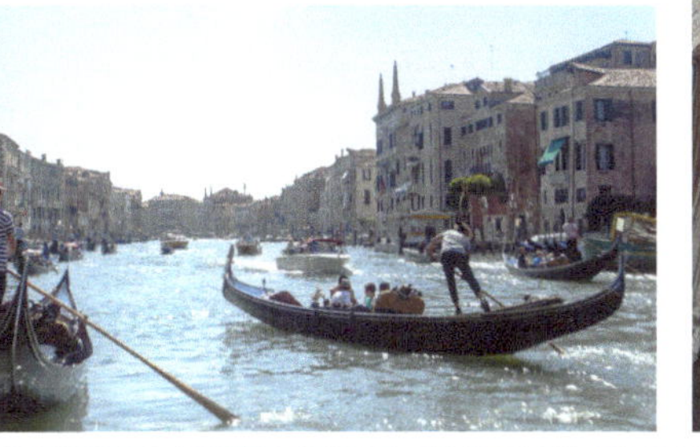

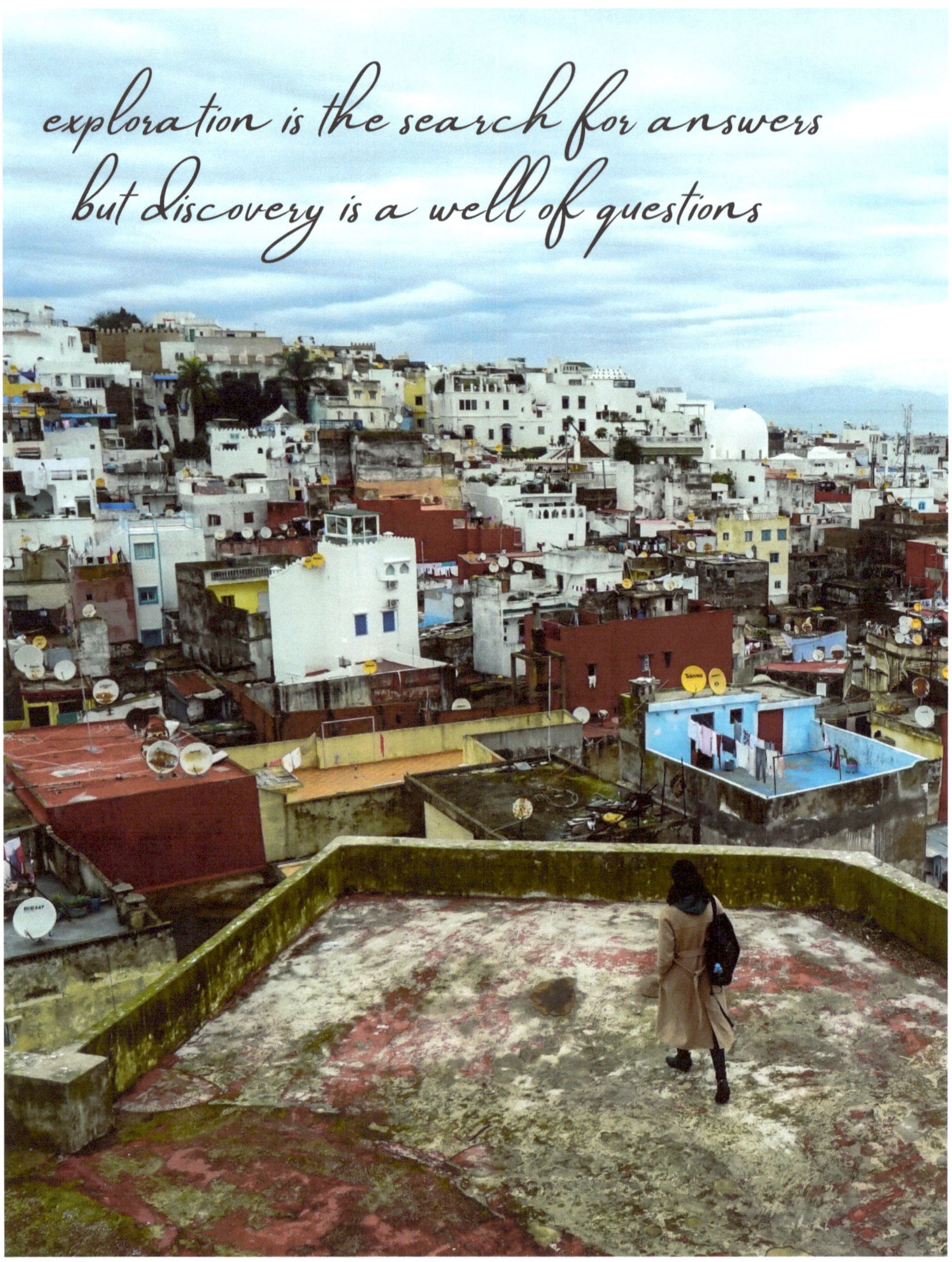
exploration is the search for answers
but discovery is a well of questions

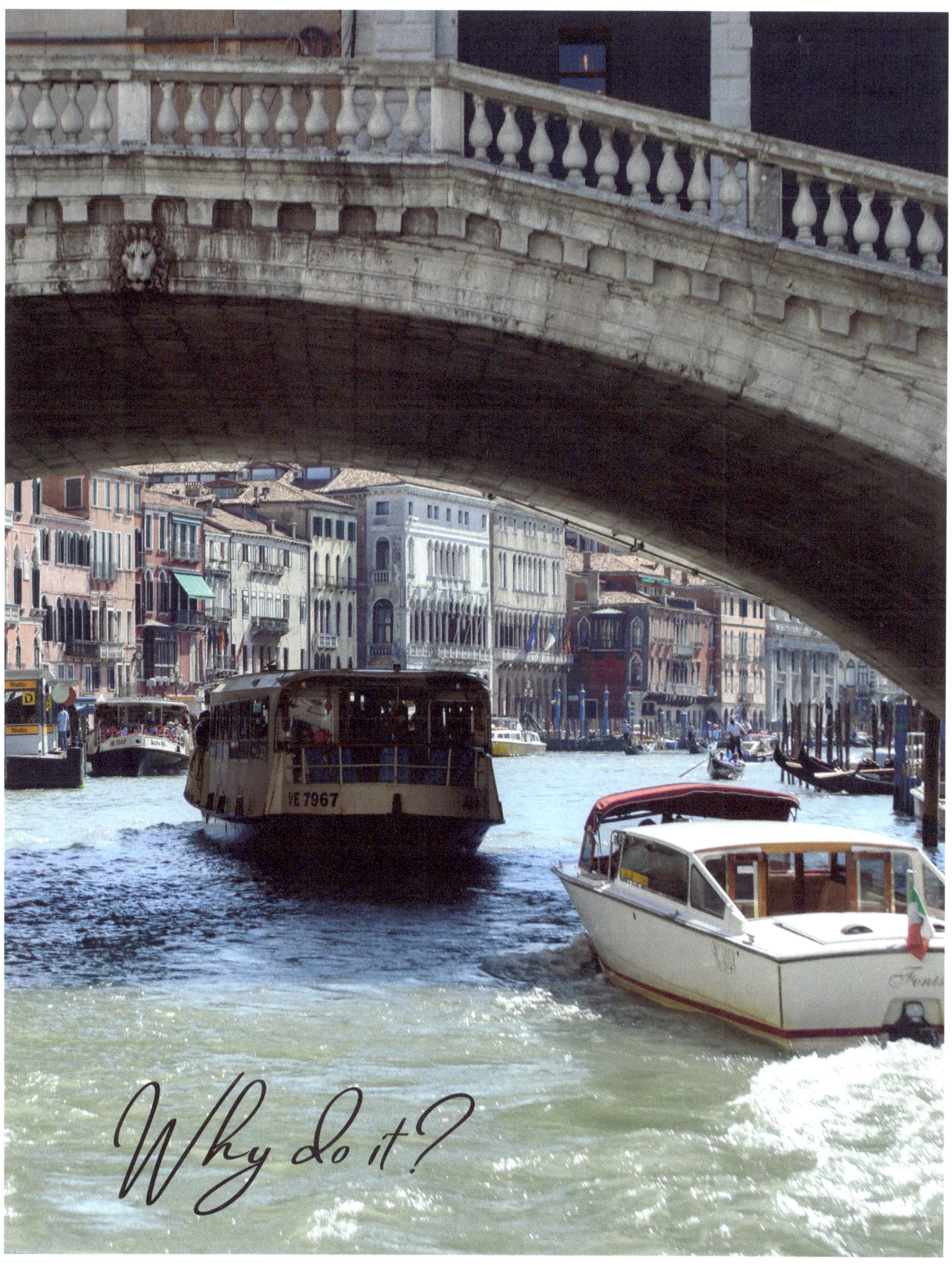
Why do it?

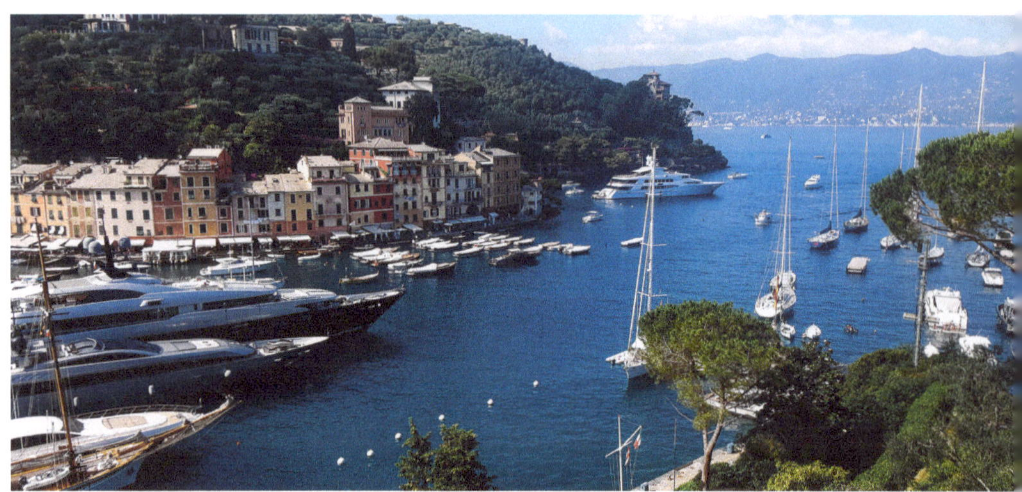

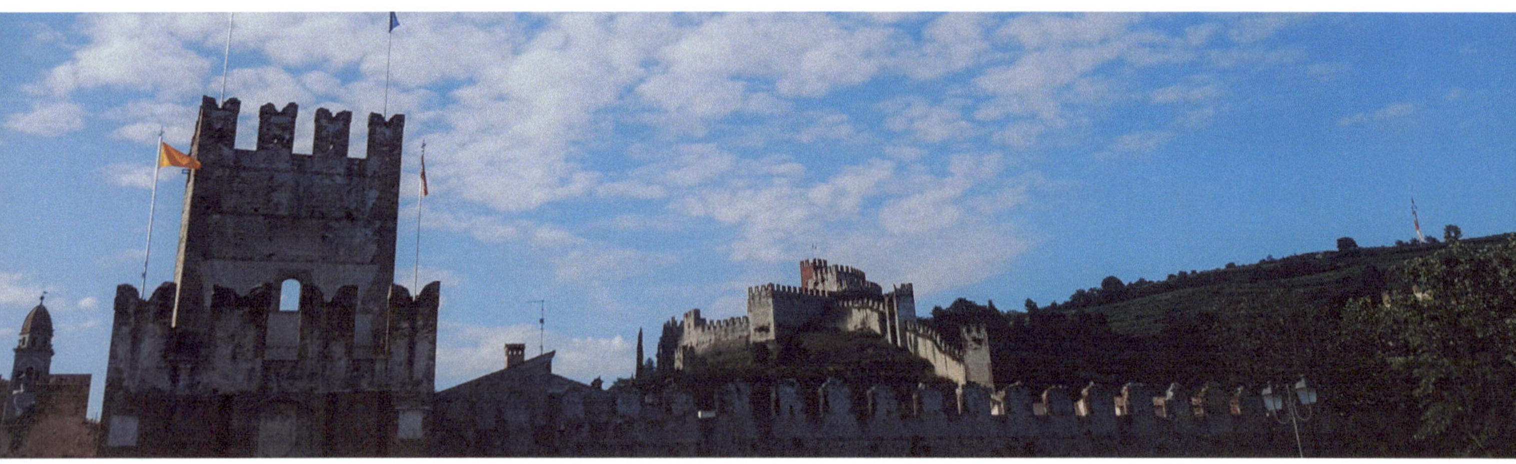

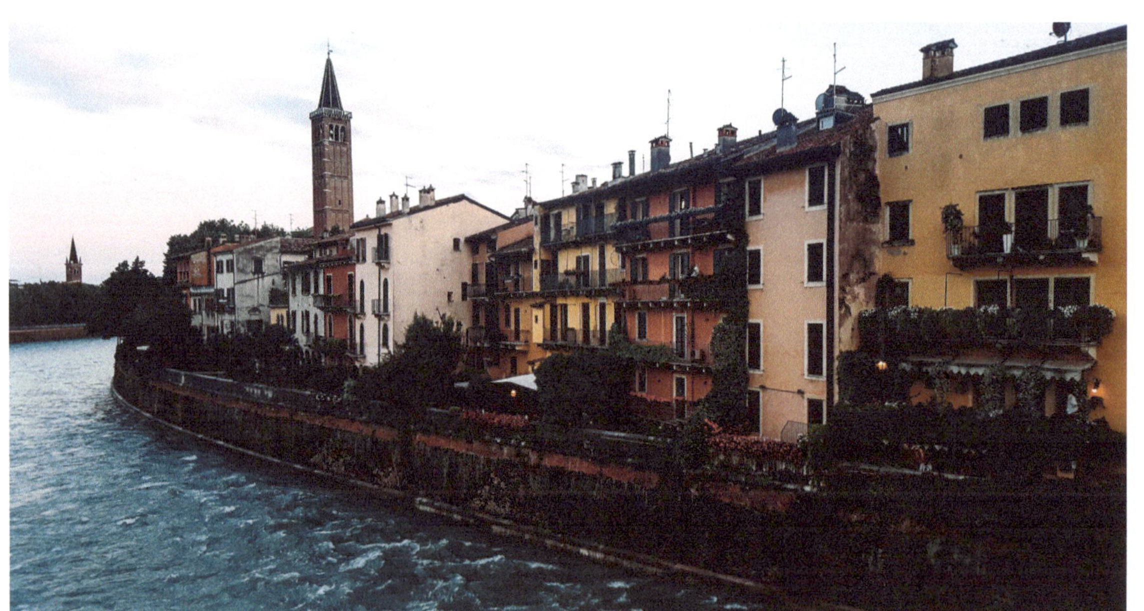

*via
Italia*

*il
mio
primo
amore*

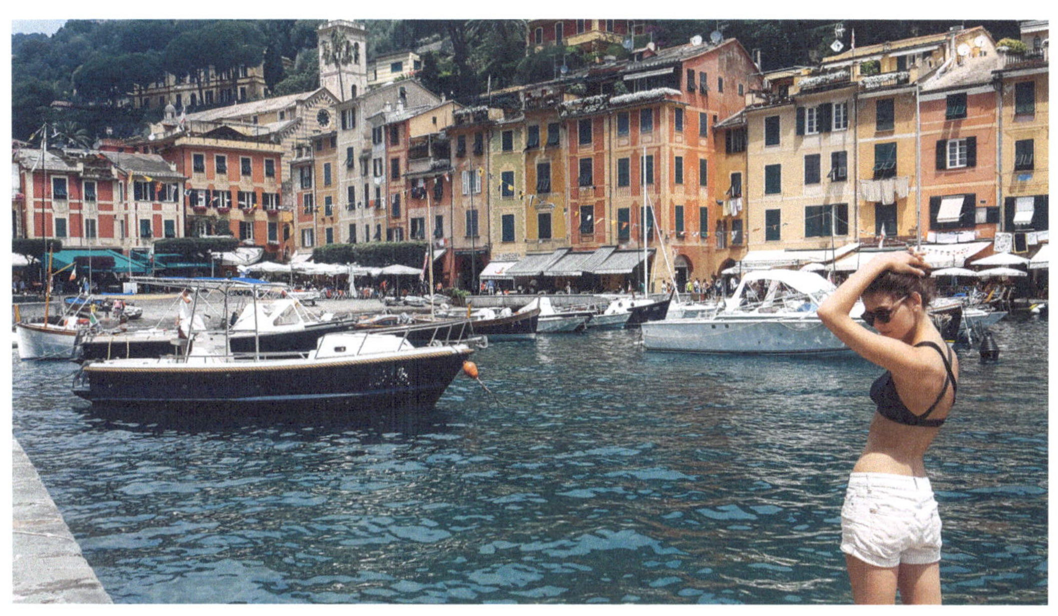

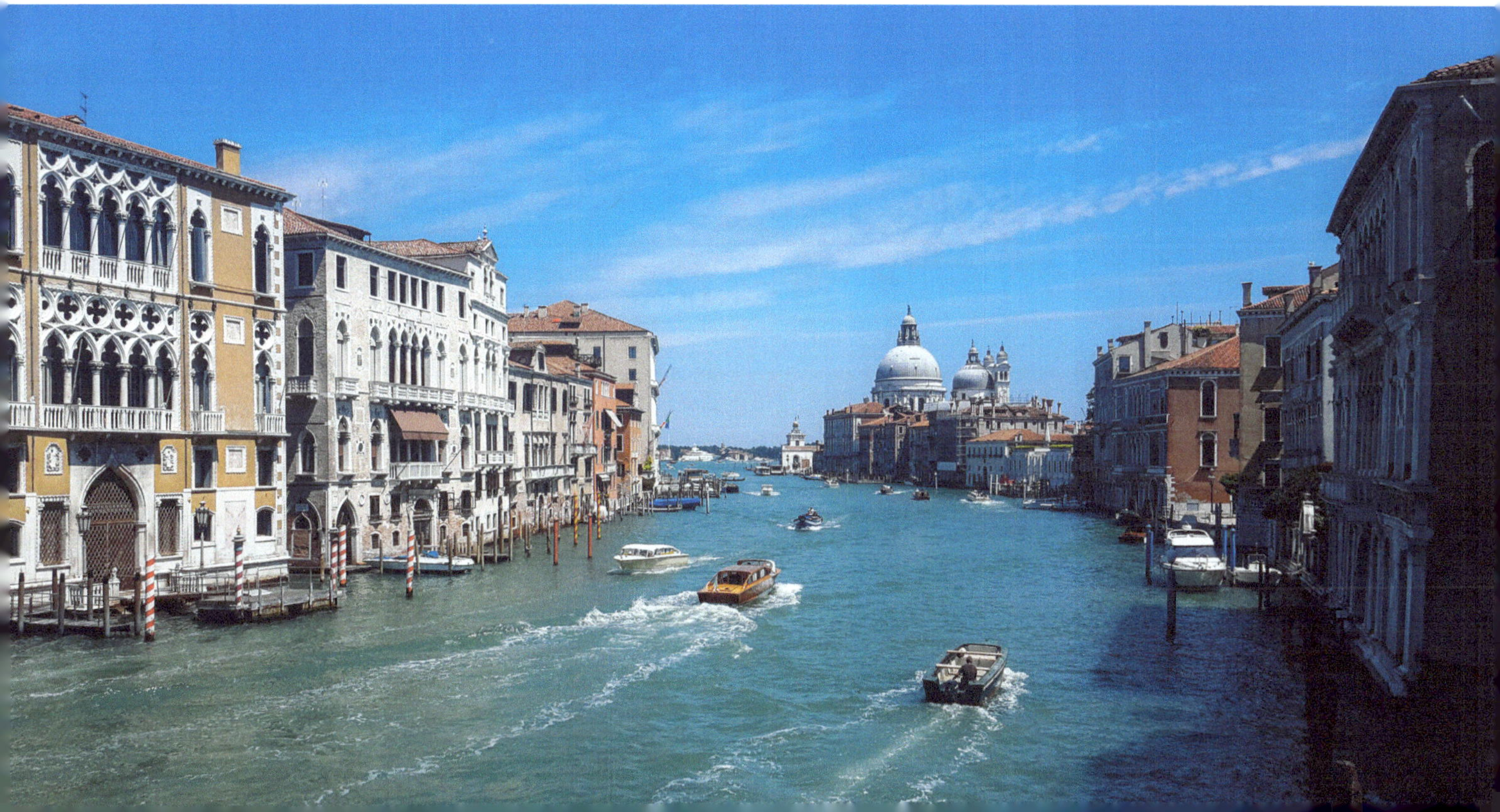

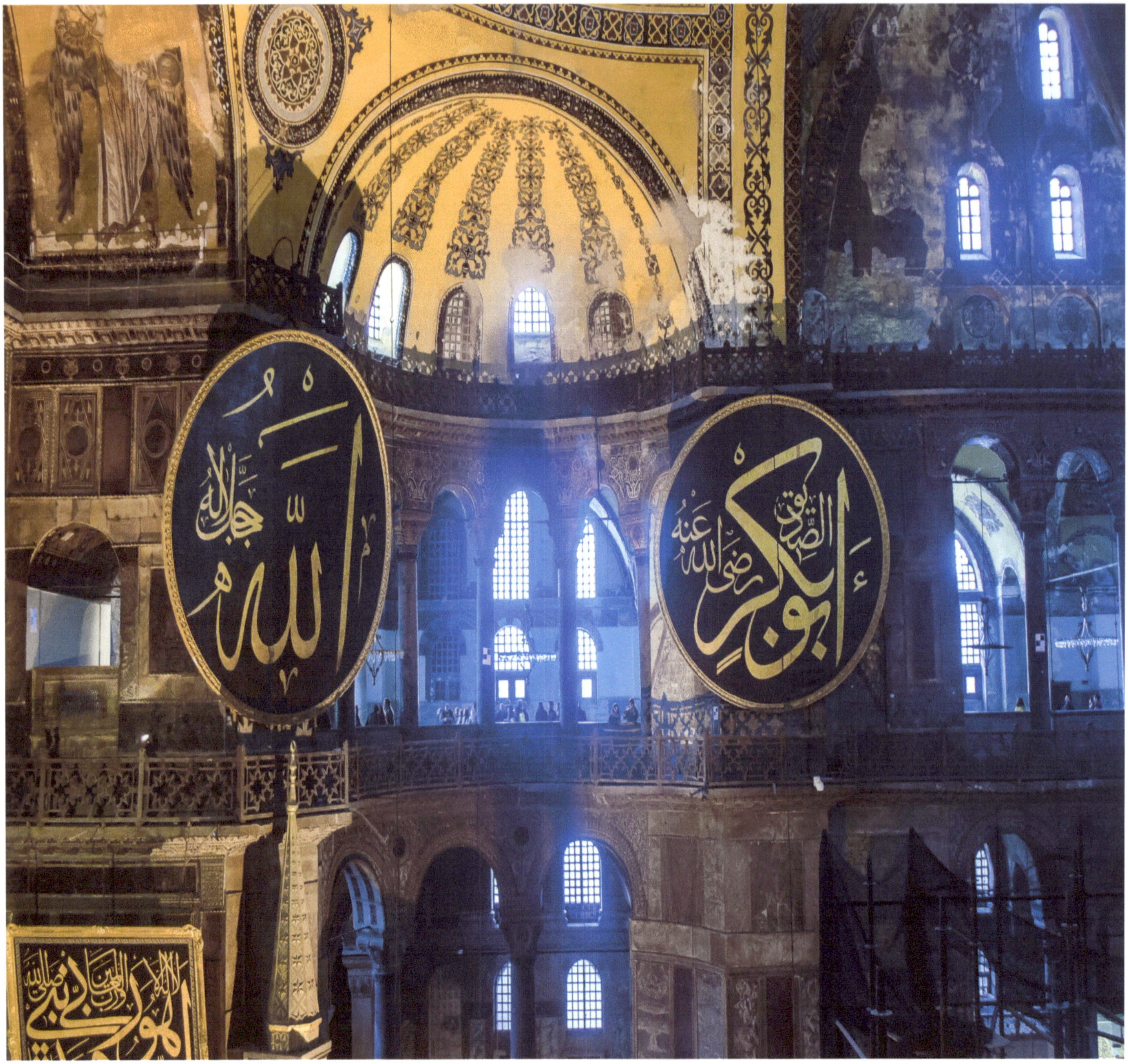

an   amulet   came
at   the   seven   hills
with   gratitude's   power
from   eastern   travels
protecting   its   bearer
from   all   evil   eyes
unlocking   the   path
in   prayers   it   binds

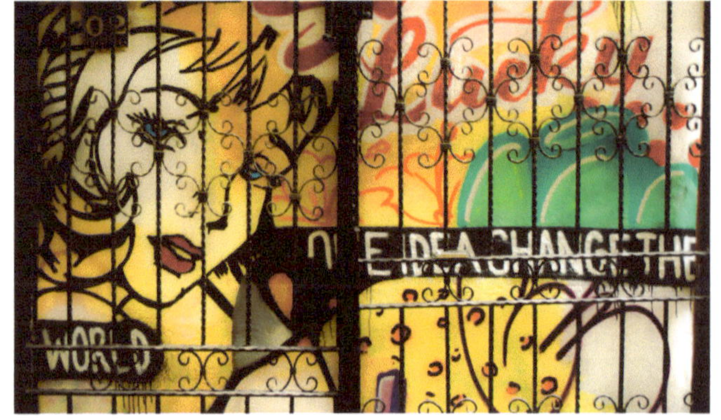

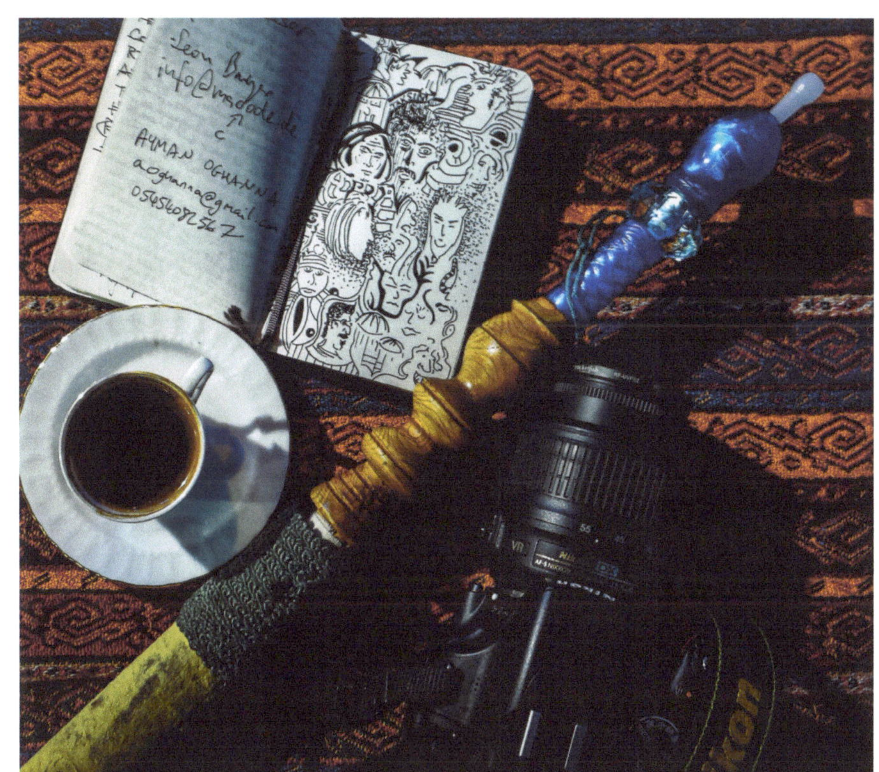

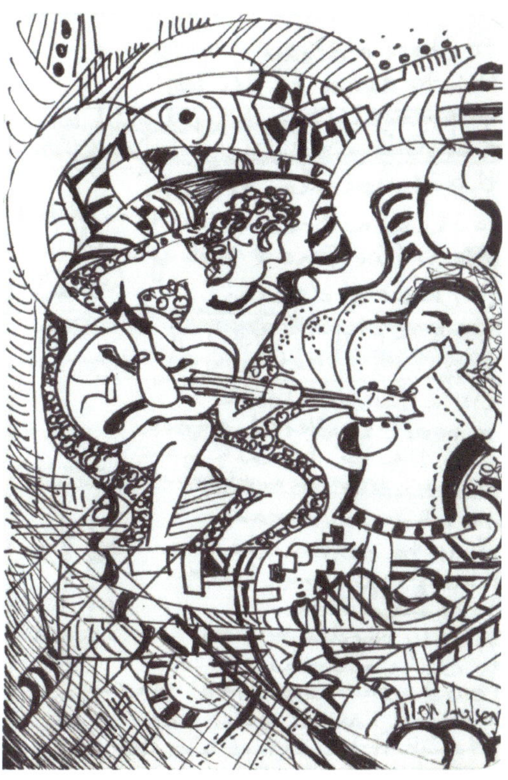

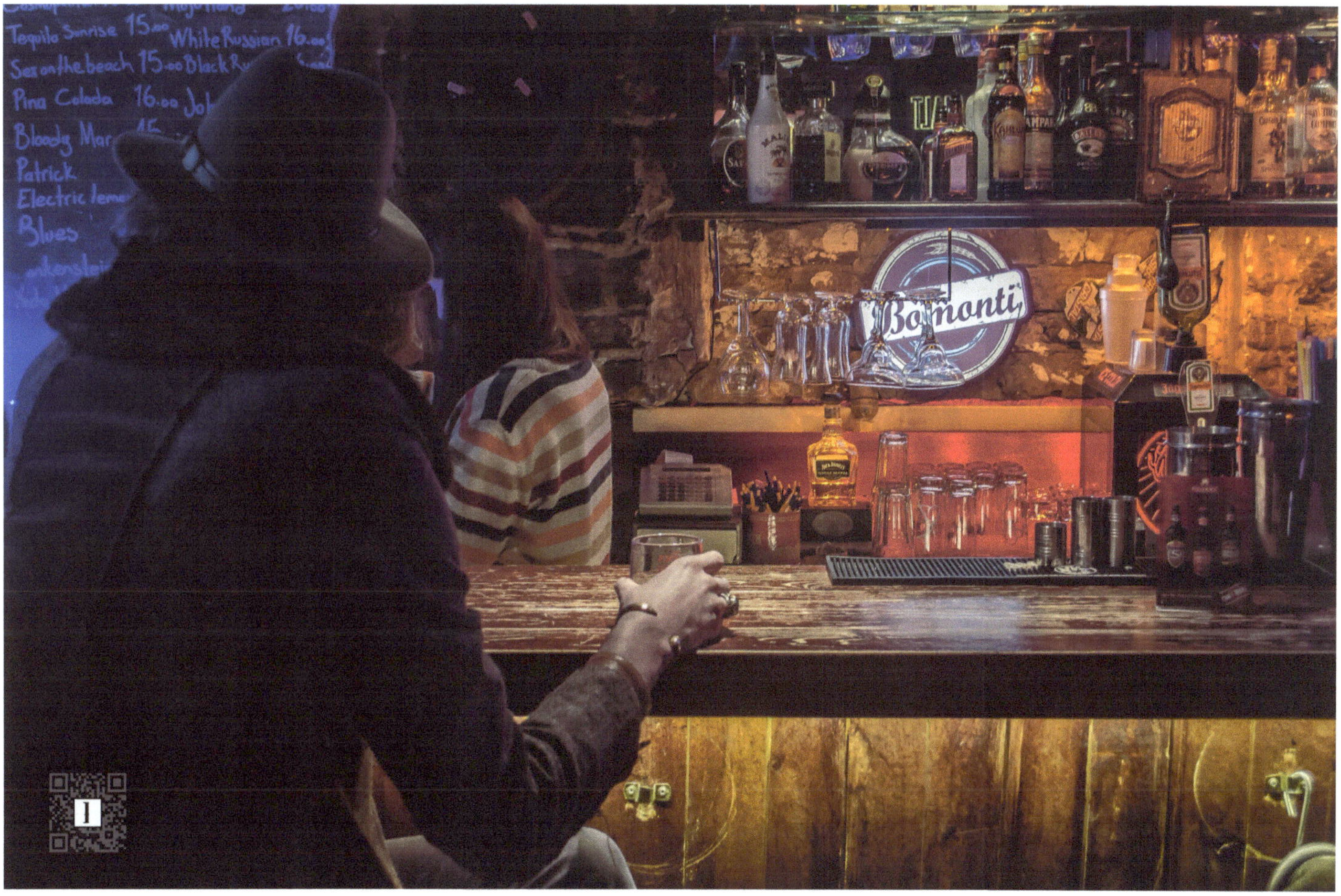

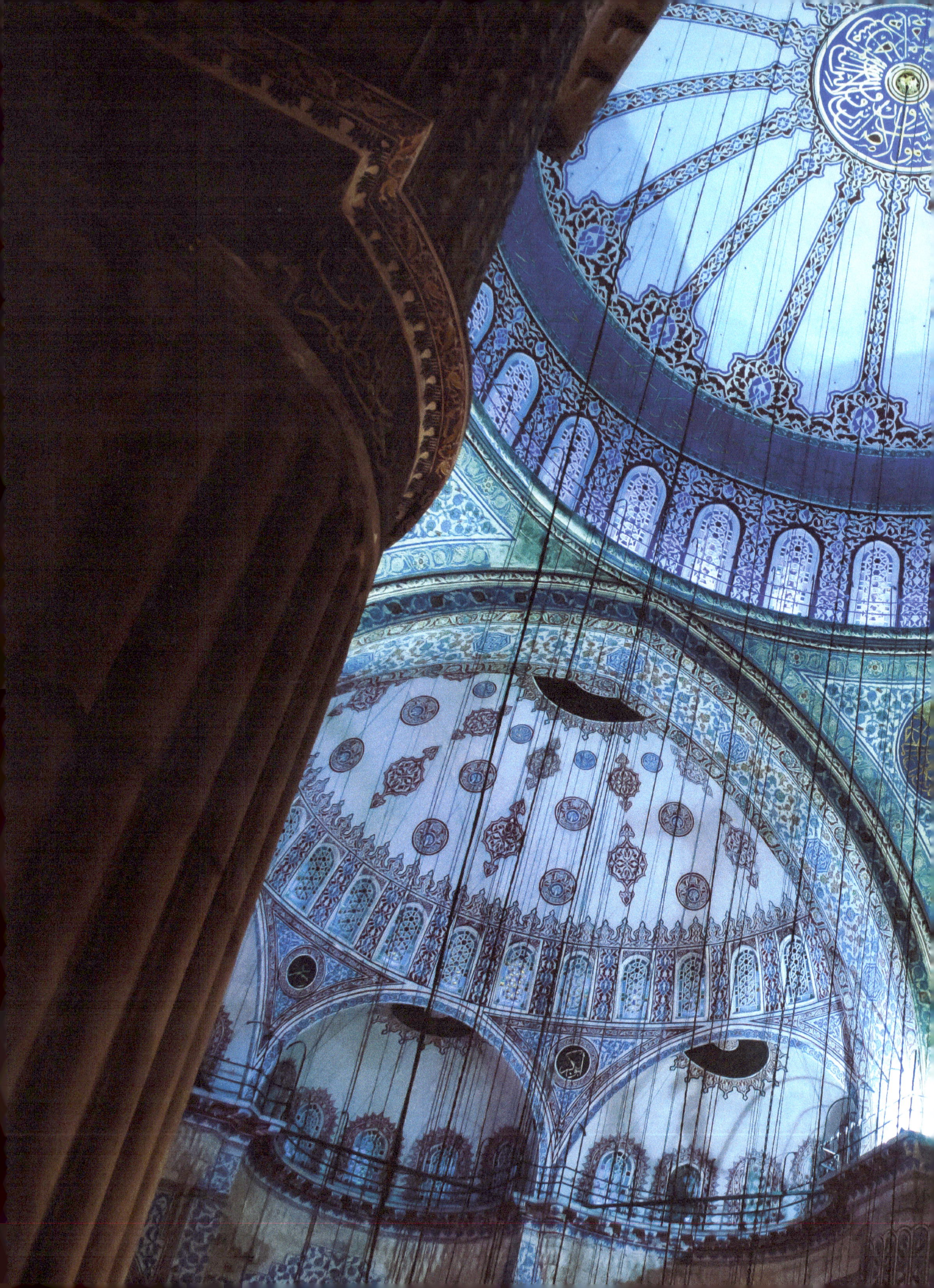

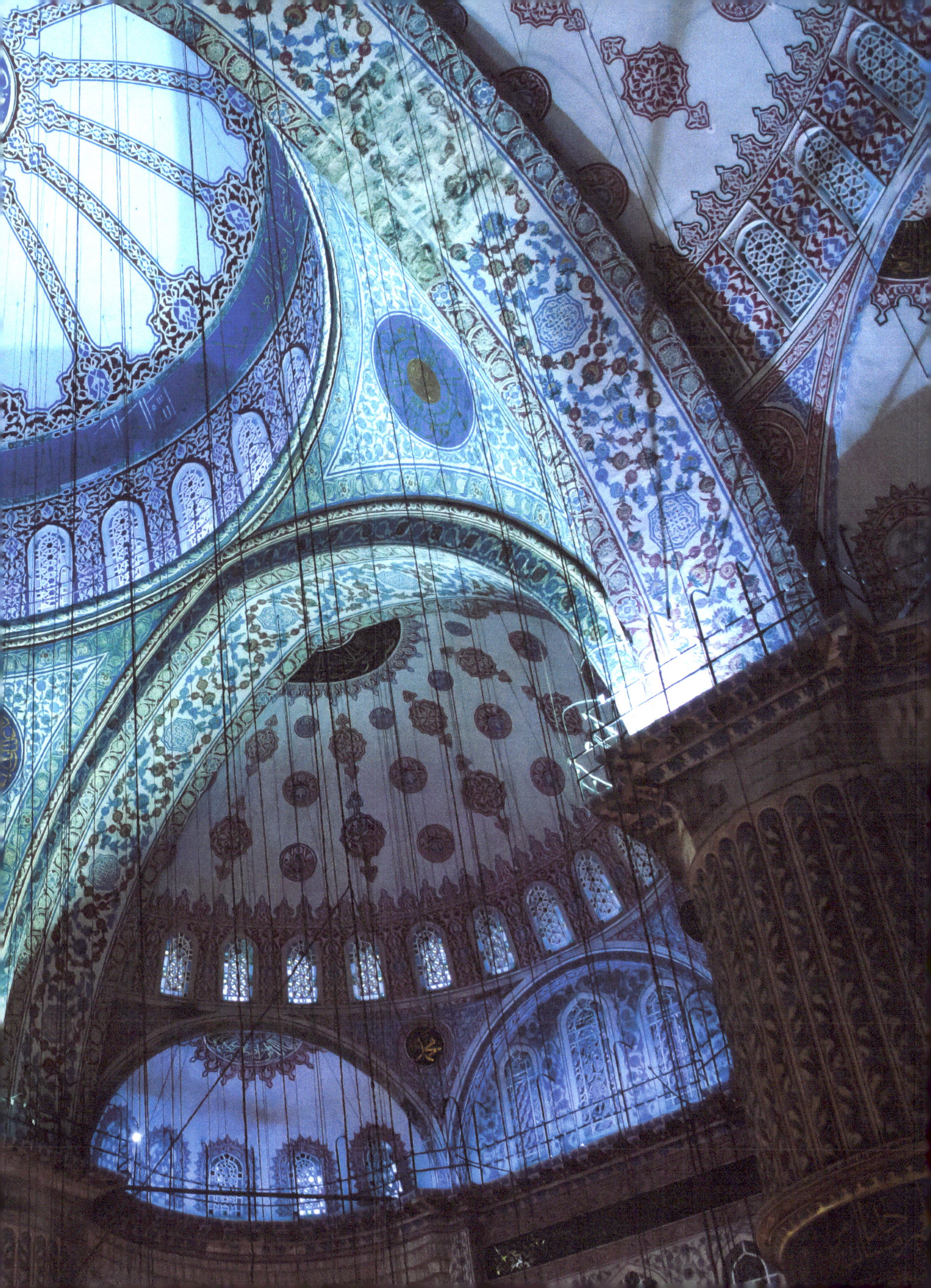

In the end, if you hated it, if I've made you mad, then I've done my duty. It's not my ambition, but repulsion suits my satisfaction. Roll your eyes, but please don't yawn.

If I've inspired any passion, I propose you ponder the mirror that puts forth. I'd need cite a million minds to try and credit the timeless wisdom that our thoughts about others often say more about ourselves.

So burn this as trash, if you wish. I will be the witch and confess to sacrilege. To perish on a pyre would be a terrible bliss worthy of Joan of Arc.

To be dull is the worst critique. I'd rather be your villain than forgotten. One man's conqueror is another's queen. If I haven't hit a nerve, then do me a favor and burn this piece of shit.

Are you listening or just reading? The metaphor of fire is not a finale, but a reckoning. It's a fact in the forest and felt in fables like the phoenix.

At Fallas, works of art a hundred feet high are burned to bits as Valencia buries its sins and sorrows in effigy. The dramatic culmination corresponds with traditions across cultures, and coincides with the coming of spring. Rebirth and resurrection.

In the end, I want you to feel it. I want you to bleed, to burn, to bare the weight of battered beliefs. Some of my biggest breakthroughs were found when I was broken.

If you want to live epic, get ready for the pits. What great story is without grief and sadness? Without tension there can be no release. For all this talk of darkness, I'm actually after the light of laughter, love, and liberty. I hold this truth to be self evident, you cannot have the day without the night. If it's Heaven you want, I recommend staying in your shitty town.

That's just basic stuff. This may be a conclusion, but the path presses on. In the end, there isn't one.

Thank you to Suus, Dirk, Judith, Michiel, Jara, Derek, Danelle, Ivo, Mark, Tamara, Rose, Stephane, Pam, Marie-Sophie, Samuel, Allen, Eka, Justine, Michael, Amy, Kevin, Danny, Lucy, Alicia, Jose Manuel, Nano, Celia, Cedric, LA, Gilles, Ghyslaine and Nicola for opening your homes to me.

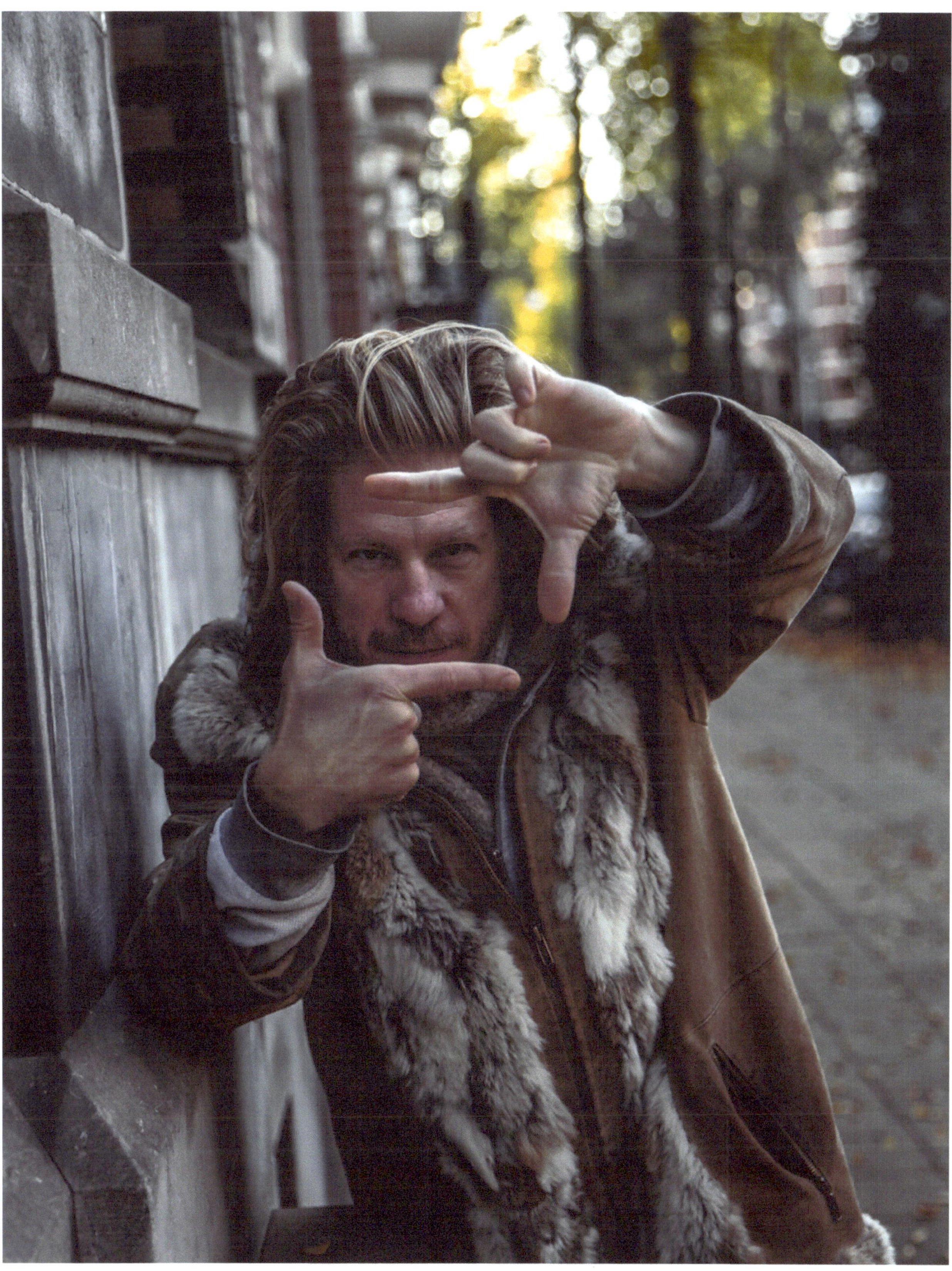